Programming Techniques for Level II BASIC

by
William Barden, Jr.

A TANDY CORPORATION COMPANY

FIRST EDITION
FIRST PRINTING—1980

Library of Congress Catalog Card Number: 80-51523

Preface

This book is meant to be a "cookbook" of Level II BASIC routines for the Radio Shack TRS-80 Model I Computer. If you have questions about the ways in which you can output graphics to the display, *Programming Techniques for Level II BASIC* can help you out. If you want to know about efficient sorting and searching, this book will show you how. If you want some concrete examples of how to interface to machine-language routines in BASIC, you can find the information and examples here. *Programming Techniques for Level II BASIC* is meant to supplement the *Level II BASIC Reference Manual;* it provides practical examples of common BASIC operations that you will want to try.

What do you need to know before using this book? You should have at least a nodding acquaintance with Level II BASIC. You should be somewhat familiar with simple BASIC program structure and Level II BASIC operations. But, if you don't know all of the details in Level II, don't be afraid to plunge right into the examples in this book. The best way to learn is by practical example, and we have attempted to provide plenty of them. You don't need a degree in computer science or mathematics, either. Most operations described here use simple straightforward logic; Level II BASIC is capable of providing advanced mathematical processing, but we have kept math discussion to an absolute minimum.

Most of all, you need to have an interest in using the power of TRS-80 Level II BASIC. We all have a tendency to become jaded as we are exposed to better and better small computer systems, but the BASIC operations provided in Level II **are** extremely powerful. This book will show you how to use them, whether your goal is accounting, games, inventory, programmed instruction, ham radio, self-education, or almost any other application.

Chapter 1 provides a review of Level II BASIC statements and commands. We'll discuss the four modes of Level II—command, execution, edit, and monitor—and the commands associated with each.

Chapter 2 discusses the types of variables provided in Level II BASIC, binary representation, and logical functions.

"Strings and Things" are discussed in Chapter 3. String formats, ASCII data, string operations, cursor control, and text editing are a few of the subjects presented.

Display of reports, columnating data, PRINT USING, line printer format, and other topics related to displaying or printing data in alphanumeric form are covered in Chapter 4.

Chapter 5 discusses the approaches to displaying graphics data on the TRS-80 video screen. We'll describe four techniques that range from display of graphs to high-speed animation.

"Tables, Chessboards, and the Fourth Dimension" (Chapter 6) discusses lists, tables, arrays, and other ways to organize data within BASIC programs.

One of the most critical areas in BASIC programming is that of searching and sorting data. Chapter 7 discusses the various methods that can be used to perform these functions.

Chapter 8 describes the built-in precision, numeric, random number, and trigonometric functions available in Level II BASIC.

Cassette tape operations are discussed in Chapter 9. Tape formats and methods for "blocking" data are described, along with file operations.

Chapter 10 discusses general problems in "debugging" BASIC programs, the error functions in BASIC, and error processing.

Level II BASIC has the ability to interface to assembly-language coding; Chapter 11 describes how you can do this to utilize the high speed of assembly language for operations that must be very efficient.

The last chapter describes the structure of Level II BASIC in regard to ROM subroutines, tokens, variable storage, and other "internals" that are not normally available to the BASIC programmer.

WILLIAM BARDEN, JR.

To Gaga and Steve

Contents

CHAPTER 4

CHAPTER 5

CHAPTER 6

CHAPTER 7

CHAPTER 8

CHAPTER 9

CHAPTER 1

A Good BASIC Foundation

This book is *applications* oriented. It is not meant to be a reference manual—the *Level II BASIC Reference Manual* is ideal for that. Here's what *Programming Techniques for Level II BASIC will* do for you:

- Provide further explanation of how Level II Commands operate in practical applications
- Show you various approaches to solving applications problems such as searching for data, high-speed graphics, and string manipulation
- Give some insight into the "internals" of Level II BASIC so you can speed up your programs and make them more efficient
- Reveal some useful programming tricks for Level II BASIC, such as assembly-language embedded in BASIC strings and repeat keys for keyboard input

The book is meant to be both a tutorial manual and a collection of modules; you can sit down and read it straight through (we are in no way assuming liability for optical damage for this feat) or you can leave it on the shelf and refer to it for various applications problems as they crop up.

All right . . . Do you have the TRS-80 plugged in and warmed up? Have you sandpapered your finger tips for optimizing your keyboard input?

In this chapter we'll present some BASIC basics. Feel free to skip the chapter if you're well-versed in aspects of Level II BASIC . . . such as program flow, statement types, variables, and the Editor. (We will, however, have an armed guard who will peri-

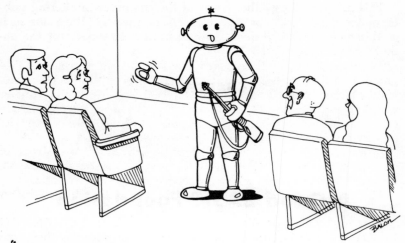

"ALL YOU BASIC READERS HAVE BEEN FOREWARNED... NOW I WANT TO HEAR SOME HIGH-LEVEL BASIC LANGUAGE... THIS IS A TEST!!"

odically be visiting our readers and testing them on the aspects of BASIC applications. Forewarned is forearmed. . . .)

I'd Like to Make a Statement

All BASIC programs are made up of BASIC lines that contain **statements**. A statement is simply a command that tells the TRS-80 to perform some action in the high-level BASIC language. A BASIC interpreter translates each BASIC statement into instructions that the Z-80 microprocessor in the TRS-80 can understand. One BASIC statement may generate hundreds of Z-80 **machine-language** instructions. Since the machine-language instructions operate in millionths of a second, each BASIC statement is interpreted by the BASIC interpreter very rapidly.

Every BASIC statement line has a statement number. These are assigned by the programmer (that's you) and may be any number from 0 to 65529. The remainder of the statement line has text that defines the BASIC statements in the statement line. A typical program is shown below. This program asks for your name and then prints a greeting and a question.

```
                                          COMMENTS
100 INPUT "NAME ";A$                      'input name
200 PRINT "HI ";A$                        'greeting
300 INPUT "ARE YOU ENJOYING THIS BOOK";B$ 'query
400 IF B$<>"YES" GOTO 300                 'go if not yes
500 PRINT "THAT'S FINE, ";A$              'proper response
```

This program shows the power of the computer in altering public opinion, as it will not accept no for an answer. (Programs such as this have been instrumental in creating survey data for the author's book promotions.)

There are five BASIC statement lines in this short program. Program execution starts at line number 100 where the BASIC statement INPUT "NAME ";A$ is encountered. The BASIC interpreter, which is a machine-language program in ROM (Read-Only-Memory) translates the "INPUT" statement into a display of NAME? and then waits for you to type in your name.

After you type your name and press "ENTER", the string of characters making up the name is assigned the **variable name** A$. Future references to A$ will refer to that string of characters.

The next statement line executed is line 200, which displays "HI " followed by your name (variable A$).

Next, line 300 causes the BASIC interpreter to print "ARE YOU ENJOYING THIS BOOK?" and wait for the answer. You then type "YES", "NO", "SOMEWHAT", or another string of characters followed by "ENTER". **This** string of characters is assigned the name B$.

Next, statement 400 tests the string of characters (variable B$) to see if it is "YES". If it is not (<>), the program **GO**es **TO** statement line 300 again where the question is again typed and waits for your response; if the answer is "YES", statement line 500 prints "THAT'S FINE, " followed by your name.

Program Flow

This short program illustrates some important aspects about BASIC (and many other programming languages). Programs flow from beginning to end with each statement line numbered in ascending order (200 follows 100, 300 follows 200, and so forth). Program flow may be altered by testing conditions within the program. The program tested for the "YES" response and altered the flow either back to statement line 300 or allowed the program to "drop through" to line 500. In a typical program, there may be dozens of these tests, and the program paths will be altered according to the results of the tests to create a type of tree structure shown in Figure 1-1.

Let's discuss the statement format again. The line numbers in the above program are in increments of 100. They could just as well have been any ascending sequence of numbers such as 101, 102, 222, 535, 65500 or 110, 120, 130, 140, 150. A common technique is to use increments of 10 (110, 120, 130, and so forth). Statement lines are then added between existing statement lines by entering

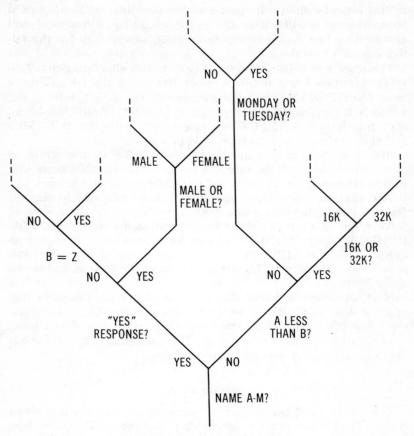

Figure 1-1. Program tree structure.

a new line with a number that is in sequence between the two existing statement numbers. If we want to add a new statement between 200 and 300, for example, we could type

```
250  PRINT "I'M A LIBRA"      'trs-80 must be an astrology nut
```

Statement line 250 would then appear between 200 and 300.

The remainder of the statement lines are the text of the statements. As you know from reading the Level II BASIC Reference Manual (*What? Guard* . . .), multiple statements may be put into one line. We could say

```
100  INPUT "NAME ";A$:PRINT "HI ";A$
```

in place of statement lines 100 and 200 above, for example. The colon (:) marks the beginning of a new statement. The advantages of this format are that it saves space in memory (data associated with the line number takes up four bytes of RAM memory) and it saves time (each new statement line is referenced by the preceding line and must be found in a list of statement lines). The disadvantage is that crowded lines make a program very difficult to read or follow. This code

```
1030 FL=1:GOSUB100:M$="BEACPSa":FORI=1TO7:IFIN$=MID$(M$,I,1)THENM=I
1035 I=7:NEXT:GOTO1037ELSENEXT:PRINTCHR$(8)::GOTO1030
1037 IF M>1ANDF=0ANDM<>7THENGOSUB9500:IFIN$="a"THEN1000
```

is almost incomprehensible to anyone not skilled in codes and ciphers. To avoid confusing you, we'll be using single statement lines in our code, with blanks and remarks. The code below shows this technique. The brackets indicate levels of **loops** (we'll cover this aspect of coding shortly); the single quote marks the beginning of a comment. Most of our lines will be commented to help you follow the program flow. **When you enter the programs, disregard remarks, since they will slow down the programs and create some differences between measured times in the book and actual times.** (The effect of using a quote for a comment is to actually create a new statement of the form :REM!) You can also leave out blanks.

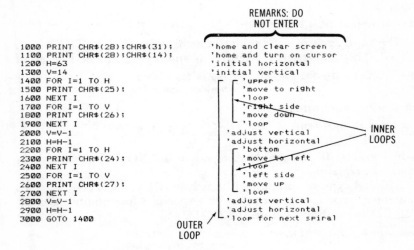

```
                                     REMARKS: DO
                                     NOT ENTER
1000  PRINT CHR$(28);CHR$(31);      'home and clear screen
1100  PRINT CHR$(28);CHR$(14);      'home and turn on cursor
1200  H=63                          'initial horizontal
1300  V=14                          'initial vertical
1400  FOR I=1 TO H                  'upper
1500  PRINT CHR$(25);               'move to right
1600  NEXT I                        'loop
1700  FOR I=1 TO V                  'right side
1800  PRINT CHR$(26);               'move down
1900  NEXT I                        'loop
2000  V=V-1                         'adjust vertical
2100  H=H-1                         'adjust horizontal
2200  FOR I=1 TO H                  'bottom
2300  PRINT CHR$(24);               'move to left
2400  NEXT I                        'loop
2500  FOR I=1 TO V                  'left side
2600  PRINT CHR$(27);               'move up
2700  NEXT I                        'loop
2800  V=V-1                         'adjust vertical
2900  H=H-1                         'adjust horizontal
3000  GOTO 1400                     'loop for next spiral
```

INNER LOOPS

OUTER LOOP

Pick a Statement, Any Statement

Now that we know the statement line format, the only other thing required to construct a program is to choose the right combinations of statement types. Not as easy as it sounds, is it? However, to help in this task we've attempted to categorize all of the Level II BASIC

13

statement types in one table called **Level II BASIC Statements and Commands** (Table 1-1). Let's go through the basic categories for review.

BRANCHes alter the sequence of a program by either a **conditional** or **unconditional** branch. GOTO 100 will **unconditionally** transfer control to statement 100. Conditional branches transfer control if the conditions are met; otherwise, the next statement line in sequence is interpreted.

There is one type of unconditional branch in Level II BASIC, the GOTO. It transfers control to the named statement number

```
100   GOTO 200        'unconditionally jump to line 200
```

There are four types of conditional branches. IF . . . THEN (line number) transfers control to a statement *if* the condition before the THEN is met.

```
100   IF A=1 THEN 200          'jump if A=1
200   IF A$="ED" THEN 300      'jump if A$="ED"
```

The first THEN above transfers control to statement line 200 if variable A is equal to 1. The second THEN transfers control to statement line 300 if the **string variable A$** is equal to "ED".

The second type of conditional branch is the IF . . . THEN action, such as

```
200   IF A=1.23 THEN PRINT "1.23"     'print value if 1.23
```

The third type of conditional branch is the IF . . . THEN . . . ELSE. This may transfer control to another statement line as in

```
100   IF A=0 THEN 200 ELSE 300     'jump to 200 if A=0
                                   'otherwise jump to 300
```

or it may cause other actions as in

```
100   IF A=0 THEN PRINT "0" ELSE PRINT     'print "0" or "NOT 0"
        "NOT 0"
```

which prints "0" if variable A equals 0 or "NOT 0" if variable A does not equal 0.

The last type of conditional branch is ON . . . GOTO. . . . This statement type transfers control to a specified line number according to the condition before the GOTO.

```
100   ON A GOTO 100,200,300     'jump to 100 if A=1, 200
                                'if A=2, 300 if A=3, next
                                'line if none
```

The above example will transfer control to line 100 if variable A is equal to 1, line 200 if A is 2, line 300 if A is 3, or will not branch if A is other than 1, 2, or 3.

Another type of statement that alters the flow of BASIC programs is the subroutine-type statement. A subroutine is a conveniently

Table 1-1. Level II BASIC Statements and Commands

LEVEL II BASIC STATEMENTS

Branches

GOTO n	Branch to line n
IF : THEN n	Conditional branch
IF : THEN . .	Conditional action
IF : THEN : ELSE . .	
ON : GOTO l,m,n, . . .	Computed GOTO

Cassette Tape

INPUT #-1, list	Read list
PRINT #-1, list	Write list

Commands

AUTO n,v	Auto line # at n with v increments
CLEAR k	Clear k bytes
CLOAD "string"	Load cassette file "string"
CLOAD? "string"	Check file "string"
CONT	Continue
CSAVE "string"	Write cassette file "string"
DELETE l-m	Delete lines l thru m
EDIT n	Invoke EDIT mode for line n
LIST l-m	List lines l thru m
NEW	Clear program
RUN n	Begin execution at line n
SYSTEM	Invoke MONITOR mode
TROFF	Turn off trace
TRON	Turn on trace

Data Tables and Arrays

DATA list	Establish data table
DIM name (dim1,dim2, . . .dimk)	Establish array
READ list	Read from data
RESTORE	Reset data pointer

Define Variable Type

DEFDBL letter range	Double precision
DEFINT letter range	Integer
DEFSNG letter range	Single precision
DEFSTR letter range	String

Error Functions

ERL	Get error line #
ERR/2 + 1	Get error code
ERROR code	Simulate error
ON ERROR GOTO n	Error trap
RESUME n	Resume execution

Functions

ABS(e)	Absolute value
ATN(e)	Arc tangent
CDBL(e)	Double precision
CINT(e)	Integer (small)
COS(e)	Cosine
CSNG(e)	Single precision

Table 1-1 cont. Level II BASIC Statements and Commands

Functions—cont.

EXP(e)	Natural exponential
FIX(e)	Truncation
INT(e)	Integer (large)
LOG(e)	Natural log
RANDOM	Reseed generator
RND(e)	Pseudo-random #
SGN(e)	Sign ($-1, 0, +1$)
SIN(e)	Sine
SQR(e)	Square root
TAN(e)	Tangent

Graphics

CLS	Clear screen
POINT(x,y)	Get -1 if on, 0 if off
POS(0)	Get cursor position
RESET(x,y)	Clear point
SET(x,y)	Set point

Input

INPUT list	Input list of items
INPUT "string";list	Print & input
INP(port)	Input value of port
INKEY\$	Get one-char string

Loop Control

FOR name = e TO e STEPe	Define loop
NEXT name	Continue and terminate loop

Machine Language

PEEK(address)	Get value at address
POKE address,v	Store v in address
USR(0)	Call subroutine
VARPTR(variable)	Get address of variable

Miscellaneous

END	End execution
LET e = e	Assignment
MEM	Get # of unused bytes
REM	Remark
STOP	Stop execution (break)
:	Multiple statements/ln

Operators

+,−,*,/	Arithmetic
↑	Exponentiation
<,>,<=,>=,<>,=	Relational and string
AND,OR,NOT	Logical
+	String concatenation

Output

OUT port,v	Output v to port

Printing

PRINT list	Print list of items
PRINT TAB(k). .	Tab
PRINT @. . .	Print at

16

Table 1-1 cont. Level II BASIC Statements and Commands

Printing—cont.

PRINT USING $,list	Formatted print
;	No tab
,	Tab

String

ASC("string")	Get ASCII code
CHR$(e)	Get one-character string
FRE($)	Get amount of space
LEN($)	Get length of string
LEFT$($,v)	Get first v characters
MID$($,p,v)	Get length v, start p
RIGHT$($,v)	Return last v characters
STR$(e)	Convert numeric to string
STRING$(v,"char")	Get string of v chr
VAL("string")	Convert string to num

Subroutines

GOSUB n	Subroutine call
ON e GOSUB l,m,n, . . .	Computed subroutine call
RETURN	Subroutine return

Variables

A-Z	
Ax-Zx where x is A-Z or 0-9	
$	String suffix
%	Integer suffix
!	Single-precision suffix
#	Double-precision suffix
D	Scientific notation suffix (double precision)
E	Scientific notation suffix (single precision)

Key:

:	Relational expression
n	Line number
. . .	Other action or n
k,v,w	Constant
"string"	Text string
l-m	Lines l-m
list	Item list
name	Var name
letter range	Initial letter from a-d,e
(x,y)	Graphics x=0 to 127, y=0 to 47 or e
$	String variable
"char"	1-chr str
e	Expression, variable, or constant
l,m,n, . . .	Line numbers

LEVEL II BASIC MONITOR MODE (SYSTEM)

SYSTEM	Invokes monitor mode
*? name	Loads object file "name"
*?/address	Execute at address (dec)
*?/	Execute at default addr

Table 1-1 cont. Level II BASIC Statements and Commands

LEVEL II BASIC EDIT MODE

EDIT n	Enter EDIT mode for line n
A	Cancel changes already made
nC	Change n characters
nD	Delete n characters to right
E	End edit, save changes
H	Delete remainder of line & I
I	Insert
nKc	Delete all characters till nth occurrence of character c
L	List remainder of line
Q	End edit and cancel all chngs
nSc	Search for nth occurrence of c
X	Display remainder, move end
n←	Backspace n spaces
shift↑	Escape from edit subcommand
nspace	Move n characters to right

LEVEL II BASIC ERROR CODES

BS	9	Subscript out of range
CN	17	Can't continue
DD	10	Redimensioned array
FC	5	Illegal function call
FD	22	Bad file data
ID	12	Illegal direct
L3	23	Disk BASIC
LS	15	String too long
MO	21	Missing operand
NF	1	NEXT without FOR
NR	18	No RESUME
OD	4	Out of data
OM	7	Out of memory
OS	14	Out of string space
OV	6	Overflow
RG	3	Return without GOSUB
RW	19	RESUME without error
SN	2	Syntax error
ST	16	String formula too complex
TM	13	Type mismatch
UE	20	Unprintable error
UL	8	Undefined line
/0	11	Division by zero

grouped set of from 1 to hundreds of BASIC statements. A **call** is made to a subroutine by a GOSUB statement, as in

```
100   A=1            'set A to 1
200   GOSUB 10000    'go to subroutine
300   B=A            'new value of A from subroutine
```

which transfers control to statement number 10000. The GOSUB's action is identical to a GOTO *except* that the *return* point of 300 is recorded by the BASIC interpreter. At the end of the subroutine a RETURN statement causes a return to the statement following the GOSUB. Let's see how this works. Suppose that we have a subroutine to skip 3 lines.

```
100     PRINT "LINE 1"      'now on line 1
200     GOSUB 1000          'skip 3 lines
300     PRINT "LINE 5"      'now on line 5

1000    PRINT               'skip line
1010    PRINT               'skip line
1020    PRINT               'skip line
1030    RETURN              'return after GOSUB
```

(The squiggly line in the above code does not mean the artist is nervous. It stands for other BASIC code that has been left out.) First statement 100 is executed. Next, the "GOSUB 1000" causes the four lines of subroutine 1000 to be executed. The last line returns control to statement 300.

Subroutines are generally used to save memory. If, for example, a program needs to skip three lines in a number of places, it would make sense to have the code for skipping three lines at one spot rather than dozens of places in the program.

The statement type ON . . . GOSUB operates exactly the same as the ON . . . GOTO except that control is returned to the statement following the one calling the subroutine.

Loops in BASIC allow a program to repeat operations, rather than coding the operations as a long repetitious list of BASIC statements. Suppose, for example, that it is necessary to fill the video display with asterisks. One way to do this would be to print an asterisk 1024 times, one for each video display position.

```
100     PRINT "*";      'print "*" at current
                        'location
200     PRINT "*";      'another
300     PRINT "*";      'and another and another . . .
        etc.
```

An easier way would be to create a loop of 1024 repetitions that would accomplish the action in a very short piece of BASIC code.

```
100     FOR I=1 TO 1024 STEP 1   ⌐'loop 1024 times
200     PRINT "*";                │'each time print "*"
300     NEXT I                   └'continue loop
```

The loop is initialized by the FOR . . . TO . . . STEP . . . statement which tells the BASIC interpreter to repeat the action from 1 to 1024 times using variable "I" to count the number of times through the loop. The NEXT statement marks the end of the loop and causes control to return to the FOR . . . TO . . . STEP statement for the next repetition of the loop. Within the loop between the FOR . . . TO . . . STEP and NEXT statements, loop action of virtually any type or range may occur. (If "STEP" is not used, an increment of 1 is assumed; we've included STEP in this example for clarity.)

BASIC programs use two types of operands—constants and variables. **Constants** are exactly that—set values that never change, for example, 3.14159 for pi and 999-99-9999 for a Social Security number. **Variables** *can* change and are simply names that the program sets aside for holding such things as index counts, subtotals, and character strings. Variable names are defined by one or two (or more) alphanumeric characters, the first of which must be alphabetic (AA, A1, Z2 are valid variable names). Variable types are related to the size and accuracy of the data that will be held in the variable.

Integer variables hold the number range −32768 to +32767 and are denoted by variables with a "%" suffix, as in A2% or A9%. **Single-precision variables** allow mixed numbers with seven decimal digits (1.234343×10^{30}) and a range of 10^{-38} to 10^{+38} (wide enough to accommodate subatomic to stellar measurements). Single-precision variables are denoted by a "!" suffix as in A2! or Z2!, or simply the variable name without any suffix. **Double-precision** variables extend the number of significant digits (all of the "accurate" digits) that may be held to 14 ($1.2343434343434 \times 10^{10}$) and are denoted by a "#" suffix as in A2# or A1#.

Variable types may also be defined by a set of DEFINE VARIABLE TYPE commands that define a range of alphabetic names that specify an appropriate variable type.

There are certain rules for the use of the proper variable types in BASIC programming. These are discussed in Chapter 2 along with the storage requirements for variable types and information relating to precision. Chapter 2 also discusses the binary numbering system and the logical operators AND, OR, and NOT.

STRING statements allow a program to handle strings of characters such as "TRS-80" or "1234 BASIC STREET, LEVEL II." You can manipulate portions of strings with the LEFT$, MID$, or RIGHT$ statements. With other statements, you can convert between strings and numeric data (ASC, CHR$, STR$, VAL). STRING$ generates a string composed of the same character repeated a specified number of times. LEN computes the length of a given string, while FRE$ finds the remaining space available in RAM for strings of all types. Strings are one of the most powerful features of Level II BASIC, and we'll cover them in Chapter 3.

PRINT statements cause an output of data to the video display.

PRINT LIST prints one or more items including variables or character strings.

```
100   PRINT "A EQUALS ";A      'print value of A
```

for example, prints "A EQUALSƄ" followed by the value of variable A. The PRINT TAB function allows a program to "tab over" to a specified column before printing another item.

```
100   PRINT TAB(50);A      'tab and print A
```

for example, moves the display **cursor** to tab position 50 and then prints the value of variable A.

PRINT @ prints at any given character position (out of 1024) on the video display.

```
100   PRINT @512, "THIS IS LINE 8"      'print at line 8
```

prints the message at line 8 of the 16 lines of the screen, starting at the extreme left.

PRINT USING $ is a somewhat complicated and powerful statement that allows you to format printing in regard to leading zeroes, decimal points, and a bunch of other goodies. We'll talk about it in detail along with the other PRINT statements in Chapter 4.

GRAPHICs statements are for those of you who want to display graphics data on the video display. Graphics means "non-character" data. The Display is divided up into a matrix of 128 by 48 elements, each one of which can be turned on (SET), off (RESET), or tested (POINT). Other graphics statements clear the entire screen (CLS) or find the current cursor position (POS). There are many techniques for displaying both character and graphics data on the video display, and we'll get to those in Chapter 5.

DATA TABLES and ARRAY-type statements define data lists (DATA) or arrays of data (DIM). Data lists are lists of constants that may be read sequentially using READ and RESTORE statements. Arrays are ordered lists of data in one or more dimensions that can be accessed in random fashion. Data lists and arrays are covered in Chapter 6. Searching and sorting data in lists and arrays, a very important topic, is covered in Chapter 7.

TRS-80 Level II BASIC includes a set of built-in FUNCTIONS. These functions are statements that perform specialized functions rather than general-purpose actions. Trigonometric functions in Level II BASIC include SIN (sine of an angle), COS (cosine of an angle), TAN (tangent of an angle), and ATN (arc tangent). Numerical and mathematical functions include ABS (absolute value), CDBL (double-precision), CINT (integer), CSNG (single-precision), EXP (natural exponential, or antilog), FIX (truncation), INT (whole number), LOG (natural log), SGN (sign of a number), and SQR (square root). RANDOM and RND allow generation of random numbers for simulation, games, and other applications. Functions and their use in various applications are described in Chapter 8.

BASIC allows cassette tape operations using two statement types, INPUT #-1 and PRINT #-1. INPUT #-1 inputs a single **record** of data for use in a program, while PRINT #-1 outputs a single record to cassette tape. Each record may contain a number of variables or constant data. Chapter 9 describes practical applications of cassette tape.

A number of statements and functions in BASIC allow for error checking in programs. Errors occur as a result of operator error, illegal operations (such as division by zero), or hardware faults. When errors do occur, Level II BASIC provides the mechanism to unravel the error and take corrective action.

ERROR lets you simulate an error condition to check out the error-handling portion of your BASIC code. ERL and ERR/2+1 return the line number at which the error occurred and the error code number, respectively. ON ERROR GOTO . . . sets up the line number of the error-processing routine, while RESUME . . . resumes program execution after an error occurs. Errors are treated in Chapter 10 (if you start making too many of them, maybe you should skip right to that chapter).

While most programmers want to program exclusively in the high-level BASIC language, there are provisions in the interpreter to interface BASIC programs with machine code. The advantages are execution speeds of up to several hundred times the BASIC interpretation speed and added versatility.

PEEK and POKE allow you to look at or change memory locations in ROM or RAM to change the action of the BASIC interpreter or just for your own enlightenment. A special USR call allows BASIC to pass control to an assembly-language routine. VARPTR finds the address of a BASIC variable for the purpose of passing **parameters** or for direct examination or modification.

Chapter 11 discusses how assembly language routines can be used in BASIC. Chapter 12 uses PEEKs, POKEs, and other statements to reveal some of the deep, dark secrets of the "internals" of the BASIC interpreter and the organization of memory.

Number Crunchies, the New Computer Energy Food

We've described most of the BASIC statements available in TRS-80 Level II BASIC, but we haven't really talked a great deal about "number-crunching" operators, the processing that BASIC can perform. Of course, BASIC can add ($+$), subtract ($-$), multiply ($*$), and divide ($/$) variables and constants, but the impres-

sive thing is that BASIC does it while automatically adjusting the number of digits and range of the number. You (the programmer) are relieved of the responsibility of remembering number ranges and decimal-point position (unlike early computers . . . may not sound like a big deal, but believe me, it is . . .). Exponentiation (↑) is also easily accomplished. Typical examples of sequences of processing operations are shown below

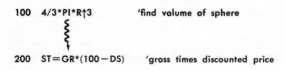

```
100   4/3*PI*R↑3        'find volume of sphere


200   ST=GR*(100−DS)    'gross times discounted price
```

We've glossed over another operator, the "=" or equivalence operator. An equals sign, of course, sets a variable on the left of the equation equal to an expression, constant, or variable on the right of the equation. The forgotten statement type "LET" may be used in conjunction with an equals sign as in

100   LET A=1.235

but the LET really only remains as an anachronism for compatibility with previous BASICs. There is really no reason to use it, and we will not in this book.

Not only can BASIC perform arithmetic and exponentiation functions, but it can also perform comparisons. Comparisons of less than ($<$), greater than ($>$), less than or equal ($<=$), greater than or equal ($>=$), equal ($=$), and not equal ($<>$) are easily performed on all types of variables including string variables. A unique **string concatenation** operator ($+$) allows two or more strings to be joined together.

100   A$="NOW IS"+" THE TIME"+" FOR . . ."

Command Performance

Up to this point in our monograph on Level II BASIC, we've been talking about BASIC program operation. As you know from the *Level II BASIC Reference Manual*, however, there are really four modes of operation—Command, Execution, Edit, and Monitor.

The Command mode is essentially a supervising mode that controls the loading of a BASIC program, some cursory editing, debugging, and listing.

A BASIC program on cassette tape is loaded by the command CLOAD and can be checked for accuracy with a program in RAM by the CLOAD? command. Another cassette-related command, CSAVE, saves the BASIC program in RAM memory on cassette tape.

The three other modes of operation are invoked by the three commands RUN (execute), EDIT (edit mode), and SYSTEM (monitor). RUN causes the current BASIC program in RAM to, well . . . , *run*, starting at the first line number, if none is specified, or at a specified line number. (RUN 10000 starts execution at line 10000.) Of course, you can stop any program that is running by pressing the BREAK key.

EDIT invokes the edit mode, which we'll discuss in a moment. (However, the Command mode allows some limited editing.) Lines can be deleted by typing the line number followed by ENTER. Lines can be modified simply by retyping the line number with the new contents. Lines can be inserted using the technique we spoke of in an earlier example—using a line number in the interval between two existing line numbers. Another delete command (strangely enough designated DELETE) deletes a range of lines (DELETE 10000-10999 deletes all program lines from 10000 to 10999). The last editing-type command is AUTO, which provides automatic line numbering, starting at a given line number and incrementing by a given value. (AUTO 100,20, for example, starts at line 100 and increments by 20 for each new line.)

The command CLEAR clears a given area for strings. Since the string area is at the top of RAM memory, the BASIC interpreter must know where the string area ends and everything else begins. (We'll discuss this topic in Chapter 3.)

The CONT command continues after a STOP statement. The STOP statement can be used to stop execution at any point, after which you can examine variables and other data to your heart's content (and then CONTinue on).

Two other commands related to debugging, TRON and TROFF (trace on and trace off), turn the trace capability on or off. The trace function displays each line number on the screen as it is executed, so you can see the program flow. The STOP statement and CONT, TRON, and TROFF commands are discussed in Chapter 10 in a general discussion of **debugging,** a nasty job of getting rid of 8-bit and other species of program bugs.

NEW is a doomsday command that wipes out the current BASIC program in RAM memory and initializes all BASIC interpreter parameters. (Use it carefully!)

The LIST command lists the current BASIC program on the screen; LLIST performs the same function on a system line printer.

The SYSTEM command invokes the monitor mode, used to load **machine-language** tapes into the system and to transfer control to machine-language routines that have been loaded. These topics are covered in Chapter 11.

Editors Are Not So Hard Bitten After All

The Edit Mode in Level II BASIC is invoked by the EDIT command. The Edit actions are well documented in the *Level II BASIC Reference Manual,* but we'll provide a recap here. Basically, the Edit Mode allows an edit of an individual line. The cursor may be positioned one position to the right on the line by typing "space" or *n* positions to the right by typing *n* space (20 "space" moves the cursor 20 positions to the right). The cursor may be moved to the left one position by typing "←" or *n* spaces by typing "n←."

Once the cursor is positioned to the proper point on the line, you can delete characters by typing "D" (or several characters can be deleted by typing "*n*D"). You can change characters by typing "C" followed by the character to be used in place of the changed character (or by "*n*C," followed by the string of characters to be used for the change). Characters can be inserted by typing "I" followed by the characters to be inserted.

The "E" character Ends the Edit and saves the changes made, while the Q command Quits the Edit and cancels all changes, leaving the line as it was before the Edit. The A command is similar to the Q except that it cancels All changes already made, but the system remains in the Edit mode. The L command Lists the entire line.

The H command Hacks off the line from the current cursor position and sets the insert mode; now you can insert additional characters. The X command is similar, but positions the cursor to the end of the line for the insert.

The K command Kills all characters up to a specified character (Kc) or kills all characters up to the nth occurrence of a specified character nKc. This last command would kill the "NOWISTHE" portion of "NOWISTHETIMEFORALLGOODPROGRAMMERS" with a command of "2KT."

The S command enables you to Search for a given character (Sc) or the nth occurrence of the character. A command of "2ST," for example, would position the cursor as follows:

NOW IS THE TIME FOR ALL GOOD PROGRAMMERS

Have you memorized the list? (*Guard . . . find out the address of that reader in Des Moines . . .*) All of this information can be gleaned from the *Level II BASIC Reference Manual,* but we've presented it here as a review. We'll be using a lot of examples in the chapters to follow. You'll be able to learn the use of some of the more exotic statements by practical example, so don't be too dismayed if you don't understand all of the commands or their applications. That's what we're here for.

CHAPTER 2

To Be Precise . . .

We'll be considering the subjects of binary numbers, BASIC variables, number ranges, and precision in this chapter. These are not as stuffy as they sound and are easier to understand than you might think. Don't let the subjects scare you off . . . (*Guard! Stop that reader from turning the page* . . .) You will be amply rewarded with BASIC programs that are faster and use up less memory, and in the bargain you may get to see some of the internal workings of BASIC.

A Long Time Ago in a Computer System Far, Far Away

Let's digress for a moment and talk about the Zzarth race of the Sirius star system. As we all know, Zzarthians have 8 hands with one finger on each hand. (Baseball umpires there have a heck of a time with signals. . . .) Back in Zzarthian antiquity when the frog-like Zzarthian speech was first developing, some of the more astute members of the tribe used fingers to denote the number of znabbeasts that were seen in the hunt. One finger meant one znabbeast, two meant two, and so forth. The limit of this was, of course, 8 znabbeasts, represented by eight arms with 8 fingers held high as shown in Figure 2-1.

Since the number of znabbeasts in a qwany varied from several to well over a hundred, this description left something to be desired. One day, however, a *strange* monolith appeared with the markings "A registered trademark of TANDY Corporation" in the lower-right hand corner. . . . The following day, one of the younger Zzarthians (by the name of Ed, if you must know) approached the elders' council and declared, "*I've just invented a new system to report on*

27

"ALL YOU READERS WHO TURNED THE PAGE ARE OUT !!"

znabbeasts." Naturally reluctant, as are all elders when approached by radicals, the elders soon became excited as the advantages of this system became apparent.

"Watch," said Ed. *"One znabbeast is represented by arm 0 with one finger held out. Two znabbeasts by arm 1 with its finger. Three by arm 1 and arm 0. Four by arm 2 only. Five by arm 2 and arm 0."*

"Wait!" cried the elders in dismay. *"Write it up and make some photocopies for us so we'll be able to understand it a little better."*

Table 2-1 is what Ed created.

The Zzarthian system became known as the binary system after the chief, Bin Ary, claimed credit for it, as elders are wont to do.

Table 2-1. Binary Representation

			Arm							
7	6	5	4	3	2	1	0			
0	0	0	0	0	0	0	0	=	0	Znabbeasts
0	0	0	0	0	0	0	1	=	1	Znabbeast
0	0	0	0	0	0	1	0	=	2	Znabbeasts
0	0	0	0	0	0	1	1	=	3	Znabbeasts
0	0	0	0	0	1	0	0	=	4	Znabbeasts
0	0	0	0	0	1	0	1	=	5	Znabbeasts
0	0	0	0	0	1	1	0	=	6	Znabbeasts
0	0	0	0	0	1	1	1	=	7	Znabbeasts
0	0	0	0	1	0	0	0	=	8	Znabbeasts
0	0	0	0	1	0	0	1	=	9	Znabbeasts
0	0	0	0	1	0	1	0	=	10	Znabbeasts
0	0	0	0	1	0	1	1	=	11	Znabbeasts
0	0	0	0	1	1	0	0	=	12	Znabbeasts
0	0	0	0	1	1	0	1	=	13	Znabbeasts
0	0	0	0	1	1	1	0	=	14	Znabbeasts
0	0	0	0	1	1	1	1	=	15	Znabbeasts
0	0	0	1	0	0	0	0	=	16	Znabbeasts
0	0	0	1	0	0	0	1	=	17	Znabbeasts
0	0	0	1	0	0	1	0	=	18	Znabbeasts
0	0	0	1	0	0	1	1	=	19	Znabbeasts
0	0	1	0	0	0	0	1	=	33	Znabbeasts
0	1	0	0	0	1	0	1	=	69	Znabbeasts
1	0	0	0	1	1	1	1	=	143	Znabbeasts
1	1	1	1	1	1	1	1	=	255	Znabbeasts

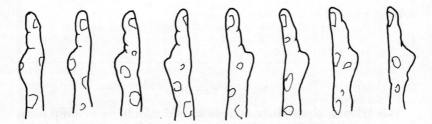

Figure 2-1. Zzarthian binary representation.

It is exactly equivalent to the system used in digital computers to-day. Each collection of 8 arms is called a **byte.** Each arm has one finger, which is either a 1 (up) or 0 (down). Each arm in effect represents a power of two just as our decimal system represents a power of ten.

The largest number that can be held in a byte is 11111111, or $128 + 64 + 32 + 16 + 8 + 4 + 2 + 1 = 255$. The smallest number is 00000000, or 0. Any number from 0 through 255 can be represented by zeros and ones in the appropriate positions.

This scheme of **positional notation** can be extended to two or more bytes. When this is done for two bytes, much larger numbers can be represented, as shown in Table 2-2. Note that the 15th **bit,** or **binary** digit, is a 0, so that in two bytes we have only 15 bits (15–0) instead of 16. We'll see why later.

Table 2-2. Two-Byte Binary Representation

Binary																Decimal
15	14	13	12	11	10	9	8	7	6	5	4	3	2	1	0	
0	0	0	0	0	0	0	0	0	0	0	0	0	0	0	0	0
0	0	0	0	0	0	0	0	0	0	0	0	0	0	0	1	1
0	0	0	0	0	0	0	1	0	0	0	0	0	0	0	0	256
0	0	0	0	0	0	0	1	0	0	0	0	0	0	0	1	257
0	0	1	0	0	0	0	0	0	0	0	0	0	0	0	0	8192
0	1	1	0	0	0	0	0	0	0	0	0	0	0	0	0	24576
0	1	1	0	0	0	0	0	0	0	0	0	0	0	0	1	24577
0	1	1	1	1	0	1	0	1	0	1	1	1	0	1	1	31419
0	1	1	1	1	1	1	1	1	1	1	1	1	1	1	1	32767

Integer Variables

This scheme of two-byte storage should enable us to store numbers from 0 (00000000/00000000) through $16,384 + 8192 + 4096 + 2048 + 1024 + 512 + 256 + 128 + 64 + 32 + 16 + 8 + 4 + 2 + 1 =$

32,767 (01111111/11111111). Let's look at the two-byte storage format in BASIC. It's called **integer** format and is defined by a variable with a % sign after it, such as A%, AA%, or Z1%.

First of all, let's verify that we can indeed store 0 through 32,767. The program below stores the input value but gives an OV (overflow) error for values greater than 32,767.

```
100  INPUT A%      'input an integer value
200  GOTO 100      'loop on input
```

By adding a VARPTR statement and some PEEK statements, we can see where in RAM memory the A% variable is stored and what it looks like. The VARPTR returns the RAM address where A% is stored. RAM, as you know, occupies from 16,384 to 32,767 (16K System), 49,150 (32K System), or 65,535 (48K System), each location containing one byte (8-arms worth) of data. Each RAM location is "addressed" by reference to an **address value** of 16,384 through 32,767 (16K), 49,150 (32K), or 65,535 (48K). PEEK retrieves the value of each byte, which is 0–255.

```
100  INPUT A%           'get integer variable
200  B=VARPTR(A%)       'find address
300  PRINT B            'print it
400  PRINT PEEK(B)      'print ls byte
500  PRINT PEEK(B+1)    'print ms byte
600  GOTO 100           'loop for next
```

The first number printed in this program is the address of A%. The next two numbers printed are the **contents** of the two bytes that make up the variable. Try inputs from 0-32767 (or above) and see what happens.

If you tried values for A% between 0 and 255, you saw that the **first byte** (ls, or least significant byte) was used to store the value, and the second was zero. For example, a value of 10 results in

10 (first byte)
0 (second byte)

and a value of 255 results in

255 (first byte)
0 (second byte)

If you tried values larger than 255, you saw that **both the second and first** bytes were used. For example, a value of 257 results in

1 (first byte)
1 (second byte)

and a value of 1000 results in

232 (first byte)
3 (second byte)

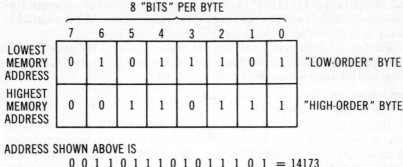

8 "BITS" PER BYTE

	7	6	5	4	3	2	1	0	
LOWEST MEMORY ADDRESS	0	1	0	1	1	1	0	1	"LOW-ORDER" BYTE
HIGHEST MEMORY ADDRESS	0	0	1	1	0	1	1	1	"HIGH-ORDER" BYTE

ADDRESS SHOWN ABOVE IS

0 0 1 1 0 1 1 1 0 1 0 1 1 1 0 1 = 14173

HIGH-ORDER   LOW-ORDER
BYTE   BYTE

Figure 2-2. Two-byte storage.

The first byte is the **low-order** byte, while the second byte is the **high-order** byte. This arrangement is true for all byte storage in the TRS-80 and is shown in Figure 2-2 for various values. We can see this better if we use some additional code to recompute the input value from the two bytes at which we've PEEKed.

```
1000 INPUT A%            'get integer variable
1100 B=VARPTR(A%)        'find address
1200 PRINT B             'print it
1300 PRINT PEEK(B)       'print ls byte
1400 PRINT PEEK(B+1)     'print ms byte
1500 C=PEEK(B+1)*256+PEEK(B)  'recompute input value
1600 PRINT C             'and print it
1700 GOTO 1000           'loop for next
```

The 1500 statement verifies that the two bytes do make up the input value by multiplying the high-order byte by 256 and adding the low-order byte, essentially converting from two 8-bit bytes into a 16-bit binary value.

As an example, suppose that we entered A% = 1000. The low-order byte (PEEK (B)) is 232, and the high-order byte (PEEK (B+1)) is 3. Multiplying 3 by 256 is 768, plus 232 equals 1000.

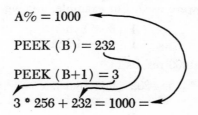

A% = 1000

PEEK (B) = 232

PEEK (B+1) = 3

3 * 256 + 232 = 1000 =

What about that 15th bit? The 15th bit is used for a **sign bit.**
Not only can we store 0 to +32767 in two bytes, but we can store
−1 to −32768. Run the program above with negative input values
and let's see what we get.

This time we displayed mysterious data. Inputting −111, for example, displays

```
?−111
145
255
65425
```

The first two values are the contents of the two bytes for variable
A%, but the next value is certainly not −111. The answer here is
that negative numbers are stored in a form called **two's complement** in binary. In this form, negative numbers are stored by finding the positive equivalent in binary and then changing all zero
bits to one, all one bits to zero, and adding one. This simplifies
hardware design and is used in almost all digital computers. To
find the equivalent negative number for A%, check the value $C =$
$PEEK(B+1) * 256 + PEEK(B)$. If it is over 32767, perform the
computation $65536 − C$, and you will have the equivalent negative
number stored.

```
1600  IF C>32767 THEN PRINT "−";65536−C ELSE PRINT C
```

The integer format is good for expressing the range of numbers
from −32768 through 0 to +32767. It always requires two bytes
and will never approximate the number, but will hold the precise
number. If you attempt to use an integer format with a result
greater than +32767 or less than −32768, an OV (overflow) error
will result, since the BASIC interpreter does not know how to
handle an integer number that requires more than two bytes.

Murphy's Rule Number 32K

At this point, we had better mention another rule which is related to the computation of negative numbers. When PEEKs and
POKES are used in this book, they will work fine if the address
argument is 32767 or less. For example,

```
100  FOR I=0 to 32767    'peek at memory loop
200  PRINT PEEK (I)      'i see you
300  NEXT I              'loop here
```

will print out all address locations from 0 through 32767. However,
if the address is 32768 or more, the value used in the PEEK or

POKE must be (ADDRESS−65536). The reason for this is that PEEK and POKE look for an integer limit of +32767. Numbers over that limit are treated as invalid numbers. PEEK and POKE must therefore be fooled into accepting addresses in the range of 32768–65535. An example of this is

```
100  FOR I=0 TO 65535      'peek at memory loop
200  IF I< 32768 PRINT PEEK(I) ELSE PRINT PEEK (I−65536)
300  NEXT I                'loop here
```

Most of the examples in this book use the lower 32K for POKE-ing values or in PEEKing at data. However, if an address in the upper 32K is involved, an OV error will result unless the computation above is performed.

The % suffix specifies integer format, but this format may also be specified by a define variable type statement such as

```
100  DEFINT A-B      'all variables A-B will be integer
```

The above example makes all variables in the range A through B automatic integer variables.

Single-Precision Variables

Obviously, we would have some difficulty in dealing only with integer variables. It would not even allow reasonable calculations on checking accounts (although the ability to express negative numbers might conceivably help in dealing with my checking account). One of the most valuable features of BASIC is that it allows us to operate with very large and very small numbers automatically, unlike machine language, the "Tiny" languages, or other less powerful languages. We are able to do this with single-precision and double-precision numbers.

Let's use the following code to define the number ranges and precision for this type of number. By the way, this format is the "default" format for variables in the system, although a suffix of "!" may also be used.

```
2000  INPUT A       'input single-precision
2100  A=A/2      ⌈ 'find smaller values
2200  PRINT A      'print
2300  GOTO 2100  ⌊ 'loop for next
```

In inputting various values of A, we can see that the smallest number that can be held in this format is 1.XXXE-38 (use "SHIFT@" to stop the display at any time). By changing statement 2100 to A = A*2, we see also that the largest number is about 5.XXXE+38. (The E format simply means that the following number is a power of 10. E−38 means 10^{-38}, and E+38 means 10^{38}.)

The complete **range** of single-precision variables, then, is about 76 powers of 10, providing the capability to express subatomic distances to the number of atoms in the universe!

The precision, however, is a different story. This format allows only seven decimal digits of precision. (BASIC will print only six of these.) Digits beyond that range are rounded off. When we multiply 123456 by 33 we should get 4,074,048, but actually get 4,074,050. Once again, the reason for this is limitations on variable storage. Single-precision variables take up four bytes of storage in RAM. About 3 bytes of that is devoted to the significant-digit part, or **mantissa**, of the number representation, while one byte is devoted to the **exponent**, as shown in Figure 2-3. The 3-byte integer provides 24 bits (one bit is always 1) to allow a range of numbers

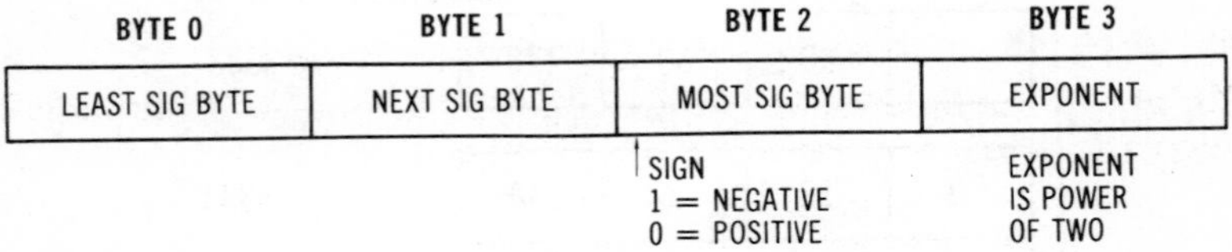

BYTE 0	BYTE 1	BYTE 2	BYTE 3
LEAST SIG BYTE	NEXT SIG BYTE	MOST SIG BYTE	EXPONENT

SIGN
1 = NEGATIVE
0 = POSITIVE

EXPONENT
IS POWER
OF TWO

Figure 2-3. Single-precision storage.

from about $-16,777,216$ to $+16,777,215$ to be expressed without loss of digits. (The exponent is a power of two allowing about 2^{-128} to 2^{+127} to be handled, or roughly 10^{-37} to 10^{+37}.) Up to a certain point, a number is held as straight binary in the 24 bits, while beyond this point the integer holds only the most significant portion of the number.

You may (if you have masochistic tendencies) care to further explore the wonderful world of floating-point formats by using the VARPTR command to retrieve and display the storage of data in a single-precision variable, as shown below (see Figure 2-4).

```
3000 INPUT A                            'input single-precision
3100 B=VARPTR(A)                        'find location
3200 PRINT PEEK(B),PEEK(B+1),           'print first 2 bytes
3300 PRINT PEEK(B+2),PEEK(B+3)          'print next 2 bytes
3400 GOTO 3000                          'loop for next
```

Double or Nothing

Because seven decimal digits are not *quite* precision enough for some calculations (imagine trying to compute federal budgets in six figures), Level II BASIC provides for a double-precision format. As the astute reader may have surmised, double-precision doubles (or more than doubles) the amount of precision available in BASIC. As a matter of fact, it allows for *17 significant deci-*

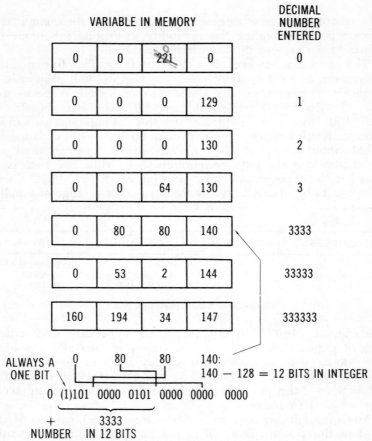

Figure 2-4. Single-precision storage examples.

mal digits (now we're finally approaching the realm of some of the smaller government agencies). Only 16 digits will ever be PRINTed.

To obtain this precision, the integer portion of the floating point variable is increased in size from 3 bytes (24 bits) to 7 bytes, as shown in Figure 2-5. Seven bytes allow 56 bits of precision, or approximately to 36,000,000,000,000,000. Note that the range of the number expressed is still limited by the exponent portion of the variable.

Double-precision variables are represented by a # suffix, as in "A#" or "Z2#". When the double precision is used in scientific notation, a "D" replaces the "E" for the exponent, as, for example, in "1.23456789D+18".

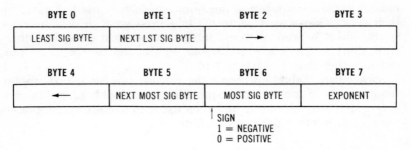

Figure 2-5. Double-precision storage.

As in the case of integers and single-precision variables, double-precision variables may be defined by a DEFDBL statement that specifies a variable range.

```
100   DEFDBL A-B      'all variables A-B will be double precision
```

specifies that all variables starting with A or B will be double-precision variables.

If you're still harboring latent masochistic tendencies (evidenced by listening to CSAVE tapes on your 150-watt stereo), you can investigate double-precision formats and storage by

```
100 INPUT A#             ┌'input double-precision
200 B=VARPTR(A#)         │'find location
300 FOR I=0 TO 7         │  ┌'set 8 time loop
400 PRINT PEEK(B+I),     │  │'print byte
500 NEXT                 │  └'loop to next print
600 GOTO 100             └'loop back to nxt input
```

When should integers be used? When should single-precision variables be used? And when should double-precision variables be used? Fortunately, the great French mathematician Blaise Pascal gave us the answer in

A Treatise on the Use of Numbers Great and Small
With Special Reference to the TRS-80

In the old days of computers, three years ago, memory was very dear. Today, one can buy a bit of memory (pun intended) for a penny or so a bit. The point is that even a parsimonious (Editor's note: *Stay away from polysyllabic words!*) programmer can afford to use single-precision (default) variables and not be very concerned about memory requirements. Double-precision can be used when required, but shouldn't be used for all variables, because, in addition to memory storage requirements, the computation speed is less efficient. The exception to the use of single-precision over integer variables is when an **array** of variables is used. Arrays, by their very nature (see Chapter 6) take up a great deal of memory space, and it is prudent to use integer variables if possible. Otherwise, don't be too concerned about widespread use of single-precision, rather than integer variables.

As a recap, Table 2-3 shows the ranges, precision, and storage requirements of integer, single-precision, and double-precision variables. Memorize this table and then eat it to avoid revealing internal secrets to other personal-computer users.

Table 2-3. Variable Ranges, Precision, and Storage

Variable Type	Range	Precision	Storage
Integer	-32768 to $+32767$	5 integer decimal digits	2 bytes
Single-precision	About 1×10^{38} to 1×10^{-38}	7 decimal digits	4 bytes
Double-precision	About 1×10^{38} to 1×10^{-38}	17 decimal digits	8 bytes

Once More Unto the Breach

I'll bet you thought we were done with discussions of binary number systems. It's our unpleasant duty to inform you that we'll have to continue the discussion (*Guard! Watch that BASIC programmer . . .*). Actually, the commands we're going to discuss here are very simple and should pose no problem in understanding. What's more, they'll enable you to manipulate data down to the bit level, which can be a very powerful capability and one that many BASIC interpreters do not provide. The three commands we'll be discussing in this section are AND, OR, and NOT.

These commands are called **logical** operators. They are used to handle logical expressions. What are logical expressions? Generally, logical expressions can be equated to true and false. True and false, of course, can be translated into a binary 1 and 0, respectively. Suppose we write a logical expression for a visit to your mother-in-law's house. We will call the end result of the expression "VISIT". If VISIT = 1, we will go on the journey; if VISIT = 0, we will not. The expression I usually work with is:

```
VISIT =  (GAS IN CAR) AND (NOT WEEKDAY) AND (NOT BEHIND
         IN WRITING BOOKS) AND (NOT TOO HOT) AND (FEELING
         OK) AND (HAVE ENOUGH MONEY)
```

This expression says that if we have gas AND if it is not a weekday AND so forth . . . then we can perform the visit. By equating each of these expressions to a 1 (true) or 0 (false), then we see that

1 = 1 AND 1 AND 1 AND 1 AND 1 AND 1

VISIT will equal 1 (true) if and only if *all* of the conditions are true.

Another logical expression might be one relating to one called OVERDRAWN. OVERDRAWN is true (1) or false (0) as follows:

OVERDRAWN = (WIFE MAKES CHECKING ACCT ERROR) OR (HUSBAND MAKES
            CHECKING ACCT ERROR) OR (UNEXPECTED BILL) OR (EXPECTED BILL)

As we can see, OVERDRAWN is almost always true (1) because one OR the other condition is probably true.

A third type of logical expression that will illustrate logical operators is

SOLVENT = NOT (OVERDRAWN)

This is easy to understand.

There is nothing magical, therefore, about logical operators or expressions. They were developed by Plato, George Boole (a 19th century mathematician), Claude Shannon (a 20th century research engineer), and others. They are really an attempt to define real-world conditions in convenient symbolic form.

The AND function, as we have seen, states that a result condition is true if one condition AND another (AND others) are true. If either of the conditions is false, the result condition is false. If we are working with two conditions, we can diagram this as:

1ST CONDITION	0	0	1	1
2ND CONDITION	0	1	0	1
RESULT	0	0	0	1

The OR function states that a result condition is true if either one OR another (OR others) is true. We can state this as:

1ST CONDITION	0	0	1	1
2ND CONDITION	0	1	0	1
RESULT	0	1	1	1

The NOT function states that the result condition is true if the input condition is false and false if the input condition is true

INPUT CONDITION	0	1
RESULT	1	0

For the most part, we spend a great deal of time in BASIC programs writing down logical conditions, most of which are embedded in IF statements

```
110 CLS                                          'clear screen
120 INPUT "VALUE 1=";A                           'input value 1
130 IF A>=0 AND A<256 GOTO 140 ELSE GOTO 120
140 INPUT "VALUE 2=";B                           'input value 2
150 IF B>=0 AND A<256 GOTO 160 ELSE GOTO 140
160 INPUT "AND, OR, OR NOT=";A$                  'input type
170 IF A$<>"AND" AND A$<>"OR" AND A$<>"NOT" GOTO 160
180 PRINT "VALUE 1 IN DECIMAL IS ";A;"IN BINARY IS";
200 C=A                                          'for subroutine
210 GOSUB 10000                                  'convert to binary
220 PRINT "VALUE 2 IN DECIMAL IS ";B;"IN BINARY IS";
230 C=B                                          'for subroutine
240 GOSUB 10000                                  'convert to binary
260 IF A$="AND" THEN C=A AND B                   'find and result
263 IF A$="OR" THEN C=A OR B                     'find or result
265 IF A$="NOT" THEN C=NOT B                     'find not result
270 PRINT "RESULT  IN DECIMAL IS ";C;"IN BINARY IS";
280 GOSUB 10000                                  'convert to binary
290 IF INKEY$="" GOTO 290 ELSE GOTO 110
10000 B0=C-INT(C/2)*2                            'find bit 0
10010 C=INT(C/2)                                 'next quotient
10020 B1=C-INT(C/2)*2
10030 C=INT(C/2)
10040 B2=C-INT(C/2)*2
10050 C=INT(C/2)
10060 B3=C-INT(C/2)*2
10070 C=INT(C/2)
10080 B4=C-INT(C/2)*2
10090 C=INT(C/2)
10100 B5=C-INT(C/2)*2
10110 C=INT(C/2)
10120 B6=C-INT(C/2)*2
10130 C=INT(C/2)
10140 B7=C-INT(C/2)*2
10150 PRINT B7;B6;B5;B4;B3;B2;B1;B0              'print binary
10160 RETURN                                     'return to calling prog
```

Figure 2-6. Binary exerciser program.

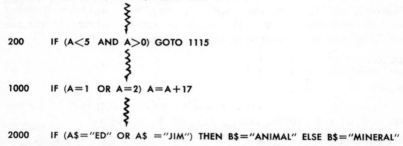

```
100     IF (A=0 AND B=0) GOTO 1000

200     IF (A<5 AND A>0) GOTO 1115

1000    IF (A=1 OR A=2) A=A+17

2000    IF (A$="ED" OR A$ ="JIM") THEN B$="ANIMAL" ELSE B$="MINERAL"
```

However, logical operators can also be used with binary values. Let's see how this works by constructing a binary exercise program. This program will illustrate binary operations by allowing you to input two 8-bit values. The values will be displayed in decimal and binary, and then you can specify an AND, OR, or NOT function to observe how the binary functions work. See Figure 2-6.

The key to this program is the decimal-to-binary conversion subroutine at 10000. It implements a conversion from decimal to binary called "divide and save remainders." To see how this works, let's convert a decimal number to binary on paper, as shown in Figure

2-7. We divide the decimal number by 2 and save remainders. The remainders in reverse order are the binary number. This method *always* works for any size of decimal number, although it does get tedious for numbers over 3 trillion. In the program, B0 is the first remainder, B1 the next, up to B7 for the last. The "INT" function finds the integer (quotient without remainder) of the divide. Multiplying the quotient by two and subtracting it from the current number gives the remainder. At the end of the subroutine, the remainders are printed in reverse order.

This program could have been made much shorter by using arrays and other clever coding, but the important thing here is to see how the binary operators work. Entering VALUE 1 = 255 and VALUE 2 = 15, and specifying an "AND", for example, results in an AND of 255 and 15. The value of 255 in binary is

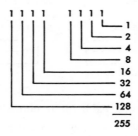

while the value of 15 is

When these two values are ANDed, each **bit position** of the eight is ANDed separately and does not affect any other bit position.

1	1	1	1	1	1	1	1
AND 0	AND 0	AND 0	AND 0	AND 1	AND 1	AND 1	AND 1
0	0	0	0	1	1	1	1

We know from the rules of logical operators that 0 AND 0 is 0, 1 AND 0 is 0, 0 AND 1 is 0, and 1 AND 1 is 1, and the result reflects this.

As another example, let's OR 170 and 112. Expressed in binary, these values are

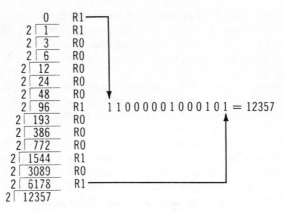

Figure 2-7. Pencil-and-paper decimal-to-binary conversion.

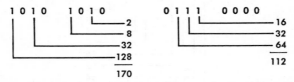

As in the case of ANDing, each bit is considered separately

1	0	1	0	1	0	1	0
OR 0	OR 1	OR 1	OR 1	OR 0	OR 0	OR 0	OR 0
1	1	1	1	1	0	1	0

We know from the rules of ORing that 0 OR 0 is 0, 1 OR 0 is 1, 0 OR 1 is 1, and 1 OR 1 is 1, and this is shown in the result.

The third example is the NOT. The NOT in this program takes the NOT function of VALUE B as the result. If the input value is 170, then the NOT looks at each bit and takes the **complement**. This is just a two-dollar word for the opposite state. If a bit is a 0, then the result bit is a 1. If a bit is a 1, then the result bit is a 0.

1	0	1	0	1	0	1	0
NOT	NOT	NOT	NOT	NOT	NOT	NOT	NOT
0	1	0	1	0	1	0	1

At this point, you're probably saying, *"Fine, we AND 255 and 15 and get 15, we OR 170 and 112 and get 250, and we NOT 170 and get 85—what's the practical application?"* (Aha . . . you *were* saying that!) The AND, OR, and NOT are not used as frequently as common BASIC operators, but they can be very valuable at times.

The AND and OR are used primarily to do **bit manipulation** of individual bits in RAM, turning specified bits on or off. We'll see some examples of applications later in the book (We promise!).

CHAPTER 3

Strings and Things

(Subtitle: Never the Twine Shall Meet)

In the last chapter we talked about the use and storage of numeric variables. In this chapter, we'll talk about another type of variable, the string variable. String variables are simply strings of alphabetic, numeric, and special characters that usually represent meaningful text data. Since there are operations that occur again and again in text processing, such as searching for given characters (such as a name) or comparing one string with another, Level II BASIC has a number of string functions built into it to make the job of processing string data easier. This chapter will describe what string variables are, how they are stored, and what types of operations can be done with the built-in BASIC string commands.

ASCII Strings

In general, all strings are made up of ASCII characters. At least that was the original intent of strings, to provide a means to group keyboard or displayable characters, such as "YES", "NO", "12345P", "TRS-80", or "*****", under a single variable name. By clever (some would say devious) means, the string definition can also include non-alphabetic, numeric, or special characters. (We'll look at those a little bit later in the chapter.)

Legitimate names for string variables include any names that would ordinarily be used for any variables, suffixed by a "$". An alternate way to define a range of string variables is by a DEFSTR command which defines all variables in the given range to be strings. DEFSTR A-B would automatically define variables such as AA, AB, and BB as string variables, and they would be synonymous with AA$, AB$, and BB$.

The first question that comes to mind is "What is an ASCII character?" ASCII stands for American Standard Code for Information Interchange. A "standards" society has established certain standards for computers. It's certainly desirable to have all computers speaking the same language. In fact, many computers *do* speak the same language when it comes to common printable characters. That language is **ASCII codes.**

ASCII is basically a seven-bit code. As we know from our comprehensive and diligent study of Chapter 2 (*Guard! Arrest that reader* . . .), seven bits of data can define 128 different codes, from 000 0000 to 111 1111. In ASCII, those 128 codes are used to represent alphabetic, numeric, and special characters, and **control codes,** as shown in Table 3-1. The control-codes portion of ASCII from 0 to 31 are somewhat non-standard from computer to computer. The 15-code used in the TRS-80 to turn off the cursor, for example, is used in another computer to shift to upper case.

The displayable portions of the ASCII codes used on the TRS-80 are from code 32 through 127, as shown in the table. These are basically grouped into special characters (space) through (/), numerics (0–9), special characters (:) through (@), upper case (A–Z), cursor controls (↑ through __), and lower case (a–z and others). The standard TRS-80 has no provision for displaying lower-case characters. Lower-case characters, however, are still usable when output to a TRS-80 system printer such as the Quick Printer I or II. They simply can't be stored in the video display memory.

The program shown below uses the INKEY$ function to get a one-character string from the keyboard and then display the key pressed in displayable form and its ASCII equivalent. Note that

7 bit code   *8th bit for graphic codes + special characters*

Table 3-1. ASCII Codes

Code	Character	Code	Character	Code	Character	Code	Character
0		32	Space	64	@	96	@
1		33	!	65	A	97	a
2		34	"	66	B	98	b
3		35	#	67	C	99	c
4		36	$	68	D	100	d
5		37	%	69	E	101	e
6		38	&	70	F	102	f
7		39	'	71	G	103	g
8	Backspace/erase	40	(	72	H	104	h
9		41	)	73	I	105	i
10	Carriage return	42	*	74	J	106	j
11	Carriage return	43	+	75	K	107	k
12	Carriage return	44	,	76	L	108	l
13	Carriage return	45	–	77	M	109	m
14	Cursor on	46	.	78	N	110	n
15	Cursor off	47	/	79	O	111	o
16		48	0	80	P	112	p
17		49	1	81	Q	113	q
18		50	2	82	R	114	r
19		51	3	83	S	115	s
20		52	4	84	T	116	t
21		53	5	85	U	117	u
22		54	6	86	V	118	v
23	32 character mode	55	7	87	W	119	w
24	←cursor	56	8	88	X	120	x
25	→cursor	57	9	89	Y	121	y
26	↓cursor	58	:	90	Z	122	z
27	↑cursor	59	;	91	↑or[	123	
28	Home cursor	60	<	92	↓or]	124	
29	Cursor to line start	61	=	93	←	125	
30	Erase to end of line	62	>	94	→	126	
31	Clear to end of frame	63	?	95	___	127	

Control Codes   **Special/Numerics**   **Upper Case**   **Lower Case**

the lower-case characters are read from the keyboard and appear in the proper ASCII code when the shift key is used (118 for lower-case v, for example, versus 86 for upper-case V), but that the video display can only display an upper-case V.

```
100 CLS                        'clear screen
200 A$=INKEY$                  'input character
300 IF A$="" GOTO 200          'back if no key input
400 PRINT @ 534,A$,ASC(A$)     'print key, ascii
500 GOTO 200                   'loop back for next chr
```

From One to Hundreds

The INKEY$ function created a one-character string when a key was pressed. Level II BASIC allows us to handle up to 255 char-

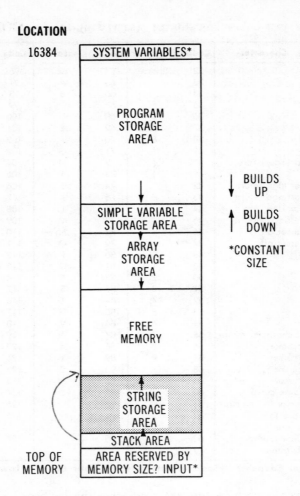

LOCATION

16384

SYSTEM VARIABLES*

PROGRAM
STORAGE
AREA

↓ BUILDS
UP

SIMPLE VARIABLE
STORAGE AREA

↑ BUILDS
DOWN

ARRAY
STORAGE
AREA

*CONSTANT
SIZE

FREE
MEMORY

STRING
STORAGE
AREA

STACK AREA

TOP OF
MEMORY

AREA RESERVED BY
MEMORY SIZE? INPUT*

Figure 3-1. String storage area.

acters in a string. Many of the strings we'll be working with will
be less than 64 characters, since that size will conveniently fit on
one display line.

String variables are stored in RAM memory above the stack, as
shown in Figure 3-1. As a matter of fact, they are up above every
other type of storage in the TRS-80. Because the BASIC interpreter must know how much storage is required for strings, a
CLEAR statement should be one of the first things that a BASIC
program specifies when strings are to be used. Performing a
CLEAR 2000, for example, clears 2000 bytes at the top of RAM

memory, just below any storage reserved by the MEMORY SIZE? input. If no CLEAR statement is specified, the BASIC interpreter, being a somewhat paranoid sort, goes ahead on the assumption you may throw in some strings anyway and reserves 50 bytes.

Each string variable occupies one byte for each character of the string, plus an additional six bytes—3 for the string name (AZ$, AA$) and 3 for the length of the string and address. As in the case of simple variables (no slur intended on their mental abilities), the VARPTR command can be used to sneak a look at the variable in RAM. When VARPTR is used with a string variable, it returns an address that points to a block containing the information shown in Figure 3-2.

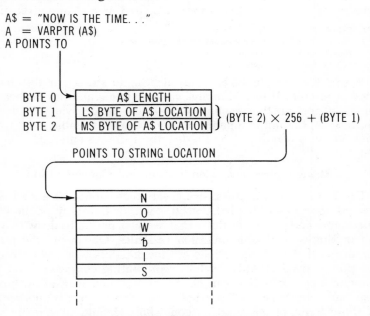

Figure 3-2. VARPTR use with strings.

You might gain some insight into string storage by running the program below, which prints out the location of the string as it is input.

```
1000 CLEAR 500          'clear string space
1100 INPUT A$           'input string
1200 B=VARPTR(A$)       'find location
1300 C=PEEK(B)          'get length
1400 D=PEEK(B+1)        'ls address byte
1500 E=PEEK(B+2)        'ms address byte
1600 PRINT "length=";C  'print length
1700 PRINT "LOCATION=";E*256+D  'print location
1800 GOTO 1100          'loop to next input
```

1750 AD= E*256+D
1800 FOR I=0 TO C-1
1850 ? PEEK(AD+I)
1900 NEXT I
1950 GOTO 1100

47

Note how the location in RAM memory where the string is stored starts off at the top of memory and decrements down for each new input of A$. BASIC uses up all available string storage space (the CLEARed area) until it does not have more available, and then goes back to "clean up" and reshuffle the string data into the CLEARed area.

This accounts for those mysterious delays that sometimes occur when one is working with large programs with many strings. The program has used up the string storage space, and the interpreter must reallocate string space to create new room.

You can check the amount of free space that is available for strings by another BASIC string function, FRE$. It reports on the number of bytes available in the CLEARed area at any given time.

```
90   CLEAR 50        'clear string space
100  PRINT FRE(A$)   'print amount of free string space
110  INPUT A$        'input a string
120  GOTO 100        'loop back to print
```

The variable used in FRE is any legitimate string variable name, used or unused. It is a "dummy" variable name and has no bearing on the report on the amount of all string space available. In the above case, the initial amount of string space available is 50 bytes. This 50 bytes is reduced by the length of the A$ entered.

String Operations: Comparison and Concatenation

Unlike numeric variables, string variables cannot be added, subtracted, multiplied, divided, ANDed, ORed, or have any of the other operations performed on them that we can normally do with integer or single- or double-precision variables. Of course, the reason for this is that such operations are meaningless when we are considering a string of ASCII values representing character data. The common operations that can be performed, however, are comparisons and concatenation. Say what? Yes, the last term is another one of those terms of computer jargon whose definition is really very simple.

Concatenation means to link together, as in a chain. (As a matter of fact, a hanging chain or other line forms a curve known as a *catenary*, hence the derivation—just thought you'd want to know.) Two separate string variables can be linked together by the string concatenation operator "+" to form a single string variable. This may occur as many times as necessary (see Figure 3-3).

A good example of concatenation uses the INKEY$ function to construct an ever-lengthening string variable. We used the INKEY$ variable earlier in the chapter, but let's discuss it a little more. INKEY$ looks at the keyboard for one instant in time. What in-

```
100  A$ = "THIS IS A MN"
200  B$ = "EMONIC DEV"
300  C$ = "ICE TO REME"
400  D$ = "MBER CONCA"
500  E$ = "TENATION!"
600  F$ = A$ + B$ + C$ + D$ + E$
```

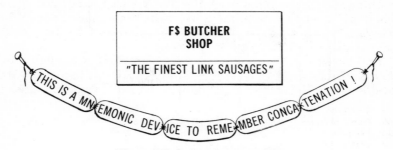

Figure 3-3. String concatenation.

stant? We can see approximately how often INKEY$ *scans* the keyboard by the program below. This code continuously uses INKEY$ to look at the keyboard. If no key is pressed, a null string (0 length) is returned. A null string corresponds to " ". If a key is pressed, a one-character string made up of the keyboard character is created. RUN the program and wait about ten seconds before pressing a key. The count of I is about 790, signifying about 79 scans per second. This means that 79 times per second, the BASIC interpreter looks at the keyboard, at least for this code. Naturally, the statements I = I+1 and IF A$=" " GOTO take some time to process, and the BASIC interpreter is not looking at the keyboard the entire time—perhaps it is looking at the keyboard ¼ of the time, as shown in Figure 3-4. However, the scanning rate is quite high and fast enough even for a prize-winning typist at 150 words per minute (13 characters per second).

```
2000  I=0              'set count to 0
2100  I=I+1            ┌─'start of loop
2200  A$=INKEY$        │ 'get character
2300  IF A$="" GOTO 2100└─'loop until chrctr
2400  PRINT A$,I       'print char,count
```

In any event, let's get back to the INKEY$ concatenation (Editor's note: *Try not to digress—these readers' attention spans are as short as my Uncle Harry who . . .*). We can do a continuous concatenation as fast as you can type using the following code, which prints the length of the string and the string while concatenating a new one-character string from the keyboard.

49

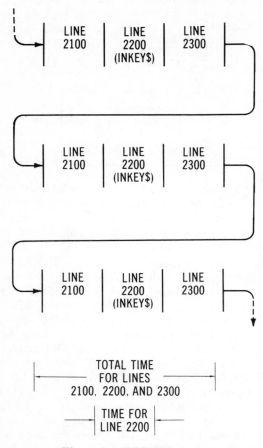

Figure 3-4. INKEY$ scan rate.

```
3000 CLEAR 260                                'clear string space
3100 A=LEN(A$)                             ┌ 'find string length
3200 A$=A$+INKEY$                          │ 'add new char to string
3300 IF LEN(A$)=A GOTO 3200 ELSE PRINT LEN(A$),A$
3400 GOTO 3100                             └ 'loop for nxt character
```

Initially, 260 bytes are CLEARed for string space to permit a maximum string length of 255 bytes to be created. Variable A is set equal to the length of the A$ string, which is initially 0. (The LEN function returns the current length of a specified string.) Next, the INKEY$ function is used to concatenate any keyboard character input. If none is input, A$ is the same as before the INKEY$ operation, as is the LENgth. The new length of A$ is then compared to the old length A. If they are equal, no new character has been input, and a return is made back to the INKEY$ function. If they are unequal, a new character has been added, and the new length and string are printed with a GOTO to the statement to set A equal to the new length for the next comparison.

Strings may be compared just as numeric variables may be compared. The same relational operators of < (less than), > (greater than), = (equal), <> (unequal), <= (less than or equal), or >= (greater than or equal) are used.

It's easy to see how one string can be equal to or not equal to another, but what is the meaning of "less than," "greater than," and the others? The answer lies in ASCII codes. Comparisons are made on the basis of ASCII codes and their binary equivalents. From Table 3-1, we can see that a space is the "lowest-valued" ASCII character, while the lower-case characters are the highest. A string of "A C" (with A, space, C) will be "less than" "AAC," and a string of "?A" will be "greater than" "=A". In a case where strings are of unequal length but otherwise identical, the shorter string is less than the longer string. "AA" is less than "AA5", for example. The code below will let you investigate the comparisons of two strings.

```
100 CLEAR 500            'clear string space
200 INPUT A$,B$          'input two strings
300 IF A$<B$ PRINT A$;"<";B$   'print if less than
400 IF A$=B$ PRINT A$;"=";B$   'print if equal
500 IF A$>B$ PRINT A$;">";B$   'print if greater than
600 GOTO 200             'loop for input
```

Printing the Unprintable

No, this is not an excursion into "blue" books, although some of you had better watch your exclamations while running some of the routines presented here. We have seen how to convert from a single printable character into the equivalent ASCII code by the ASC ("A") command, but how do we convert the other way, from a code to a character? The CHR$ lets us do just that. CHR$ is extremely powerful since it lets us embed all kinds of unusual characters in a character string, characters that simply can't be input from the keyboard! The **argument** of CHR$ is a numeric value from 0 to 255, or an expression that is equivalent to those values. The code below displays all characters from 32 to 191. The ASCII codes from 192 to 255 are not printed, as they are tabs for 0 to 63 spaces and scroll the display off the screen. The codes from 0 to 31 are also not displayed, as some of them cause screen clearing, line clearing, and so forth.

```
1000 CLS                          'clear screen
1100 FOR I=32 TO 191              ┌'ascii codes
1200 PRINT CHR$(I);               ['print character
1300 NEXT I                       └'loop for next
1400 GOTO 1400                    'loop here for display
```

The interesting thing about the display is that not only are characters displayed that can't be generated from the keyboard (such as ↓, ←, and →), but the graphics character codes are also displayed. It is possible, then, to incorporate graphics character codes from 128–191 into a character string! This is an exciting concept because strings are printed very rapidly, and we may be able to use this to advantage to get "high-speed" graphics. We'll discuss this concept further in Chapter 5.

The CHR$ function can be used to compare any non-printable character in the program. A backspace, for example, does not result in a displayable "←", but rather is converted into a code of 8. We can look for that code using a CHR$ (8) function:

```
2000 B$=INKEY$                    ┌'get character
2100 IF B$="" GOTO 2000           │'try again if null
2200 IF B$<>CHR$(8) GOTO 2500     │'go if not bs
2300 PRINT "BACKSPACE"            │'backspace found
2400 GOTO 2000                    │'get next character
2500 A$=A$+B$                     │'concatenate
2600 PRINT A$                     │'print current string
2700 GOTO 2000                    └'get next character
```

Left, Right, Left, Right, Mid, Right . . .

We're allowed to link or concatenate two strings, but are not allowed to truncate a string into a shorter string directly. How do we then access parts of strings? There are several approaches to a problem such as this. The ways in which Level II BASIC approaches it are from the right, from the left, and from the middle. (*I know, I know . . . I just couldn't resist.*) The three methods are implemented by the LEFT$, RIGHT$, and MID$ functions. They allow all or a portion of a string variable to be accessed starting from the right or left, or by taking a portion out of the middle, as shown in Figure 3-5.

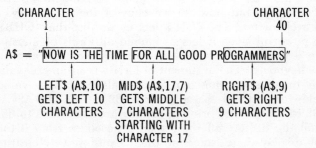

Figure 3-5. Accessing strings.

The LEFT$ function gets the first *n* characters from the left of the string variable. B$ = LEFT$("A MAN A PLAN A CANAL PANAMA",5) would set B$ equal to "A MAN".

The RIGHT$ function gets the last *n* characters from the right of the string variable. B$ = RIGHT$("A MAN A PLAN A CANAL PANAMA",5) would set B$ equal to "ANAMA". The following routine shows how this can be used to retrieve characters from the right or left.

```
3000 A$="A MAN A PLAN A CANAL PANAMA"    'palindrome!
3100 FOR I=1 TO LEN(A$)                  ┌'outer loop
3200 PRINT LEFT$(A$,I)                   │ 'print from left
3300 FOR J=0 TO 50                       │  ┌'inner loop
3400 NEXT J                              │  └'for delay
3500 NEXT I                              └'larger and larger
3600 FOR I=1 TO LEN(A$)                  ┌'outer loop
3700 PRINT TAB(LEN(A$)-I);RIGHT$(A$,I)   │ 'print from right
3800 FOR J=0 TO 50                       │  ┌'inner loop
3900 NEXT J                              │  └'for delay
4000 NEXT I                              └'larger and larger
```

The MID$ function is used to take a portion of a string out of the middle. MID$ specifies a string variable, a starting location (from the left), and the number of characters to be retrieved. B$ = MID$("A MAN A PLAN A CANAL PANAMA",10,5) would create B$ = "LAN A". The following code creates two strings, one made by concatenating single characters starting from the left, and the other made by concatenating single characters starting from the right; both use the MID$ function.

```
50 CLEAR 400                             'clear string space
100 A$="A MAN A PLAN A CANAL PANAMA"     'read it sdrawkcab
200 FOR I=1 TO LEN(A$)                   ┌'loop for mid
300 B$=MID$(A$,I,1)+B$                   │ 'from left
400 C$=MID$(A$,LEN(A$)-I+1,1)+C$         │ 'from right
500 NEXT I                               └'continue
600 PRINT B$                             'print left string
700 PRINT C$                             'print right string
```

The STRING$ String

One of the remaining string functions that we haven't mentioned yet is the STRING$ function. With STRING$, you can create a string of identical characters. The format of STRING$ is STRING$ (*n*,"c"), where *n* is a value from 0 to 255 and "c" is **either a string or value** (or expression). The character or value represented will be replicated *n* number of times. For example, PRINT STRING$ (20,"#") prints 20 pound signs and PRINT STRING$(32,63) prints 32 question marks (63 is the ASCII code for "?").

The value in STRING$ may be any value from 0 to 255, including graphics characters. (The graphics potential for STRING$ is discussed in Chapter 5.) STRING$ is especially handy for printing headings, filling in display fields with **fill characters**, or filling in strings with fill characters.

Numeric to Strings and Back Again

We have two more string functions to investigate before trying our hand at a generalized input routine, cursor control, text editing, and some other functions. If you'll bear with us (*Guard, that gun is not necessary* . . .), we'll complete this discussion of string functions by looking at two powerful functions, STR$ and VAL.

STR$ converts a given numeric value or expression into a string. The string can then easily be edited and processed for printing or display.

PRINT STR$(12.34)

for example, converts the single-precision variable 12.34 into the string variable " 12.34", six characters long, and

PRINT STR$(1E−06)

converts the single-precision variable 1×10^{-6} into the string variable " 1E−06", six characters long. A leading blank appears before the numeric value in the string to allow for a possible minus sign as in

PRINT STR$(−9999)

which would generate "−9999", five characters long.

VAL operates in reverse fashion from STR$; it converts a string variable or expression into a numeric value—eVALuates it. The string variable must be either numeric characters, a decimal point, or exponent (E or D). Evaluation stops on the first (non-E or D) alphabetic or special character encountered.

Expression	Result
VAL("12.34")	12.34
VAL("12E−06")	1.2E−05
VAL("99999999")	9999.9999
VAL("12D−06")	1.2D−05
VAL("TEXT100")	0
VAL("100TEXT")	100

Note that if the string starts with a non-numeric character, it evaluates as zero.

VAL can be used to convert a string of numeric data to a more compact numeric variable form. This saves memory for large amounts of numeric data, but more importantly, it drastically reduces the amount of processing time required.

A Thousand Cursors Upon You, Effendi!

Knowing what we now know about the manipulation of strings, large and small, it should be a simple matter to produce some useful general-purpose text-handling routines. Some of the things we'll be discussing in the remainder of this chapter will be cursor control, generalized string inputs, and text editing.

Just how do we manipulate the cursor? If we look at Table 3-1 again we see that there are indeed cursor control characters that can be output to the screen. These are backspace cursor (24), advance cursor (25), down cursor (26), up cursor (27), home cursor to character position 0, line 0 (28), and move to beginning of line (29). In addition to these, we can turn the cursor on (14), and off (15).

As an example of how we can implement these cursor codes, look at the routine below. It moves the cursor to the home position (CHR$(28)), clears the screen (CHR$(31)), moves back to home (CHR$(28)), and turns on the cursor (CHR$(14)). The cursor is then moved in spiral fashion until it retreats to the screen center.

```
1000 PRINT CHR$(28);CHR$(31);      'home and clear screen
1100 PRINT CHR$(28);CHR$(14);      'home and turn on cursor
1200 H=63                          'initial horizontal
1300 V=14                          'initial vertical
1400 FOR I=1 TO H                  ┌  'upper
1500 PRINT CHR$(25);               │  'move to right
1600 NEXT I                        └  'loop
1700 FOR I=1 TO V                  ┌  'right side
1800 PRINT CHR$(26);               │  'move down
1900 NEXT I                        └  'loop
2000 V=V-1                         'adjust vertical
2100 H=H-1                         'adjust horizontal
2200 FOR I=1 TO H                  ┌  'bottom
2300 PRINT CHR$(24);               │  'move to left
2400 NEXT I                        └  'loop
2500 FOR I=1 TO V                  ┌  'left side
2600 PRINT CHR$(27);               │  'move up
2700 NEXT I                        └  'loop
2800 V=V-1                         'adjust vertical
2900 H=H-1                         'adjust horizontal
3000 GOTO 1400                     'loop for next spiral
```

The above code is more than a little showy and not too useful (unless you're a spiral freak). However, it does show that we have complete control over the cursor and related screen control characters in our BASIC programming. We can use this fact to advantage in writing a good generalized input routine.

The Universal Gee Whiz Input

This routine is meant to exercise our string capabilities, but also to provide a general-purpose keyboard input routine. On input, it is desirable to have a routine that will accept string input from any of the 1024 input positions. A "fill" string of blanks or an existing character string such as "MM/DD/YY" should be available to initialize the input area. Another nicety is the ability to move the cursor within the field to any position to permit modification of previ-

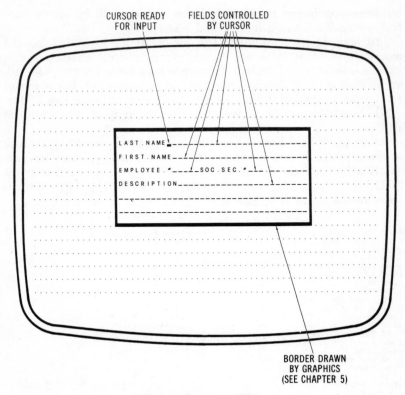

CURSOR READY
FOR INPUT

FIELDS CONTROLLED
BY CURSOR

LAST.NAME
FIRST.NAME
EMPLOYEE.   SOC.SEC.
DESCRIPTION

BORDER DRAWN
BY GRAPHICS
(SEE CHAPTER 5)

Figure 3-6. Form fill-in.

ously input or existing text. Also, control characters that might create ambiguous conditions, such as down cursor, must be ignored.

A generalized input routine such as this allows easy form fill-in as shown in Figure 3-6. The form is made up of several fields, each of which may be controlled by the input routine. Another example would be modification of existing strings under cursor control rather than by retyping the entire string.

The program shown in Figure 3-7 provides all of these features. The subroutine is CALLed with string variable ZA$ containing the fill string to be used. The "@" location for the string is contained in variable ZC (0–1023). When the subroutine is CALLed, the fill field will be printed at the spot designated, and data may then be entered from the keyboard. *The fill field must be all on one line for proper operation.* The cursor may be moved without destroying the data by "←" and "→". The cursor may not be moved past the start of the field or past the end of the field. When the data has

```
40 REM CLEAR SCREEN AND CALL SUBROUTINE
50 CLS
100 ZA$="**************"
200 ZC=512
300 GOSUB 20000
400 PRINT ZA$
500 GOTO 40
19000 REM PRINT FILL FIELD AND BACKSPACE CURSOR TO START
20000 PRINT @ZC,ZA$;CHR$(14);
20010 FOR ZF=1 TO LEN(ZA$)
20020 PRINT CHR$(24);
20030 NEXT ZF
20035 REM SET CURSOR POSITION TO 1 AND GET KEY PRESS
20040 ZG=1
20050 ZH$=INKEY$
20060 IF ZH$="" GOTO 20050
20065 REM TEST FOR LFT CURSOR,RT CURSOR,ENTER, AND VALID CHAR
20070 IF ZH$=CHR$(8) OR ZH$=CHR$(9) OR ZH$=CHR$(13) GOTO 20080
20075 IF ZH$<CHR$(32) GOTO 20050
20080 IF ZH$<>CHR$(8) GOTO 20120
20085 REM LEFT CURSOR ROUTINE. DONT GO PAST START
20090 IF ZG=1 GOTO 20050 ELSE PRINT CHR$(24);
20100 ZG=ZG-1
20110 GOTO 20050
20120 IF ZH$<>CHR$(9) GOTO 20160
20125 REM RIGHT CURSOR ROUTINE. DONT GO PAST END
20130 IF ZG>=LEN(ZA$) GOTO 20050 ELSE PRINT CHR$(25);
20140 ZG=ZG+1
20150 GOTO 20050
20160 IF ZH$<>CHR$(13) GOTO 20190
20165 REM ENTER ROUTINE. PRINT FINAL STRING AND RETURN
20170 PRINT @ZC,CHR$(15);ZA$
20180 RETURN
20185 REM VALID CHARACTER ROUTINE. PRINT CHARACTER, ADJUST CURSOR
20190 ZG=ZG+1
20200 IF ZG>LEN(ZA$)+1 PRINT CHR$(24);
20210 IF ZG>LEN(ZA$)+1 ZG=ZG-1
20220 PRINT ZH$;
20230 ZA$=LEFT$(ZA$,(ZG-2))+ZH$+RIGHT$(ZA$,LEN(ZA$)-ZG+1)
20240 GOTO 20050
```

Figure 3-7. Universal Gee Whiz Input.

been properly input, the "ENTER" key causes a return to the calling program. The subroutine is shown with a short driver program illustrating its use. **For maximum input speed, this code should be compressed by removing REMark statements, using multiple statement lines, and locating it with "low-valued" line numbers.**

Within the subroutine, ZG is used to mark the current cursor position within the field. ZG will always contain a value of 1 to LEN (ZA$). ZG is adjusted for left cursor (8), right cursor (9), or for any new character. Control characters other than 8, 9, or ENTER (13) are ignored. Whenever a new character is entered, the subroutine finds the portion of the field string left of the cursor, concatenates the input character ZH$, and concatenates the portion of the field string right of the cursor to create a new string equivalent to the display on the screen. This string is passed back to the calling code as the updated string and is also left on the screen after the cursor is turned off and the display restored.

In spite of the heading, this input routine does not contain all the "bells and whistles" that could be put in. However, it should suffice for many applications.

Text Editing

Strings are a natural format for **text editing** applications programs. Text editing is also called **word processing**. Text editing allows a user to manipulate text for manuscripts, letters, and other appearance-oriented printing. A comprehensive text editor provides for deletion and insertion of characters, words, paragraphs, and blocks, automatically justifies (creates an even margin), counts the words in a block, and performs other sophisticated functions. We can't create a complete text editor in this chapter, but we can illustrate some of the ways a BASIC text-editing program could be implemented.

Three common operations in text editing are searching, deleting, and inserting. Most text editors allow a user to search a string for a given string contained within it. We can make full use of the comparison capabilities for string variables to implement a search. The code in Figure 3-8 inputs a string of text that creates a text

```
1000 CLS                                       'clear screen
1010 CLEAR 1000                                'clear string space
1020 INPUT "TEXT BASE:";A$                     'input text to search
1030 INPUT "SEARCH STRING";B$                  'input string to find
1040 CLS                                       'clear screen
1050 PRINT @ 512,A$                            'print string to be searched
1060 FOR I=1 TO LEN(A$)-LEN(B$)+1             ┌'setup loop for search
1070 IF MID$(A$,I,LEN(B$))=B$ GOTO 1105       │'go if string found
1080 NEXT I                                   └'continue search
1090 PRINT B$;" NOT FOUND"                      'string not found here
1100 GOTO 1100                                 'loop here
1105 I=I-1                                      'adjust for computation
1110 PRINT CHR$(14);CHR$(28);                   'turn on cursor and home
1120 FOR J=0 TO 7+INT(I/64)                    ┌'setup loop to find line
1130 PRINT CHR$(26);                           │'down cursor
1140 NEXT J                                    └'continue till line fnd
1145 IF I-INT(I/64)*64=0 GOTO 1180             'go if character position 0
1150 FOR J=1 TO I-INT(I/64)*64                 ┌'setup loop to find char
1160 PRINT CHR$(25);                           │'advance cursor
1170 NEXT J                                    └'continue till char fnd
1180 GOTO 1180                                  'loop here at end
```

Figure 3-8. String search operations.

base and then inputs a search string to be found within the text base. Obviously, the search string must be shorter than the text base. If the string is found, the cursor is moved to the position of the string. The cursor movement portion of the program has to consider the number of lines to move down (7 to get to @ 512 plus INT($I/64$) to get to the proper text line [there are 64 characters to a line]) and the number of positions to the right after the proper line is found (I-INT($I/64$)).

Deletions of characters within text normally cause the remaining text to "snake up" into the space left by the deleted characters, as shown in Figure 3-9. BASIC code to implement the delete function (not shown) might reconfigure the string with the current cursor

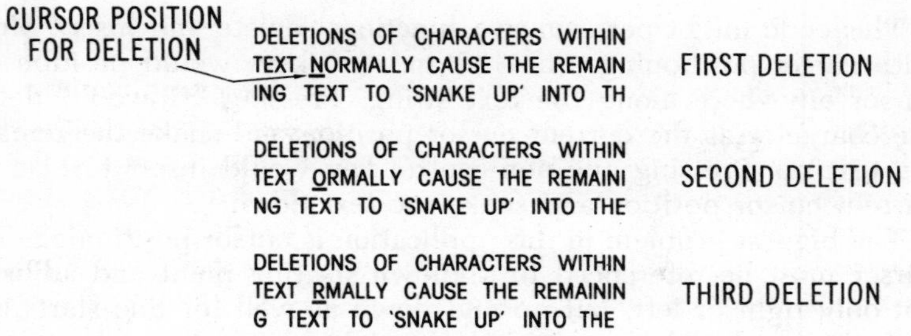

CURSOR POSITION
FOR DELETION

DELETIONS OF CHARACTERS WITHIN
TEXT NORMALLY CAUSE THE REMAIN
ING TEXT TO 'SNAKE UP' INTO TH

FIRST DELETION

DELETIONS OF CHARACTERS WITHIN
TEXT ORMALLY CAUSE THE REMAINI
NG TEXT TO 'SNAKE UP' INTO THE

SECOND DELETION

DELETIONS OF CHARACTERS WITHIN
TEXT RMALLY CAUSE THE REMAININ
G TEXT TO 'SNAKE UP' INTO THE

THIRD DELETION

Figure 3-9. Deleting characters in text.

character deleted and print it at the same screen position. The code
could insert by reconfiguring the string with an insert character
inserted at the current cursor position and "snaking" the string
down as characters are inserted. These operations are shown in
Figure 3-10.

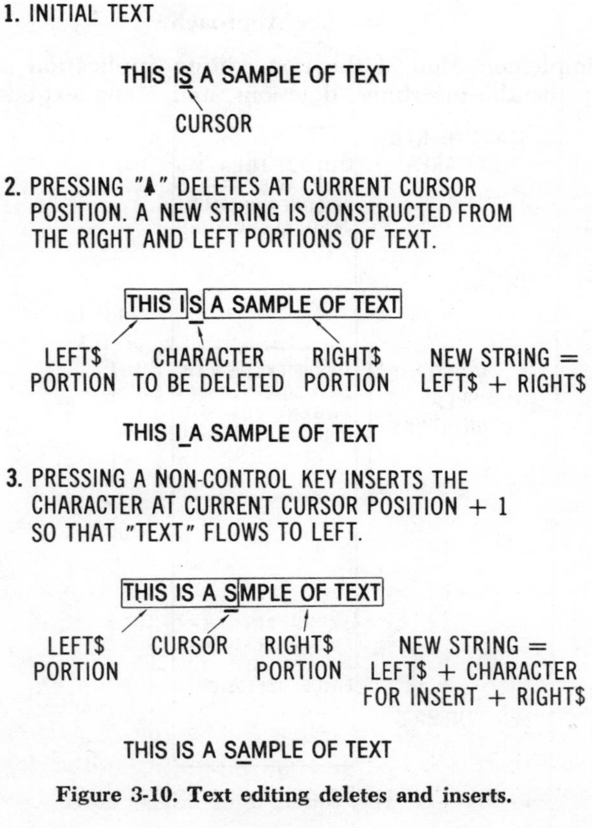

1. INITIAL TEXT

THIS IS A SAMPLE OF TEXT

CURSOR

2. PRESSING "▲" DELETES AT CURRENT CURSOR
POSITION. A NEW STRING IS CONSTRUCTED FROM
THE RIGHT AND LEFT PORTIONS OF TEXT.

THIS I|S| A SAMPLE OF TEXT

LEFT$ CHARACTER   RIGHT$ NEW STRING =
PORTION   TO BE DELETED   PORTION   LEFT$ + RIGHT$

THIS I A SAMPLE OF TEXT

3. PRESSING A NON-CONTROL KEY INSERTS THE
CHARACTER AT CURRENT CURSOR POSITION + 1
SO THAT "TEXT" FLOWS TO LEFT.

THIS IS A S|MPLE OF TEXT

LEFT$ CURSOR   RIGHT$ NEW STRING =
PORTION   PORTION   LEFT$ + CHARACTER
                                    FOR INSERT + RIGHT$

THIS IS A SAMPLE OF TEXT

Figure 3-10. Text editing deletes and inserts.

This code might perform two functions—delete and insert, along with cursor positioning. The "←" and "→" keys would position the cursor anywhere along the text string. Pressing "↑" would delete the character at the current cursor position and snake the remaining text up. Pressing any non-control key would insert text at the current cursor position and snake the text down.

The biggest problem in this application is cursor positioning. The cursor must be referenced to a known starting point and adjusted not only right or left, but up and down as well for line starts and ends. For each delete, a new string might be constructed from the left and right portions of the current string with the character removed at the current cursor position. For each insert, a new string might be constructed from the left and right portions of the current string with the character at the current cursor position embedded between the two strings; the cursor could then be moved over one position to the right so that the text is built from left to right.

Another Approach

The implementation of the text editing application above used strings to handle insertions, deletions, and other text-editing func-

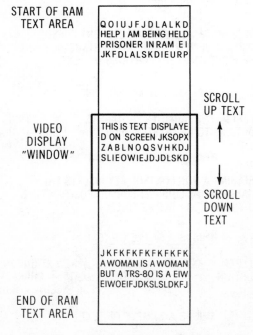

Figure 3-11. Text editing using display memory.

tions. Another approach to the problem is to treat the entire video display memory as several huge strings. The screen is actually a memory that will store displayable (and graphics) characters, so it is an excellent way to implement such an application. Insertions of characters can be handled by moving blocks of screen memory down from the current cursor position to the end of screen memory (16383). Deletions can be handled by moving a block of screen memory up. The screen represents a "window" of a much larger text area in this case, with the window scrolling up and down to allow display and text editing functions on various portions of the text (see Figure 3-11). We'll discuss display applications more fully in Chapter 5, and the reader may be able to get a better picture (pun intended) of the types of things that can be done in working with the display memory.

CHAPTER 4

Our Latest Report Indicates

In this chapter, we'll provide some information about printing reports on the screen and on the system line printer. We'll also discuss in detail the use of PRINT USING, a powerful statement for formatting string and numeric values.

Why do we want to format reports? First, there's the aesthetic aspect. Nobody likes to see sloppy, uncolumnated reports coming out of a powerful computer system. The processing involved may be spectacular, but the effect of a cluttered report may be disastrous. (Or vice versa. I once saw several vice presidents of an aircraft manufacturer literally enthralled by meaningless data *nicely printed* on a system they had ordered that wasn't *quite* ready.) Secondly, to produce *useful* reports, displays, and other graphics, the programmer is forced to define some format for the report to follow with pagination (new pages), columnization (putting data in proper columns), and menus (lists of choices to prompt the user).

One From Column A and One From Column B

The PRINT statement is easy to understand. A PRINT statement with a single item and no comma or semicolon at the end prints the item at the start of the next line on the screen and then moves the cursor position to the start of the next line as shown in Figure 4-1.

```
100   PRINT 4.55      'print 4.55 and move to next line
200   GOTO 200        'loop here
```

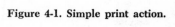

Figure 4-1. Simple print action.

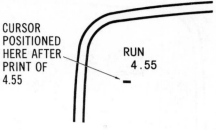

The data printed in this first case is ♭4.55♭; because the number was a positive number, a blank is printed in place of a "+" sign. If the number is a negative number, such as −8.95, then the negative sign is printed, followed by the magnitude of the number. In both cases, the number also has a **trailing** blank in addition to the leading blank or negative sign. You can see this by the code below, which uses a semicolon to specify that the cursor is **not** moved to the next line, but remains where it is after the print. The cursor in this case normally must be imagined, as it is not active during execution of the program unless we turn it on in the program. We've turned it on before doing the PRINT, using the cursor-on code (14) that we discussed in Chapter 3 (see Figure 4-2).

```
100   PRINT CHR$(14)      'turn on cursor
200   PRINT  −4.5;4.5;     'print two values
300   GOTO 300            'loop here
```

Notice that the format is −4.5♭♭4.5; each print is five character positions on the screen, one for the sign, three for the "4.5," and a trailing blank.

The unfortunate thing about printing in this fashion is that variables are not fixed-length. When variables are printed, leading and trailing zeroes are always suppressed as in the display from this code

```
100   FOR I=0 TO 1000   ⌈ 'loop 1001 times
200   PRINT I↑1.1;       | 'print I to the 1.1 power
300   NEXT               ⌊ 'continue
```

How do we go about columnating data in this simple case? One way to do it, of course, is by using a comma instead of a semicolon to tab to the next print zone. The print zones on the video display are positions 0, 16, 32, and 48, and using a comma after each print item will print data in four nice, neat little columns.

```
100   FOR I=0 TO 1000
200   PRINT I↑1.1,        'use tab on prints
300   NEXT
```

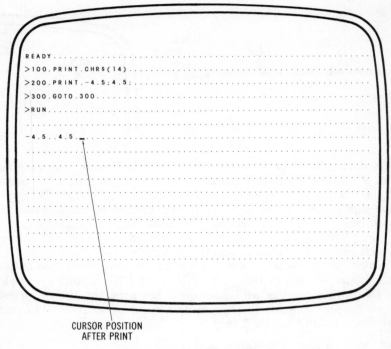

```
READY . . . . . . . . . . . . . . . . . . . . . . . . . . . . . . . . . . . . . . . . . . . . . . . . .
>100 . PRINT . CHR$ ( 14 ) . . . . . . . . . . . . . . . . . . . . . . . . . . . . . . . . .
>200 . PRINT . - 4 . 5 ; 4 . 5 ; . . . . . . . . . . . . . . . . . . . . . . . . . . . . . . .
>300 . GOTO . 300 . . . . . . . . . . . . . . . . . . . . . . . . . . . . . . . . . . . . . . .
>RUN . . . . . . . . . . . . . . . . . . . . . . . . . . . . . . . . . . . . . . . . . . . . . . . .

- 4 . 5 . . 4 . 5 . ▄
```

CURSOR POSITION
AFTER PRINT

Figure 4-2. Variable printing.

This is definitely an improvement, but there are still problems
with the appearance of the data—namely, the decimal points don't
line up. There are other problems with this type of columnization,
also. The world is not always a four-column world, as evidenced
by the new tax-return formats. Sometimes, we would like to
squeeze eight columns of data onto the screen, especially if we
know that the variables will be limited to six digits plus sign and
trailing blank. And how about the case of dollars and cents data?
We would like to see the .00 cents displayed instead of being suppressed in cases when we're dealing with the almighty dollar.

The first problem of additional columns may be partially solved
by a PRINT TAB statement. PRINT TAB moves the cursor position to a specified character position along the line from 1 to 64.
PRINT TAB may be used to produce a display of more than the
four print-zone columns by tabbing over to the next column after
printing a data item. This works, providing the length of the data
item is known to be less than the width of the column plus 2.
Suppose, for example, the data items to be printed are three digits.
Adding one trailing blank and one leading blank defines a column

of five characters and a total of 12 columns, as shown in the code
below and in Figure 4-3.

```
100 FOR I=1 TO 60 STEP 5          ┌ ┌'tab 5,10,15,...
200 PRINT TAB(I);123;             │ │ 'print dummy value
300 NEXT I                        │ └ 'loop
400 PRINT                         │ 'line feed
500 GOTO 100                      └ 'next set
```

Here we've "dummied up" the value to guarantee that we have
three digits each time. When we use values that may be any number of digits from 1 to 4, we get the same problem as previously:
columns that are not right justified, as shown in Figure 4-4.

```
1000 FOR I=1 TO 60 STEP 5         ┌ ┌'tab 5,10,15,...
1100 PRINT TAB(I);RND(999);       │ │ 'print tab and 1-3 chars
1200 NEXT I                       │ └ 'loop
1300 PRINT                        │ 'line feed
1400 GOTO 1000                    └ 'next set
```

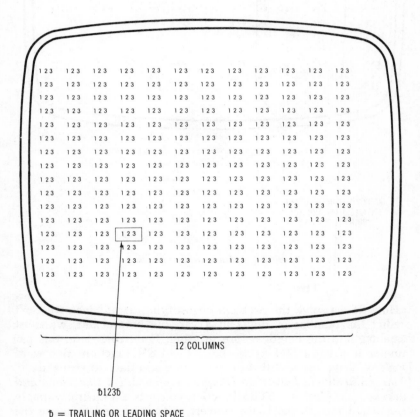

12 COLUMNS

ƀ123ƀ

ƀ = TRAILING OR LEADING SPACE

Figure 4-3. Columnating example 1.

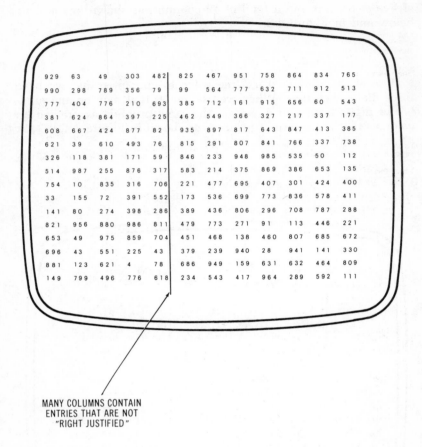

Figure 4-4. Columnating example 2.

There's No Justification for This . . .

How do we solve the problem of justifying data? Since we can't predict the number of digits in a variable beforehand, we must somehow find the length before printing. For string data, this parameter is easy to find as we have the LEN function. But wait! Don't we have the ability to convert numeric data to string data? (*You really should have read Chapter 3. Guard, get that name and address . . .*) Yes, the STR$ function converts a numeric variable or constant to a string. If we convert to a string and then use the LEN function to find the string length, we can handle justification of columns. Let's see how it works.

```
2000 INPUT "JUSTIFY Y/N";A$        'input justify action
2100 FOR I=1 TO 55 STEP 6      ┌─ 'tab 1,7,13,...
2200 A=RND(9999)               │  'get 1-4 digits
2300 IF A$="N" THEN PRINT TAB(I);A; ELSE GOTO 2500
2400 GOTO 2800                 │  'for next loop
2500 B$=STR$(A)                │  'convert to string
2600 C=LEN(B$)                 │  'find length
2700 PRINT TAB(I+5-C);B$;      │  'tab and print
2800 NEXT I                    └─ 'loop
2900 PRINT                        'get next line
3000 GOTO 2100                    'again
```

The program above first asks for a decision on justification. If the answer is "N", then ten columns of 1–4 digits are printed as we have been doing—each variable is printed with a leading blank (for sign) and a trailing blank plus 1 to 4 digits, making a column entry three to six digits. If the answer is a "Y", then the 1 to 4 digit value from RND(9999) is converted to a string by STR$(A). Note that STR$ converts the numeric value with a leading blank for positive values (or a minus sign) and **no** trailing blank. The length of the string is therefore 2 to 5 digits. The tab position to be used is the extreme left of the column for a five-character string

$$TAB=I+5-5=I,$$

three positions over for a string of 2 digits

$$TAB=I+5-2=I+3,$$

or intermediate positions for strings of four or three characters (see Figure 4-5). Our display in this case definitely gets an "A" for neatness.

Dollars and Cents

Changing a numeric to a string by means of STR$ may be done for all types of numeric data so that the length of the field may be computed before printing. When the numeric data includes a decimal point, the decimal point will also be converted.

```
100  PRINT STR$(111.77)     'convert and print
```

will print "111.77". However, we still have the same problem with the decimal point! If the variable is 111.5000, it will be printed as "111.5" rather than a dollars and cents value of 111.50. Also, 111.00 will be printed as "111" and 111.234 will be printed as "111.234"! How do we make cents out of such a value? One way to accomplish this is to scan the resulting string variable after the STR$ conversion for the decimal point and to add a decimal point and trailing zeroes as required. The following subroutine takes an input variable ZZ and converts it to a dollars and cents format in string variable ZZ$.

```
10000 ZZ$=STR$(ZZ)                        'convert to string
10010 FOR I=1 TO LEN(ZZ$)                 ['look for dec pnt
10020 IF MID$(ZZ$,I,1)="." GOTO 10060     ['go if found
10030 NEXT I                              ['loop
10040 ZZ$=ZZ$+".00"                       'not fnd-add cents
10050 RETURN                              'return to calling prog
10060 IF I=LEN(ZZ$)-2 RETURN              'return if ##.##
10070 IF I<>LEN(ZZ$)-1 GOTO 10100         'go if not ##.#
10080 ZZ$=ZZ$+"0"                         'convert to ##.##
10090 RETURN                              'return to calling prog
10100 ZZ$=LEFT$(ZZ$,I+2)                  'use only 2 cents digits
10110 RETURN                              'return to calling prog
```

There are five cases in the above subroutine. ZZ may be converted to a string of the form ##, with no decimal point and no characters for the cents. In this case, the search for the decimal point using MID$ is not successful, and a new ZZ$ is created by adding ".00" to the original string. The second case occurs when

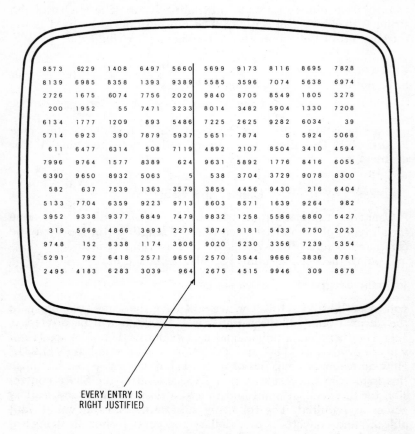

EVERY ENTRY IS
RIGHT JUSTIFIED

Figure 4-5. Use of STR$ function for columnating.

ZZ$="##.##", a string with a decimal point and two cents characters. In this case (I=LEN(ZZ$)−2), nothing must be done and a RETURN is made. The third case occurs when ZZ$="##.#". In this case (I=LEN(ZZ$)−1), only a "0" needs to be added. The fourth case occurs when ZZ$="##.###. .", a string of more than two cents digits. In this case, we must shorten the string by taking only the first two cents digits and taking the left-hand side of the string up to the decimal point plus two digits. Three notes on the technique used above:

1. The case "##." never occurs because the decimal point would always be deleted.
2. The technique of **truncating** the digits to the right is not necessarily the best way to handle the fractional cents. Millionaire programmers have been produced when such fractional cents have gone into other checking accounts.
3. The code above could be replaced by two statements. (*Extra! Extra! Writer Mobbed by Angry Readers!*)

All right! I know that you're angry with me for going through the code above when it could have been replaced by two instructions. However, I just wanted to show you how powerful that one instruction was. The instruction is . . . (may I have the envelope please?) . . .

PRINT USING!

The entire code above could have been replaced by

```
10000   PRINT USING "####.##";ZZ      'print dollars, cents
10010   RETURN                        'return
```

In the PRINT USING statement above, the "#" characters defined a digit position for a numeric field, and the decimal point defined the decimal point location within the field. If the value in ZZ had more than two digits to the right of the decimal point, they would have been "rounded off" to produce only two digits; if the ZZ value had fewer than two digits to the right of the decimal point, then the remaining digit positions would have been filled with zeroes. If the numeric value had fewer than four digits to the left of the decimal point, the remaining positions would have been filled with spaces. Neat, eh?

Let's look at some of the other capabilities of the PRINT USING statement. Another "field specifier" character that may be added in the definition string is a comma. Since the PRINT USING is used primarily for accounting-type applications, an obvious use of a comma is to provide the comma for large dollar amounts.

```
50    INPUT A                      'provide input
100   A$="###.###.##"             'define string
200   PRINT USING A$;A             'print using A$ string
300   GOTO 50                      'return to input
```

The PRINT USING statement above should handle many of the reader's weekly paychecks and provide a printout of such amounts as 1,232.77, 66,327.00, and 121,067.99. The comma and decimal points may be inserted anywhere within the string, but such string field specifiers as #.#,.## are not too meaningful and may confuse the BASIC interpreter.

How about dollar signs? I'm glad you asked. *One* dollar sign used as a field specifier will cause a dollar sign to be printed at the left with intervening print positions filled with spaces. PRINT USING "$####.##" will enable printouts such as $1000 00, $ᴃᴃᴃ1.23, and $ᴃᴃ77.79, $ᴃᴃᴃ0.36. *Two* dollar signs used as field specifiers will **float** the dollar sign and put it directly before the first digit printed. PRINT USING "$$####.##" produces printouts such as $1111.77, $13.24, $1.77, and $0.34. Note that dollar amounts less than one dollar are printed with a leading 0 for the dollar amount in both the floating and non-floating dollar-sign case.

Have any of you ever altered your paychecks to increase your weekly wage—no, of course not (*Guard, let's get those names . . .*). One safeguard against such action is the use of asterisk characters before the printing of the dollar amount. When a **$ field specifier is used in PRINT USING, asterisks will occupy all field positions before a floating dollar sign. PRINT USING "**$####.##", for example, will produce amounts such as ****$11.11, **$1000.99, *$10000.10, and $100000 00. Note that the maximum amount that "**$####.##" can hold is $999999.99 with seven characters including "$" to the left of the decimal point.

Accounting type information sometimes uses a trailing minus sign after the amount. When the field specifier "−" is used at the end of a field, a minus will be printed if the amount is negative.

```
100   A$="#####.##−"    'define string
200   PRINT USING A$;A             'print using A$
```

prints 22.23− when A is negative or 22.23 when A is positive.

When an initial + or − sign is required, a + sign placed at the beginning of the field results in a "+" character for positive numbers or a "−" character for negative numbers. PRINT USING +##.## produces +12.22, +1.22, +0.22, −12.22, −1.22, or −0.22.

The % and ! field specifiers are used to denote string fields that must be printed. When the first character of a string must be printed, "!" is used.

```
100   A$="1234"          'string
200   PRINT USING "!";A$          'print first character
```

Table 4-1. PRINT USING Field Specifiers

Specifier	Description	PRINT USING A$; N		
		A $	N	Result
#	Numeric field	###	13	ƀ13
		###	2	ƀƀ2
		###	−2	ƀ−2
.	Decimal point	##.##	1.2	ƀ1.20
	position	##.###	1.2	ƀ1.200
		##.###	−1.2	−1.200
+	Leading or trailing	+#.#	−1.123	−1.1
	sign	+#.#	1.123	+1.1
		#.#+	−1.123	1.1−
		#.#+	1.123	1.1+
−	Trailing sign	#.#−	−1.123	1.1−
	if negative	#.#−	1.123	1.1ƀ
**	Leading asterisks	**#.##	23.53	*23.53
		**#.##	2.53	**2.53
$$	Floating dollar	$$##.##	123.53	$123.53
	sign	$$##.##	12.53	ƀ$12.53
		$$##.##	1.25	ƀƀ$1.25
**$	Leading blanks,	**$##.##	123.53	*$123.53
	floating dollar	**$##.##	12.35	**$12.35
		**$##.##	1.23	***$1.23
↑↑↑↑	Exponential format	#.##↑↑↑↑	51235	0.51E+05
	(scientific notation)	##.##↑↑↑↑	51235	ƀ5.12E+04
!	Single character	!	"1234"	1
	of string	!	"ABCD"	A
%%	First two characters	%%	"ABCD"	AB
	of string			
%..%	First two + spaces	%ƀƀƀ%	"ABCDEFG"	ABCDE
	of string			

for example prints "1". The % field specifier prints either the first two left characters of a string, as in

```
100  A$="1234"              'string
200  PRINT USING "%%";A$     'print first two characters
```

which prints "12", or two plus the number of spaces between the % characters, as in

```
100  A$="1234"
200  PRINT USING "%   %";A$
```

which prints "1234".

Table 4-1 shows all PRINT USING field specifiers and examples of their use.

When more than one variable is to be printed, then each variable of the list uses the same field specifiers.

```
100 A$="##.##"              'using string
200 A=11.11                 'dummy
300 B=2.22                  'another
400 C=.33                   'and another
500 D=4.44                  'still another
600 PRINT USING A$;A,B,C,D   'print all four
```

will print "11.11̸52.22̸50.33̸54.44". Note that even though a comma was specified, the form of the printout used a five-character field with no leading or trailing blanks or tabs; four characters were the # field specifiers and one was the decimal point. When the string field specifiers "%" and "!" are used, then it is possible to construct complex formats for printing, such as the code below which takes the first two characters of string A$ and prints them, prints a ".", and then prints the first three characters of string B$.

```
1000 A$="1234"              'first string
1100 B$="5678"              'second string
1200 PRINT USING "%%.% %";A$,B$   'print PORTIONS OF BOTH
```

In this example, the field specifiers were used one at a time in conjunction with the variable list to define the printing. A weird operation? Yes, but we will *never* say that such operations will not find widespread use for fear of letters from Boise, Idaho, that start out "I don't see how you can say that multiple string field specifiers are not used often! I use them all the time in my hog breeding program! Furthermore, your gross humor is irritating and . . ."

PRINT USING can be used with double-precision variables to provide formatted printing of variables to 14 digits of dollar amounts and two cents digits, which should handle receivables for most of the current TRS-80 business applications.

PRINT USING provides a very convenient means to produce formatted printing of variables and saves a great deal of special coding to accomplish this formatting, as we saw earlier in the chapter. Conservative estimates by recent industry experts indicate about 100,737 lines of code annually saved as a direct result of the PRINT USING statement. And there are those who say BASIC is not very powerful!

$4.50 for a Slice of Cheesecake?

Menus are used not only in posh restaurants, but in posh computer software. You've seen menus on Radio Shack software, but let's illustrate the use of them to jog your memory. Suppose that we have written an applications program to process weather data. When the program is first loaded, it may display a menu of functions that may be selected, as shown in Figure 4-6. If entry 4 is desired, then the user types a "4", and a new menu of items related to "annual weather data" is displayed for further selection. This type of implementation is termed **"menu-driven."** Menus provide an easy-to-use format that is very descriptive. This section should *definitely* be interpreted as a plug for menu use. (I have a brother-in-law in the menu-printing business.) Menu printing is easy, of

Figure 4-6. Menu use.

course, and may be implemented by a series of TABs and text, followed by a PRINT @ and INKEY$ input as shown below.

```
1500 CLS                          'clear screen
1510 PRINT TAB(15);"1 ENTER NEW WEATHER DATA"
1520 PRINT TAB(15);"2 MODIFY WEATHER DATA"
1530 PRINT TAB(15);"3 CHANGE WEATHER DATA"
1540 PRINT TAB(15);"4 ANNUAL WEATHER DATA"
1550 PRINT TAB(15);"5 SAVE WEATHER DATA"
1560 PRINT TAB(15);"6 LOAD WEATHER DATA"
1570 PRINT @ 656,"ENTER SELECTION"
1580 A=VAL(INKEY$)                  'get value
1590 IF A=0 OR  A>6 GOTO 1570 ELSE ON A GOTO 2000,3000,4000,5000,6000,7000
```

The code above first clears the screen and then prints the menu selections. A TAB is done for each selection to center the selection. After the selections are displayed, the **prompt** message "ENTER SELECTION" is displayed at a convenient place *beyond* the menu selections. The input choice is detected by an INKEY$ statement which will return a one-character string of the key pressed or a null if no keys are pressed. If no keys are pressed or *if no numeric key is pressed,* VAL(INKEY$) will equal 0, and a GOTO back to the PRINT @ is made to display the selection message and to look for the next input. In some respects, this procedure is very bad. It does not inform an inexperienced operator that he has pressed the wrong key—it simply ignores it. Oh, I know—what idiot would choose anything but the right key? Still, it is always best to attempt to make things "idiot proof," to avoid "cuteness," and to be as informative as possible for this type of interactive input. (Sad to say, I was once jailed for damage to capital equipment when attempting to use a program with a bug that ignored my correct input and kept repeating "DUMMY! CAN'T YOU READ? NOW ENTER AGAIN AND DO IT CORRECT! [sic].") A better response might be

```
1500 CLS                                        'clear screen
1510 PRINT TAB(15);"1 ENTER NEW WEATHER DATA"
1520 PRINT TAB(15);"2 MODIFY WEATHER DATA"
1530 PRINT TAB(15);"3 CHANGE WEATHER DATA"
1540 PRINT TAB(15);"4 ANNUAL WEATHER DATA"
1550 PRINT TAB(15);"5 SAVE WEATHER DATA"
1560 PRINT TAB(15);"6 LOAD WEATHER DATA"
1570 PRINT @ 656,"ENTER SELECTION"
1580 A$=INKEY$                                  ┌'get character
1590 IF A$="" GOTO 1580 ELSE A=VAL(A$)          │'convert if not null
1600 IF A<>0 AND A<7 GOTO 1660                  │'go if correct
1610 PRINT @ 718,"INCORRECT RESPONSE"           │'notify user
1620 FOR I=1 TO 200                             │  ┌'delay loop
1630 NEXT I                                     │  └'loop
1640 PRINT @ 718,"                           "  │'blank error msg
1650 GOTO 1580                                  └'try again
1660 PRINT "CORRECT RESPONSE"                   'action for correct input
1670 END                                        'additional code here
```

More work? Sure, but much more responsive to inexperienced operators. (When made into a subroutine, it really does not create a great deal of additional work or code, either.)

74

All the Data That's Fit to Print
(And Some That Isn't)

If you've made it through the above sermon, you're about to be rewarded with some interesting material about line printers. Level II BASIC has built-in provisions for printing to line printers, of course.

The two commands that are used to print to a line printer are the command LLIST and the statement LPRINT. LLIST is normally used to list a BASIC program on the system line printer, while LPRINT is used within a BASIC program to print data in much the same way as a standard PRINT is used. Operation of the LLIST is very straightforward—the format is identical to the LIST command for screen display.

LLIST 100-300

for example, would list program lines 100 to 300 on the system line printer.

LPRINT may be used in similar fashion to PRINT, but you should consider the characteristics of the system line printer. The number of tab positions on the display is 64, but the number of tab positions on some line printers is limited, either physically or under software control, to fewer than 64 (20 or 40). In this case, existing code that specifies tabs greater than line-printer print positions will have to be modified for proper columnization and report printing. Conversely, some printers allow more than 64 print positions on a line, and you may use the expanded line to include more information on reports. TABs are produced by "padding" text with enough spaces to move to the proper tab position.

One of the differences between PRINT data on the display and LPRINTing on the system line printer is that the display is always "ready," but the line printer may not be in a ready condition due to being out of paper or being "off-line." When this "not ready" condition exists, the BASIC interpreter will continuously monitor the state of the line printer until it becomes ready. The ready state of the line printer may be determined by the following code

100 IF PEEK(14312)<>63 THEN PRINT "NOT READY" ELSE PRINT "READY"

The code above looks at the line printer by **addressing** location 14312. This system address is *not* memory, but is the line-printer address (37E8 in hexadecimal). The PEEK effectively reads a byte of status from the line printer. If the line printer is not connected in the system, this status will be 11111111; otherwise, the status bits will be as shown in Figure 4-7. Although you could detect each bit by ANDing values and comparing the results, it is sufficient to simply make the test above and print out an appropriate error message to

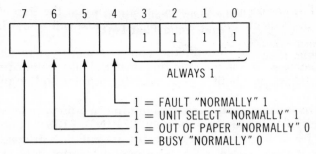

Figure 4-7. Line-printer status bits.

the system user. Here again, this error message may be used to inform an inexperienced operator of the line-printer condition.

Another difference between the display and line printer concerns pagination. The display lines **scroll off** the screen as new lines are printed, and this is adequate for many applications where hard copy is not required. The line printer operates in identical fashion to the display except, of course, that all printed lines are saved on the continuous scroll of line-printer paper. If the material covers more than one page, it is not conveniently spaced for reproduction or for "bursting" the pages for notebooks. The solution to pagination is built into Level II BASIC at memory locations 16424 and 16425. RAM location 16424 holds the number of lines per page, while 16425 holds a current line count. The number of lines per page is initialized to 67, and the line count is initialized to 0. As each line is printed, the line count is increased by 1. If the line count equals the number of lines per page, then the line count is reset to 0. You can see this by the following code, which displays the line number after each line is printed.

```
100   LPRINT "LPTEST"    ⌐  'print line
200   PRINT PEEK(16425)  |  'display line number
300   GOTO 100           ⌐  'loop back
```

On many printers, the number of vertical lines per inch is six. If the print area is to be 10 inches, we'll have 60 lines per page and a margin of three lines (½ inch) on the top and three lines on the bottom. The code below is in the form of a subroutine that looks at the current line number and skips six lines if the line number is 60, to provide a suitable margin for top and bottom. To use the subroutine for printing, set the current line count to 0 before using the line printer by

```
100   POKE 16425,0    'reset current line count
```

At the same time, adjust the line printer to "top of form" by positioning the paper to three lines down from the top. Every time an

LPRINT is performed, call the subroutine so that the "top of form" may be implemented at the 60th line. A typical call would be

```
1200   LPRINT "VALUE=";ZZ
1210   GOSUB 10000
1220   GOTO 1200
```

The code follows

```
10000  ZZ=PEEK(16425)          'get line count
10010  IF ZZ<>60 RETURN        'return if not time
10020  FOR ZI=1 TO 6         ┌─ 'loop for 6 lines
10030  LPRINT " "             │  'print line (WITH BLK)
10040  NEXT ZI               └─ 'loop
10050  POKE 16425,0             'clear line count
10060  RETURN                   'return to calling prog
```

Another difference between the line printer and display is that the character sets of each are different. In most cases, the characters from ASCII 32 to ASCII 127 are identical, or very similar. This range defines special characters, numerics, special characters, upper case, special characters, and lower case, in that order (refer to Table 3-1). The codes 128 through 191 are graphics codes and tab codes that will probably not be accepted by the line printer, or will cause printing of (somewhat) unpredictable line-printer characters. The codes from 0 to 31 will vary with the line printer. Some line printers have programmable character and line widths, and others have programmable line spacing and things such as the BEL code. (The BEL [bell] codes are used on teletypewriters to attract the operator's attention for such things as important wire-service news stories.) Here, I will give standard writing ploy number 127—refer to your system line printer operating manual for specific instructions.

We'll be looking at some of the other aspects of using the line printer in Chapter 12 ("POKEing Around in Memory") when we discuss the video display and line-printer device control blocks (DCBs).

CHAPTER 5

Graphic Examples

We'll be discussing one of the most interesting features of Level II BASIC in this chapter, the ability to create displays of graphics data. The graphics character set allows us selectively to turn on and off 6144 picture elements on the screen of the TRS-80. Graphics allows us to create graphs, forms, and animated pictures. There are several techniques for using graphics, and we'll be discussing each, including a technique of high-speed graphics using strings.

Back to the Books . . .

Before we discuss the techniques, however, let's discuss the mechanics of how graphics are implemented on the TRS-80. (*Guard, stop that reader from sneaking off. . . .*) We know from previous chapters that there are 1024 print positions on the display screen, as shown in Figure 5-1. Each of the 1024 print positions is represented by one byte in video-display memory as shown in the figure. The electronics in the TRS-80 automatically and continuously cycles through each of the 1024 video display memory bytes 30 times per second. If a byte holds a value of less than 128 (less than 10000000 in binary), then the logic in the video display electronics says, "Aha, I detect a displayable character!" It then converts the character code into a displayable character of 5 by 7 dots as shown in Figure 5-2 (the top row is always blank). The dots are configured to represent the ASCII character set shown in Table 3-1.

However, if the video-display memory byte for any print position of the 1024 is greater than 127, the logic in the video-display electronics says, "Another one of those darn graphics characters—

"Come Back! ... He said Implement... *Not* Execute!"

troublemakers, every one. Let's see now, how does that scheme work again?" The scheme that befuddles the logic also befuddles many BASIC programmers. If the code in video-display memory is greater than or equal to 128, the first two bits are ignored, as shown

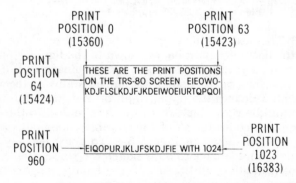

PRINT
POSITION 0
(15360)

PRINT
POSITION 63
(15423)

PRINT
POSITION
64
(15424)

THESE ARE THE PRINT POSITIONS
ON THE TRS-80 SCREEN EIEOWO-
KDJFLSLKDJFJKDEIWOEIURTQPQOI

PRINT
POSITION
960

EIQOPURJKLJFSKDJFIE WITH 1024

PRINT
POSITION
1023
(16383)

(XXXXX) = VIDEO DISPLAY MEMORY BYTE

Figure 5-1. Screen print positions.

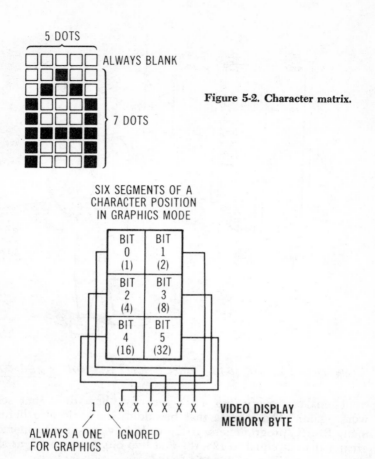

Figure 5-2. Character matrix.

Figure 5-3. TRS-80 graphics format.

in Figure 5-3. The next six bits represent the on/off condition of six segments of the character position, as shown in the figure.

The logic here is readily understood by the binary code in the six bits. The first bit (bit 0) defines the on/off status of the upper left segment, bit 1 defines the upper right, bit 2 defines the middle left, bit 3 the middle right, bit 4 the lower left, and bit 5 the lower right. The graphics codes for *all* of the possible combinations from 128 through 191 are shown in Figure 5-4. To construct any combination, though, all you have to do is sketch the six segments, indicate the on/off condition, and then add the binary weights to 128 to get the corresponding graphics code for the character, as shown in Figure 5-5. The example in the figure produces the code 128+1 (upper left) + 8 (middle right) + 16 (lower left) = 153.

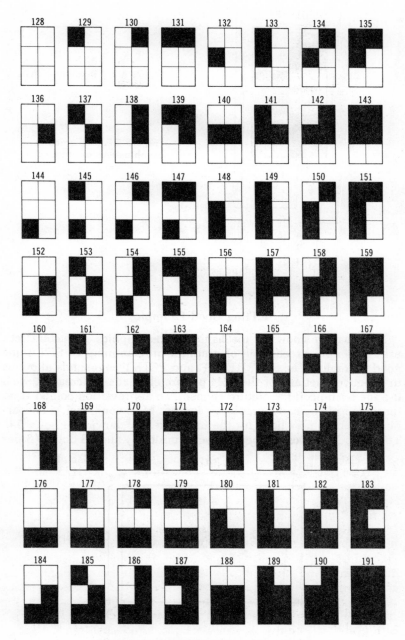

Figure 5-4. TRS-80 graphics characters.

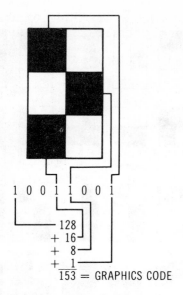

Figure 5-5. Constructing combinations of graphics.

1 0 0 1 1 0 0 1

```
    128
  + 16
  +  8
  +  1
  ‾‾‾
   153 = GRAPHICS CODE
```

SETting Good Examples

Now that we know the mechanics of the graphics characters, let's use the simplest technique of graphics programming to SET some good examples. The SET, RESET, and POINT commands allow us to selectively set any of the 6144 picture elements. (Hereafter, we'll use the term **pixel** for picture element, an abbreviation coined from the name of an early graphics pioneer, Max von Pixel.) The arrangement we now have for the 6144 pixels is shown in Figure 5-6. There are 128 across (2 per character position) and 48 down (3 per

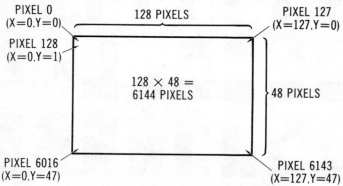

Figure 5-6. Display pixels.

character position) for a total of 128 × 48 = 6144. Numbering is from left to right with a range of 0 through 127, and from top to bottom with a range of 0 through 47. The format of the SET, RESET, and POINT command is

SET(x,y)
RESET(x,y)
POINT(x,y)

SET and RESET, of course, **set** or **reset** the specified pixel. POINT returns the value of the pixel, 0 for off, or -1 for on. Is POINT useful? Does the TRS-80 sleep in the woods? (*Wait a minute, how did sleeping in the woods get into the act . . . ?*) Since the video display *is* a memory, it stores the current on/off status of each point. This can be very useful in determining the point status without referring to another memory location. More on that later.

One of the more common things that is done to the display is to "white it out." The following code whites out the display by two nested loops that use the SET statement. Run the program, but before you do, get out that old trusty stopwatch you were using in your jogging program (you've just got to do something about that paunch . . .). Record the time it takes to white out the screen and save it for comparison with some high-speed techniques we'll be using later.

```
100 CLS                    'clear screen
110 FOR X=0 TO 127         ┌─'outer loop
120 FOR Y=0 TO 47          │ ┌─'inner loop
130 SET (X,Y)              │ │ 'set point
140 NEXT Y                 │ └─'go down columns
150 NEXT X                 └─'and then across
160 GOTO 160               'for nice screen display
```

Got it? I have about 49 seconds. (Some of the later techniques will cut down on that time by a factor of 100!)

Plotting Along With SET/RESET

The SET/RESET technique of graphics is a slow method for displaying patterns, but it does lend itself very well to plotting graphs. As a matter of fact, it is probably the fastest method for displaying graphs of any we'll be discussing.

If you recall those happy days of high-school algebra, you may remember that the "standard" convention for graphs was as shown in Figure 5-7. X is along the horizontal axis, and y is along the vertical axis. X increases toward the right, and y increases toward the top. We have a somewhat different situation with the x,y coordinates for the TRS-80 display. X increases to the right, but the x axis is at the *top* and the y axis increases toward the bottom. Prob-

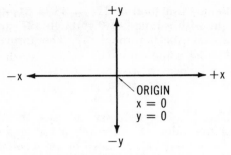

Figure 5-7. "Standard" graphing.

lem: How do we **translate** from the standard graph to the TRS-80 display? Let's plot a simple function to see how we can do this.

Guns Versus Butter

Suppose that we take a classic problem of Guns versus Butter. In this example, we will attempt to solve the economic problems that have been perplexing our country for some time. To make the problem more visible, we'll graph it on the ol' TRS-80.

Guns cost $40 each, while butter costs $4 per pound. If we have $200 to spend, we may divide it up between guns and butter. First of all, let's define the **limits** of the graph. If we buy 5 guns, then we've used up our $200, and we have 0 pounds of butter. If we buy 50 pounds of butter, then we can't afford guns. It looks suspiciously, then, as though the number of guns ranges from 0 through 5 and the number of pounds of butter ranges from 0 through 50. We can now set up the layout of the graph we'd like to draw on the video display (see Figure 5-8).

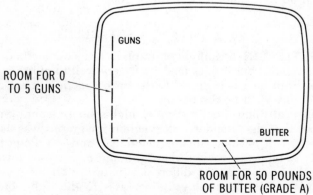

Figure 5-8. Graph skeleton example.

Like most graphing problems of this type, we can divide the work into two parts, drawing the **skeleton** of the graph, and drawing the points themselves, or **plotting**.

The skeleton of the graph can be drawn by drawing one horizontal line and one vertical line. The vertical line runs from y=0 through 47, and we can draw it by

```
200 FOR Y=0 TO 47          ┌'setup loop
300 SET (0,Y)              ├'draw column
400 NEXT Y                 └'continue
```

The horizontal line runs from x=0 through 127 on line 47, and we can draw it by

```
500 FOR X=0 TO 127         ┌'setup loop
600 SET(X,47)              ├'draw row
700 NEXT X                 └'continue
```

To complete the skeleton, we need some way of marking the increments of guns and butter and some labels. We'll use a blank spot every 2 points for butter, and a blank spot every 9 points for guns. (We chose these increments because the maximum value of 50 pounds of butter would be at x=100 and the maximum value of 5 guns would be at y=45; neither value would cause illegitimate x or y values.)

The following code would clear the tick marks and label each of the axes.

```
800 FOR X=2 TO 100 STEP 2      ┌'setup tick loop
900 RESET (X,47)               ├'blank tick mark
1000 NEXT X                    └'continue
1100 FOR Y=47 TO 2 STEP -9     ┌'setup tick loop
1200 RESET (0,Y)               ├'blank tick mark
1300 NEXT Y                    └'continue
1400 PRINT @ 5,"GUNS";          'vertical title
1500 PRINT @ 936,"BUTTER";      'horizontal title
```

The skeleton we have now looks like Figure 5-9. All we need to do at this point to solve the world's economic problems is to do some meaningful plotting. The problem resolves into

$$\# \text{ GUNS } * \$40 + \# \text{ LBS BUTTER } * \$4 = \$200$$

One way of implementing this problem is to step the number of guns from 0 through 5, since we know that this is the range of the number of guns. The code below does this and computes the number of pounds of butter for each quantity of guns.

```
1600 FOR G=0 TO 5          ┌'setup computation
1700 B=(200-G*40)/4        ├'compute butter
1800 NEXT G                └'continue
```

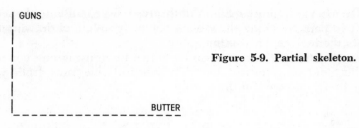

Figure 5-9. Partial skeleton.

The only remaining thing to do is to plot the points for each set of guns and butter. The horizontal distance or **displacement** for the x value defining the number of pounds of butter is found by taking B, the number of pounds of butter, and multiplying it by 2 (there are two increments for every pound of butter). The vertical distance for the y value defining the number of guns is found by multiplying G, the number of guns, by 9 (there are 9 increments for every gun). Putting this calculation in the above code produces

```
1600 FOR G=0 TO 5        'setup computation
1700 B=(200-G*40)/4      'compute butter
1720 X=B*2               'x displacement
1740 Y=47-G*9            'y displacement
1760 SET (X,Y)           'set point
1800 NEXT G              'continue
```

With the addition of a screen clear at the beginning, the completed program looks like this

```
100 CLS                      'clear screen
200 FOR Y=0 TO 47            'setup loop
300 SET (0,Y)                'draw column
400 NEXT Y                   'continue
500 FOR X=0 TO 127           'setup loop
600 SET(X,47)                'draw row
700 NEXT X                   'continue
800 FOR X=2 TO 100 STEP 2    'setup tick loop
900 RESET (X,47)             'blank tick mark
1000 NEXT X                  'continue
1100 FOR Y=47 TO 2 STEP -9   'setup tick loop
1200 RESET (0,Y)             'blank tick mark
1300 NEXT Y                  'continue
1400 PRINT @ 5,"GUNS";       'vertical title
1500 PRINT @ 936,"BUTTER";   'horizontal title
1600 FOR G=0 TO 5            'setup computation
1700 B=(200-G*40)/4          'compute butter
1720 X=B*2                   'x displacement
1740 Y=47-G*9                'y displacement
1760 SET (X,Y)               'set point
1800 NEXT G                  'continue
1900 GOTO 1900               'loop here for display
```

The most important point (no pun intended) in the above program is that the usual graphic y value must be converted to the screen graph y system by subtraction from 47. This must always be done for a graph with y coordinate at the bottom of the display.

```
1740  Y=47-G*9      'y displacement
```

The Guns and Butter graph illustrates the general approach that you should take in graphing a particular **function**, or set of points that define a graphical relationship.

1. Determine the appropriate ranges of both the x and y variables.
2. Draw the skeleton of the graph and mark off the horizontal and vertical axes with appropriate tick marks to cover the range. Numeric values, of course, may be put on or near the axes.
3. Compute the function and get x,y values.
4. Convert the x,y values to the TRS-80 video coordinates by using the same x value, but by finding a new y value by subtracting the old value from 47.
5. Plot the point by a SET.
6. Repeat for all points.

In the above example, we used values for x and y that were somewhat contrived. X and y turned out to be integer values only; that is, none of the x and y values were mixed numbers containing integers and fractions. What happens if we do use mixed numbers for x and y? If we attempt to set, say, x=12.7 and y=13.5, the x,y values are **truncated** to x=12 and y=13. This means that x and y can be computed without worrying about invalid values, unless x is less than 0, x is greater than or equal to 128, or y is greater than or equal to 48.

A Moving Experience

The SET and RESET commands can be used together to give the illusion of motion for dots, lines, starships, flying rolling pins, and other items. Let's take the simplest case first, a moving dot. To make a dot appear to move, the dot must be SET in one position, RESET in that position, and then SET in the next position. The timing should be such that the motion appears fluid (see Figure 5-10).

The simplest code for this is shown below. The speed of the single dot moving across line 24 is about 1½ seconds per crossing.

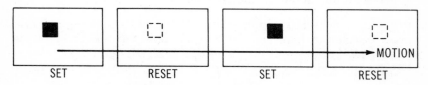

Figure 5-10. Simple animation.

This is about the maximum speed for a SET/RESET approach. The dot can be *slowed down* by inserting "time wasters" at statement 350. Try various "time wasters" such as 350 REM or 350 A=0 or 350 A=1*2 to see how they affect the speed of the dot.

```
100 CLS              'clear screen
200 FOR X=0 TO 127   ┌'animation loop
300 SET (X,24)       │'turn dot on
400 RESET (X,24)     │'turn dot off
500 NEXT X           └'continue
```

The same principle of animation may be applied to more complex figures. The more complex the figures, of course, the more difficult it is to know which dots to turn on and off. We'll show some more examples of animation later in this chapter when we discuss some of the faster graphics methods.

Good Points to Consider

What the heck is the purpose of the POINT command? Beats me —let's go on to the next subject. . . .

But seriously, folks . . . the POINT command is a way of checking each of the 6144 pixels on the video display to see whether they are turned on or off. But don't we know at all times whether or not the pixels are on or off? Not necessarily. We could keep track of all pixels that are on in a long **table**, and then search that table to find out the state of the pixel in question. But why not use the POINT command to check the pixel without spending a lot of time searching through a table of values? After all, each pixel is really a one-bit (0 or 1) memory in itself. The POINT command makes it possible to check the state of any one of the 6144 bits that represent the pixels on the screen.

There are times when it's very convenient to use the POINT command in place of keeping a long list of turned-on pixels. Suppose that we have turned on points at random and now wish to check whether a pixel is on. The code below shows a simple example of the approach. It searches the video **memory** by a POINT command to find the one pixel that has been turned on by a random selection. The random selection was made by the RND command, which we'll talk about a little later on.

```
1000 CLS                              'clear screen
1100 X=RND(127)                       'find random x 1 to 127
1200 Y=RND(47)                        'find random y 1 to 47
1300 SET (X,Y)                        'turn on point
1400 FOR X=0 TO 127                   ┌'setup outer loop
1500 FOR Y=0 TO 47                    │┌'setup inner loop
1600 IF POINT(X,Y)=-1 PRINT X,Y       ││┌'print if point on
1700 NEXT Y                           │└'continue search
1800 NEXT X                           └'continue with outer
```

Notice that a −1 was returned for the POINT in only one case, the case in which the pixel was found to be ON. All other pixels caused the POINT to return a zero, indicating that they were OFF.

The POKE Graphics Method

The second approach to graphics that can be used is the POKE method. We know that video-display memory is exactly that, a set of 1024 memory locations. The addresses of the 1024 locations range from 15360 to 16383. This area is in the first 16K (16 × 1024) locations of the TRS-80 memory address range. The video-display memory shares this memory along with Level II BASIC and some dedicated addresses for the line printer and other devices (see Figure 5-11).

LOCATION

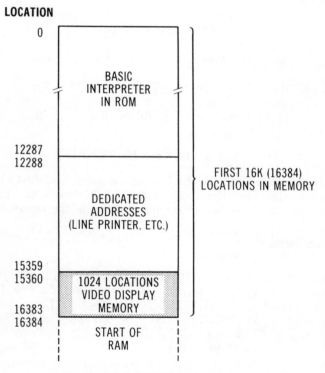

Figure 5-11. Video-display addresses.

To address any of the 1024 print positions, all that we must do is find the displacement of the print position from the start of video-display memory as shown in Figure 5-12. Since there are 64 char-

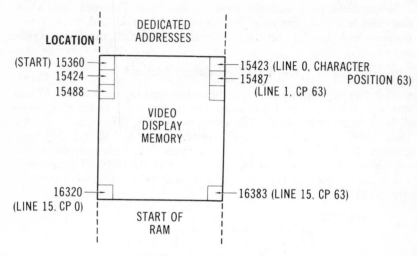

Figure 5-12. Finding the print-position displacement.

acters per line and 16 lines per display, the video-display memory address for any character position is 15360 + (line number *64) + (character position in line). To address line 8, character position 10, for example, we find

$$15360 + 64 * 8 + 10 = 15882$$

Here, we were using 0 as the first line number and first character position on the line. Referring to our ASCII codes of Table 3-1, we can store a "1" on that character position on the screen by

```
100   CLS              'for set
200   POKE 15882,49    'set pixel
300   GOTO 300         'loop here
```

The POKE method is very useful when we must fill the same graphics character across an entire line or portion of a line. Did you save the timing of the SET/RESET "white-out"? Let's compare it with one using the POKE method. The following code whites out the display by POKEing a 191 (10111111) into each of the 1024 character positions of the video display. The value 191 represents all ones for the six pixels and a one bit to signify graphics. For the fastest speed, don't enter the comments!

```
10 CLS                        'clear screen
20 FOR X=15360 TO 16383      ⌈'screen memory limits
30 POKE X,191                ⌊'all 6 pixels on
40 NEXT X                     'continue
50 GOTO 50                   'looks nice
```

90

Seven and a half seconds! Quite a difference between the POKE and SET/RESET methods!

Of course, any of the 64 patterns shown in Figure 5-4 may be output as a line or portion of a line using the POKE technique. The following code draws a stop light using the POKE method. When the areas involved are small, the method is fast enough that you can at least think about animation techniques.

```
90  DATA 191,131,131,191,191,131,131,191
92  DATA 191,131,131,191,131,171,151,131
94  DATA 128,170,149,128
100 CLS                              'clear screen
110 FOR I=0 TO 4                    ┌─'setup row loop
120 FOR J=0 TO 3                    │ ┌─'setup column loop
130 READ A                          │ │ 'get graphics value
140 POKE 15360+350+J+I*64,A         │ │ 'poke into row,column
150 NEXT J                          │ └─'go for next column
160 NEXT I                          └─'go for next row
170 FOR I=0 TO 2                  ┌─┌─'setup light output
180 POKE 15360+351+I*64,167        │ │ 'flash light
190 POKE 15360+352+I*64,167        │ │ 'in two positions
195 IF I=1 THEN K=300 ELSE K=1000  │ │ 'use short value for yel
200 FOR J=0 TO K                   │ │ ┌─'timing loop
210 NEXT J                         │ │ └─'for light
220 POKE 15360+351+I*64,131        │ │ 'now turn off light
230 POKE 15360+352+I*64,131        │ │ 'in two positions
240 NEXT I                         │ └─'continue
250 GOTO 170                       └─'loop for next cycle
```

How about addressing the 6144 pixels randomly using the POKE technique? I was afraid you'd ask. . . . While it's easy to compute the address of a character position for the POKE, it's rather difficult to compute the address of a pixel. Furthermore, computing the pixel address and performing a POKE for the pixel bit actually takes longer than the equivalent SET/RESET. For those masochistic programmers out there who wish to try it anyway. . . .

To find the POKE address for a given x,y, perform the following steps.

1. Divide x by 2 and save the quotient as XQ. $XQ=INT(X/2)$
2. Save the remainder as XR. $XR=X-(XQ*2)$
3. Divide y by 3 and save the quotient as YQ. $YQ=INT(Y/3)$
4. Save the remainder as YR. $YR=Y-(YQ*3)$
5. The POKE address is given by $A=15360+YQ*64+XQ$.

To SET a bit using POKE,

1. Get the value at the POKE address by $B=PEEK(A)$.
2. OR in a bit value as follows: $B=B \text{ OR } 2\uparrow(YR*2+XR)$.
3. Make certain the most significant bit is set by ORing in 128. $B=B \text{ OR } 128$
4. POKE the value back in the address. POKE A,B

To RESET a bit using POKE, change the value in step 2 to $255-2\uparrow(YR*2+XR)$ and AND instead of ORing.

$$B=B \text{ AND } (255-2\uparrow(YR*2+XR))$$

String Graphics and the Chattanooga TRS-80

Do you still have that stop watch available? Execute the following program to "white-out" the screen, and time its duration.

```
100 CLEAR 500          'clear string space
200 CLS                'clear screen
300 A$=STRING$(64,CHR$(191))  'get graphics string
400 FOR I=1 TO 16      ┌'setup loop
500 PRINT A$;          │'print line
600 NEXT I             └'loop
700 GOTO 700            'for display
```

This time the screen white-out took less than a second! Obviously, this method is the fastest of any so far—75 times as fast as the SET/RESET method and 10 times faster than the POKE implementation. This method uses one of several methods to establish a string variable. Once the string has been established, it can be PRINTed very rapidly because it requires no computation; the string values are just simply printed as they appear!

To see another example of this method, let's establish a display other than a continuous string of the same pattern. We'll use an old-time locomotive as the pattern we want, as shown in Figure 5-13. The choo-choo is made up of 36 character positions with 6 pixels in each character position, as shown in the figure.

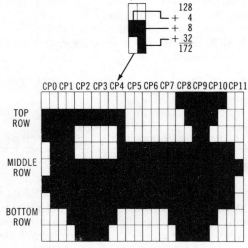

Figure 5-13. Choo-choo pattern.

We must take each of the 36 character positions and translate them into a proper graphics code by referring to Figure 5-4. When we do this, the codes are

TOP ROW   188,188,140,140,172,128,128,128,139,191,135,128
MIDDLE ROW   186,191,188,188,190,191,191,191,191,191,191,157
BOTTOM ROW   130,139,191,191,135,131,131,139,191,191,135,129

Just to be certain that we have the proper codes, let's draw the figure in the center of the screen. We'll use three strings, one for each row in the figure.

```
100 CLEAR 1000                          'clear string space
200 CLS                                 'clear screen
300 A$=CHR$(188)+CHR$(188)+CHR$(140)+CHR$(140)+CHR$(172)+CHR$(128)+CHR$(128)+CHR$(1:
400 B$=CHR$(186)+CHR$(191)+CHR$(188)+CHR$(188)+CHR$(190)+CHR$(191)+CHR$(191)+CHR$(1°
500 C$=CHR$(130)+CHR$(139)+CHR$(191)+CHR$(191)+CHR$(135)+CHR$(131)+CHR$(131)+CHR$(1:
600 PRINT @ 538,A$;                     'print first row
700 PRINT @ 602,B$;                     'print second row
800 PRINT @ 666,C$;                     'print third row
900 GOTO 900                            'loop here for display
```

To make the choo-choo move, we'll move it a character position at a time. If we add leading blanks to the strings, we will get an automatic erase of the old image. With the addition of some smoke, we've completed the animation

840 IF RND(3)=1 GOTO 850 ELSE PRINT @ I−54,"0";

```
100 CLEAR 1000                          'clear string space
200 CLS                                 'clear screen
300 A$=" "+CHR$(188)+CHR$(188)+CHR$(140)+CHR$(140)+CHR$(172)+CHR$(128)+CHR$(128)+CHF
400 B$=" "+CHR$(186)+CHR$(191)+CHR$(188)+CHR$(188)+CHR$(190)+CHR$(191)+CHR$(191)+CHF
500 C$=" "+CHR$(130)+CHR$(139)+CHR$(191)+CHR$(191)+CHR$(135)+CHR$(131)+CHR$(131)+CHF
600 FOR I=512 TO 563                   ─'setup loop for movement
650 PRINT @ I,A$;                        'print first row
700 PRINT @ I+64,B$;                     'print second row
800 PRINT @ I+128,C$;                    'print third row
825 FOR J=1 TO 20                       ┌'delay for effect
830 NEXT J                              └'loop
840 IF RND(3)=1 GOTO 850 ELSE PRINT @ I-54,"0";
850 NEXT I                               'move to the right
900 GOTO 900                           └'loop here for display
```

Note that in the above code, we used a timing loop (FOR J=1 TO 20: NEXT J) to actually *slow down* the animation! We're making progress in speeding up our graphics! Another trick we could have used would be to add cursor characters in the string so that A$, B$, and C$ would be concatenated into one super string. Adding STRING$ (13,CHR$(24)) and CHR$(26) would move the cursor left 13 positions and down one position, in preparation for the next row. You might like to work that out on your own (reviewing cursor positioning in Chapter 3 will help refresh your memory about cursor movement).

String Graphics Using Dummy Strings

There is an additional technique that we can use to implement string graphics, the technique of "dummy strings." For this method, we use a dummy string equal in length to the desired string and then fill in the graphics characters required. When a number of strings are used for graphics, this technique saves on string initialization and string storage requirements, and is easier to use. We'll see how this works using one large string with cursor control movements.

```
1000 CLS                              'clear screen'
1100 A$="THIS IS A DUMMY STRING TO BE FILLED WITH GRAPHICS AND CURSOR CHARS!"
1200 DATA 128,188,188,140,140,172,128,128,128,139,191,135,128
1250 DATA 26,24,24,24,24,24,24,24,24,24,24,24,24
1300 DATA 128,186,191,188,188,190,191,191,191,191,191,191,157
1350 DATA 26,24,24,24,24,24,24,24,24,24,24,24,24
1400 DATA 128,130,139,191,191,135,131,131,139,191,191,135,129
1500 B=VARPTR(A$)
1600 C=PEEK(B+2)*256+PEEK(B+1)         'find actual address
1700 FOR I=C TO C+66               ⌐'setup loop to fill string
1800 READ A                        │'get one byte value
1900 POKE I,A                      │'poke into string
2000 NEXT I                        └'loop
2100 FOR I=512 TO 560              ⌐'setup loop to move
2200 PRINT @ I,A$;                 │'print one long string
2300 FOR J=1 TO 30                 │  ⌐'delay for effect
2400 NEXT J                        │  └'loop
2450 IF RND(3)=1 GOTO 2500 ELSE PRINT @ I-54,"0";
2500 NEXT I                        └'move to right
2600 GOTO 2600                      'to retain display
```

Unlike the other string graphics mode, no CLEAR is necessary, since the BASIC interpreter will use the string text in the A$ statement for PRINTing the string. The dummy string is established by using any text string *that is equal to the number of graphics characters to be printed*. Next, the graphics characters themselves are constructed using a DATA statement. The first two rows have the cursor control characters 26 (down cursor) and 24 (left cursor) appended to move the cursor back to the beginning of the next row.

We know from Chapter 3 that the VARPTR function will find the address of the string variable parameters for A$ in the following order:

(B) = A$ length
(B+1) = Least significant byte of A$ address
(B+2) = Most significant byte of A$ address

C is computed to contain the address of A$. This address, unlike a string that has been constructed from CHR$ or concatenation, is the address of the string within the A$ statement itself. The READ loop reads each of the DATA values and puts them into the dummy string. Now we have a string for A$ made up of the actual graphics characters we require. This is used in the PRINT@ statement in the same fashion as the other string graphics mode, except that we now have one large string.

The speed of this graphics method is about the same or slightly faster than the previous string method, once the dummy string has been filled with the proper characters. The program below "whites out" the screen using this method.

```
3000 A$="                            '64 spaces here!
3100 B=VARPTR(A$)                    'get string block locn
3200 A=PEEK(B+2)*256+PEEK(B+1)       'get address of string
3300 FOR I=A TO A+63                 ┌'set fill loop
3400 POKE I,191                      │'fill with all on chrs
3500 NEXT I                          └'loop
3600 CLS                             'clear screen
3700 FOR I=1 TO 16                   ┌'setup loop for lines
3800 PRINT A$;                       │'fill line
3900 NEXT I                          └'loop
4000 GOTO 4000                       'loop for appearance
```

One important point about this method: Do not attempt to edit the lines after they have been initialized!

Graphics Review

We've discussed four graphics methods: the SET/RESET method, the POKE method, the string method, and the dummy string method.

Let's just recap how to apply these methods: Use SET/RESET for plotting graphs and random data. This method is useful any time points must be displayed that are not in the same area, or that do not have a similar pattern. The POKE method is used as a simple, direct way to draw horizontal or vertical line segments that have an identical pattern or for drawing blocks of patterns (and it's much faster than the SET/RESET method). The string methods are used when animation is to be performed. They're extremely fast but require a great deal of work in translating the graphics patterns to be output into corresponding data values. The dummy string method is perhaps the easiest for setting up a large number of graphics data, but it does require a means to move the data into the dummy string.

Is there a faster graphics method? Yes, there is a method that is even a hundred times faster than the string method. The kicker is that this method uses **machine language.** We'll be describing some of the interfacing techniques to machine-language subroutines in a later chapter, but we cannot cover the subject in less than another book! Take a look at our *TRS-80 Assembly-Language Programming* (62-2006) if you're interested in learning how to create machine-language programs.

How to Draw a Straight Line

Drawing a straight line on the video display is not always easy to do. The TRS-80 video screen is divided into 128 by 48 picture elements, as we have seen. Now, the more pixels that there are on a display, the finer the **resolution** of the display, and the straighter the lines that can be drawn. Compare the line drawn on a portion of a screen that has 100 pixels (10 by 10) with one that has 400 (20 by 20) (see Figure 5-14).

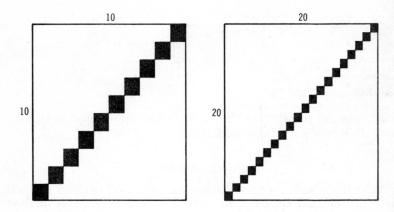

Figure 5-14. Drawing straight lines.

In attempting to draw a straight line between two points, a certain amount of "jaggedness" has crept in. This jaggedness is unavoidable, and the 6144 pixels on the TRS-80 represent a good compromise between a reasonable resolution and a manageable number of points. (Remember, each point takes a discrete amount of time to process, and painting a white screen with 128 by 128 pixels would take about 2⅔ times as long as 6144 pixels.)

How can we draw a reasonably straight line between two points? One way this could be done, of course, would be to work with the equation of a straight line for a graph. Everyone knows that this is $Y=MX^*C$. Or is it $Y=MX/C \ldots$? Or, wait a minute . . . I've got it here in my notes. . . .

On second thought, let's look at a way that is just as efficient (probably more so) and that takes very little math and no analytic geometry. Suppose that we have two points that must be connected by a straight line. We've shown the number of points between the two points in Figure 5-15.

The following code draws a straight line between the two points by determining the minimum number of points to *fill every pixel* between the two points. The code tries to minimize SETting the same pixel ON more than once, since this is an obvious waste of time. On the other hand, it makes certain that every pixel of the jagged line between the two points is SET that must be SET. Of

X2—X1 IN THE x OR HORIZONTAL DIRECTION
Y2—Y1 IN THE y OR VERTICAL DIRECTION

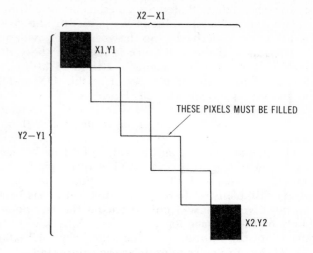

Figure 5-15. Connecting two points.

course the code is a subroutine and must be called using something such as:

```
100   INPUT X1, Y1, X2, Y2    ┌  '2 points
110   GOSUB 10000             │  'call line subroutine
120   GOTO 100                └  'loop
```

```
10000 IF ABS(X2-X1)<ABS(Y2-Y1) GOTO 10200
10005 DY=(Y2-Y1)/ABS(X2-X1)              'get delta Y
10010 IF X2>X1 GOTO 10070                'go if X2 TO RIGHT
10020 FOR I=X1 TO X2 STEP -1          ┌ 'X2 to left
10030 SET (I,Y1)                      │ 'set point
10040 Y1=Y1+DY                        │ 'add delta Y
10045 IF Y1<0 THEN Y1=0               │ 'may happen once
10050 NEXT I                          └ 'continue loop
10060 RETURN                             'return to calling prog
10070 FOR I=X1 TO X2                  ┌ 'X2 to right
10080 SET (I,Y1)                      │ 'set point
10090 Y1=Y1+DY                        │ 'add delta Y
10095 IF Y1<0 THEN Y1=0               │ 'may happen once
10100 NEXT I                          └ 'continue loop
10110 RETURN                             'return to calling prog
10200 DX=(X2-X1)/ABS(Y2-Y1)              'find delta x
10205 IF Y2>Y1 GOTO 10300                'go if Y2 below
10210 FOR I=Y1 TO Y2 STEP -1          ┌ 'Y2 above
10220 SET (X1,I)                      │ 'set point
10230 X1=X1+DX                        │ 'add delta x
10235 IF X1<0 THEN X1=0               │ 'may happen once
10240 NEXT I                          └ 'continue loop
10250 RETURN                             'return to calling prog
10300 FOR I=Y1 TO Y2                  ┌ 'Y2 above
10310 SET (X1,I)                      │ 'set point
10320 X1=X1+DX                        │ 'add delta x
10325 IF X1<0 THEN X1=0               │ 'may happen once
10330 NEXT I                          └ 'continue loop
10340 RETURN                             'return
```

The code above functions as follows: It compares the distance in the y direction with the distance in the x direction. If the x distance is greater, then the code will step x in increments of 1 from X1 to X2. For each x step, a "delta" value of y is added to the current Y1 value. The DY value is derived from the y distance divided by the number of steps in x. If the x distance is less than the y distance, then the code will step y in increments of 1 from Y1 to Y2 and vary X1 by adding a delta x. In the process of adding DX or DY, it is possible to go over Y1=47 or X1=127. However, as we saw earlier, an x or y value that is fractionally over is truncated. Given sufficient precision, X1 and Y1 will never be equal to or greater than 128 or 48, respectively.

A different situation exists when the value of X1 or Y1 decreases. Because the delta is fractional, X1 or Y1 may become very small negative numbers. Because of this, a check is made for negative X1 or Y1, and the variable is set to 0 if a negative value has been computed. The negative value will only occur on the last point to be SET and only on the extreme top (Y) or left (X).

A test driver for the subroutine in the code below will allow you to input X1, Y1, X2, Y2 values to exercise the subroutine.

The subroutine may be used as the lines are required, or it may be used to draw an initial pattern by setting up values in a DATA statement or array and by READing the values with a call to the subroutine for each set of four as shown below. A convenient way to detect the end of the data is by an illegal set of points such as −1, −1.

```
100  DATA 20,20,30,20
200  DATA 30,20,30,30
300  DATA 30,30,20,30
400  DATA 20,30,20,20
500  DATA 20,20,30,30
600  DATA 20,30,30,20
700  DATA -1,-1,-1,-1
750  CLS                      'clear screen
800  READ X1,Y1,X2,Y2         ┌'read two point definitions
900  IF X1=-1 GOTO 900        │'loop for aesthetics
1000 GOSUB 10000              │'draw that line
1100 GOTO 800                 └'loop for next line
```

CHAPTER 6

Tables, Chessboards, and the Fourth Dimension

In this chapter and the next, we'll be talking about how to organize data. In the jargon of computer science, organization of data is treated under the name **data structures.** The three data structures we'll discuss in this chapter are **lists, tables,** and **arrays.** In the next chapter, we'll talk about how to maintain the order of tables and arrays, and about a third type of data structure called a **linked list.** We'll limit our discussion to those data structures used commonly in BASIC programs and forget about such esoteric structures as the Flying Buttress Array, the Catenary String, and the Starboard List, all of which cause computer science students many sleepless midterm nights.

The simplest form of a data structure is a **list** of items. A list represents a set of data that is probably related in some fashion. An example might be a shopping list for the grocery store:

1 lb butter
1 qt milk
3 sm tomatoes
1 can orange juice
1 qt oil
1 can peas

All the items are related except one. Which one? Exactly—the 3 sm tomatoes are the only items that are not packaged! This only points to the fact that lists can include any number of related or non-related items at the user's discretion.

BASIC DATA Lists

We have a built-in provision in Level II BASIC for creating a list. The DATA statement allows us to build a list as long as the memory we have available. The DATA statements below build our list.

```
10 DATA "1 LB. BUTTER"
12 DATA "1 QT MILK"
14 DATA "3 SM TOMATOES"
16 DATA "1 CAN ORANGE JUICE"
18 DATA "1 QT OIL"
20 DATA "1 CAN PEAS"
```

We can **read** the list by performing a READ command. The code shown below continuously READs the list we established in statements 10-20 until it runs out of data. At that point, the BASIC interpreter, having looked throughout the current BASIC program unsuccessfully for more DATA statements, prints the message "OD

ITEM 1	"1 LB BUTTER"
2	5
3	3.7
4	"1 QT OIL"
5	377258
6	.005
7	2

Figure 6-1. Example of DATA list.

ERROR IN 1000". In the case of this list, each string (such as "1 LB BUTTER") was one **item** in the list. Every time a READ was performed, the next item from the list was read.

```
1000   READ A$
1010   GOTO 1000
```

We can have any number of items in the DATA list as long as we either have a data statement for each one or separate the items by commas. The types of items in the list can also be mixed—we can intersperse strings with numeric data of several types. BASIC automatically makes each entry a separate item. The statements

```
100   DATA "1 LB BUTTER",5,3.7,"1 QT OIL"
110   DATA 377258,.005,2
```

would create a list of 7 items arranged as shown in Figure 6-1. Every time a READ was performed, the next item in the list would be read. Of course, we could *not* have tried reading a *string* with a "100 READ A". If we had, an error would have resulted.

We mentioned earlier that the list could be as long as the memory available. When using DATA statements, there is only **one** list. And that list includes **every** DATA statement in the current program, the same way that the Lord High Executioner's list in the *Mikado* included all of his enemies.

```
DATA   "PEOPLE WHO HAVE FLABBY HANDS AND IRRITATING LAUGHS"
DATA   "PERSONS WHO IN SHAKING HANDS WITH YOU SHAKE HANDS
        WITH YOU LIKE THAT"
DATA   "THE BANJO SERENADER AND THE OTHERS OF HIS RACE"
```

When we have three DATA statements in a 2000 statement program, one at the beginning, one at the middle, and one at the end, such as

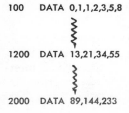

```
100   DATA 0,1,1,2,3,5,8



1200   DATA 13,21,34,55



2000   DATA 89,144,233
```

```
100 CLS                                 'clear screen
110 PRINT "height vs weight"             'print title
120 INPUT "input height in inches";IH    'input height
130 IF IH<50 OR IH>72 GOTO 120           'try again if off scale
140 RESTORE                              'reset pointer
150 READ HT,WT                           'read ht,wt from list
160 IF HT=IH PRINT "FOR HEIGHT OF";HT;"WEIGHT SHOULD BE";WT ELSE GOTO 150
170 GOTO 120                             'go for next ht
180 DATA 50,65,51,67,52,75,53,88,55,95,56,101,57,106,58,111
190 DATA 59,120,60,125,61,131,62,136,63,144,64,148,65,156,66,161
200 DATA 67,167,68,172,69,180,70,184,71,253,72,197
```

Figure 6-2. DATA list program.

then we've created a fourteen-element list of items. The data statements can be put anywhere; the BASIC interpreter will skip over them in the normal flow of execution and simply note where they are and that they constitute **the one and only** data list.

READs and RESTOREs

Every time a READ is executed, another item in **the** data list is read, and an imaginary pointer is adjusted to point to the next DATA item. Actually, the pointer is not so imaginary. There *is* a pointer used in the BASIC interpreter, but it is not accessible to John Q. Programmer, except via the RESTORE statement. The RESTORE resets the pointer to the beginning of the DATA list. Any time we want to start at the beginning of the DATA list, we can take advantage of the RESTORE.

A good example is shown in Figure 6-2, where we have a program to access the DATA list to find the average weight for a given height. In this case, the data is arranged in groups of two, height (in inches) followed by average weight (in pounds). Every READ reads two items, height into HT and weight into WT. When the height matches a given input height, then the weight is printed. A RESTORE then resets the pointer in preparation for the next input. Note that a **multiple** READ has been done with two variables. We can read as many variables as we can pack into each READ statement.

Mixing It Up

Having one huge DATA list of mixed variables is a mixed blessing. It's a convenient way to establish a long list of *constant* data, but it does not allow an easy way to set up independent data lists. If we read three different sets of data, as in this example,

```
100 REM LIST OF TELEPHONE NUMBERS
110 DATA "555-1212","999-8000","999-1234"
```
↓
```
1200 REM LIST OF DISTANCES IN MILES
1210 DATA 1.2,3.6,5.7,9.2,11.8
```
↓
```
1830 REM LIST OF LISTS
1840 DATA "STARBOARD","PORT","BOTTOMS UP"
```

then we wind up with one integrated list of 11 items. How do we locate each group conveniently? We *could* be aware of the number of items in each group. That way, to get to the third group, the list of lists, we could execute

```
2000 RESTORE                    'reset pointer
2100 FOR I=0 TO 2              ┌'setup for first group
2200 READ A$                   │'read and throw away
2300 NEXT                      └'loop
2400 FOR I=0 TO 4              ┌'setup for 2nd group
2500 READ A                    │'read and throw away
2600 NEXT                      └'loop
2700 REM WHEW! FINALLY MADE IT!
```

This code bypasses the first two groups by READing and discarding DATA items. Two separate READs must be made because the first group is a string list while the second group is a numeric list.

Another way to find the proper group is to insert a unique code at the beginning of each group and then search for that code to set the pointer to the proper data. This technique is shown in Figure 6-3,

```
1000 DATA -1
1010 DATA 23,5,6,78,115,5,4,6,89,101
1020 DATA -2
1030 DATA 5,6,7,45,666,77,89,17,3
1040 DATA -3
1050 DATA 3,4,5.6,7.8,3.01,5
1060 RESTORE                    'reset data pointer
1070 READ A                     'search for -2
1080 IF A<>-2 GOTO 1070         'read again if not -2
1090 REM NOW POSITIONED AT SECOND LIST
```

Figure 6-3. Using multiple DATA sets.

where a search is made for −2, which is the second group of data. When −2 is found, the data in the second group can be accessed. Obviously, a −2 cannot be a DATA item anywhere in the DATA list, nor can any of the other values that are used for codes that mark the position. Clearly, we have reached the end of our list in noting the usefulness of the DATA, READ, and RESTORE commands. Let's move on to more useful data structures, but remember the DATA list as a powerful data structure for short programs, and, as we shall see, a means for **initializing data** in another data structure called an **array**.

Array of Hope

One of the more powerful data structures we have in Level II BASIC is the **array**. What's an array? Thought you'd never ask . . . an array is an ordered list. The list may be one-dimensional, two-dimensional, three-dimensional, or many-dimensional. The number of dimensions relates to how data in the list is accessed or obtained.

One-Dimensional Arrays

A good example of a one-dimensional array is a shopping list. Wait a minute . . . didn't we go through this some other time? I have a feeling of deja vu. . . . Actually, the shopping list presented earlier under DATA statements *is* a one-dimensional array, as are the other examples of DATA statements. The primary differences, however, are that the DATA statement produced a list of constant data that could not be modified and could not be easily accessed except in **sequential** fashion, starting from the beginning. A one-dimensional array, on the other hand, may be easily modified and accessed.

As an illustration of a one-dimensional array, let's set up an array called AG (**AG**e) that will hold the ages of 100 people. The equivalent DATA statement approach would be

```
100  DATA 33,50,12,2,7,105,969
```

where the ages are known beforehand. (We have included Methuselah's age for contrast.) Using a one-dimensional array, though, we **reserve** space for the 100 ages by a **DIM**ension statement.

```
100  DIM AG(99)
```

Note that the DIM statement specified an upper limit of 99. The number of items, or **elements,** in the array is 0–99 or 100. The number specified in the DIMension statement is always one less than the number of elements in the array.

When the BASIC interpreter encounters a DIM statement such as the one above, it reserves, or **allocates,** an area in RAM memory for array AG made up of 100 elements. What is in the elements? Initially, zeroes. It is up to the programmer to fill it with meaningful data. (That's usually the hardest part of programming.)

The array is represented in Figure 6-4. It is stored in RAM memory as a **contiguous** (consecutive) block, with the first element (0) at the start (lowest RAM) location, and the last element at the highest RAM location. Now let's fill in those elements with meaningful data. . . .

To access any element in the array, we simply give the name of the array, AG, and a number from 0 to 99 representing the array element. Of course, the number may be represented by a variable or expression, also. To INPUT a number of ages and fill in the array, for example, we can execute the code shown below.

```
3000 CLS                        'clear screen
3100 I=0                        'index=0
3200 INPUT "ENTER AGE";A        ┌ 'input age in years
3300 AG(I)=A                    │ 'store in array
3400 I=I+1                      │ 'point to next array el
3500 GOTO 3200                  └ 'go for next age
```

104

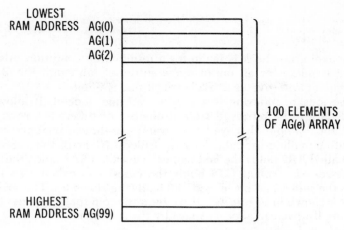

Figure 6-4. Example of one-dimensional array.

This code will fill array AG forever, especially since there is no provision for ending the INPUT process. Initially, I is set to 0, and the first entry is made by AG(0)=A after A has been set equal to the INPUT value. Each time through the loop, I is incremented by one to point to the next element of the array. If more than 100 entries are made, a "BS ERROR" or "bad subscript" results.

To access any element of the array, all that's necessary is to specify AG(n), where n is any value 0 to 99. To find the 50th age, for example, we may say

```
100  B=AG(49)      'get 50th age
```

Look It Up in the Index

Arrays group similar items of data, and the elements of one-dimensional data are accessed using an **index value.** In the case of the age array above, the index of 0–99 represented the number of the age entry. The first entry was at AG(0), the next at AG(1), and so forth. This positional index is always maintained in arrays and makes them much more powerful than DATA lists, where data is accessed in sequential fashion from beginning to end. In the age array above, we stored the ages in sequential fashion as they were received. In many cases, however, the position in the array is related to other than chronological order. Suppose that we had a 100-element one-dimensional array representing ages from 0 to 99 years—DIM AG(99) (you old-timers don't get riled up, now!). We could tabulate a count of ages by incrementing the proper array element (corresponding to an age) quite easily as shown below.

105

```
4000 CLS                         'clear screen
4100 INPUT "ENTER AGE";A          ┌─'input age
4200 AG(A)=AG(A)+1                │ 'increment age count
4300 GOTO 4100                    └─'loop
```

Here again, no check is made for a terminating condition. Also, no check is made for an out-of-range subscript, although the BASIC interpreter will give us a "BS" error if one is input.

The idea of indexing is a very useful one, indeed. It allows related data to be retrieved from a number of different arrays. Suppose, for example, that we have several one-dimensional arrays representing mailing-list data. An array called LN$ holds the last names, one called FR$ holds the first names, one called SA$ holds the street addresses, one called CT$ holds the cities, one called ST$ represents the states, and one called ZP$ holds the zip codes. This arrangement is shown in Figure 6-5. If we require room for 100 names in the mailing list, we can allocate space by the statements

```
5000 CLEAR 5000                  'clear for strings
5100 DIM LN$(99)                 'last name array
5200 DIM FR$(99)                 'first name array
5300 DIM SA$(99)                 'street address array
5400 DIM CT$(99)                 'city address array
5500 DIM ST$(99)                 'state address array
5600 DIM ZP$(99)                 'mr. zip array
```

By splitting up the data on each entry in the mailing list, we've accomplished several things. First of all, we've made it easier to access each element of an entry in the mailing list. If we want to obtain the city, for example, we don't have to search a large string such as "PASCAL,BLAISE,123SORBONNE,PARIS,FRANCE,1623" to find "PARIS". Instead, we can simply pick up "PARIS" from the CT$ array with the proper index such as CT$(52). Secondly, we've made the speed of access faster. String manipulation is one of the slowest parts of *any* software. To anyone who has spent hours watching a mailing-list sort only to have the line power go off about 3.2 seconds from the end of the task, this is a large benefit. To print the mailing-list label, we can do

```
6000 LPRINT FR$(I);" ";LN$(I)            'print first,last name
6100 LPRINT SA$(I)                       'pRint street address
6200 LPRINT CT$(I);" ";ST$(I);" ";ZP$(I)  'print city,state,zip
```

Tables and the Boarding House Reach

This is probably a good time to talk about **tables.** Tables are another type of data structure closely related to one-dimensional arrays. A good example of a table is a shopping list. (What? You say we've used this example eight times already?!) A table is, like a one-dimensional array, a collection of data arranged in convenient

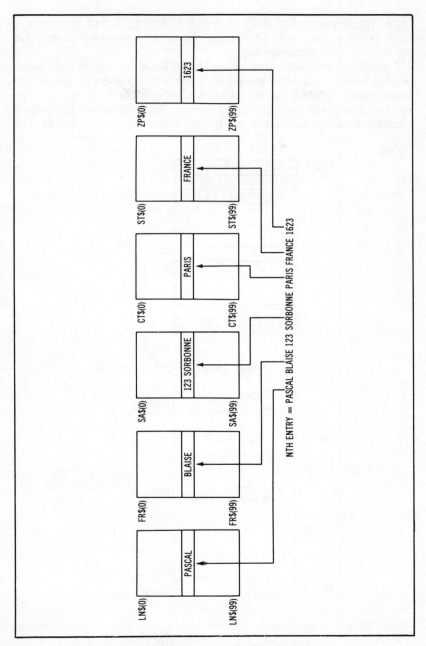

Figure 6-5. Related one-dimensional arrays.

form. While we tend to think of arrays as being a list of very similar data (such as "states"), a table may have sub-groupings of data for each entry, and a master **key**.

Let's take the mailing-list example and build a table to hold mailing-list entries. (Excuse me while I get a programmer's plane and some binary glue. . . .) All right, a typical table is shown in Figure 6-6. Each table is made up of **entries**. An entry is usually a fixed length—so many characters or bytes. Each entry may be broken

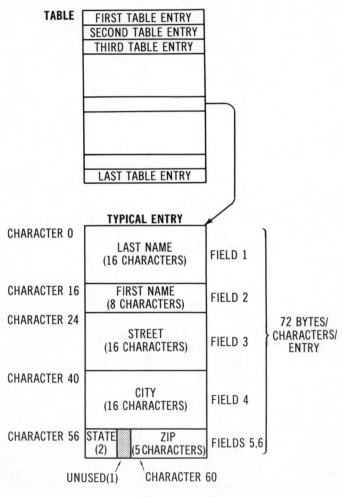

Figure 6-6. Table structure.

down into **fields,** each field representing a piece of data associated with the entry. One (or more) of the fields may be a **key,** which is the data item that is searched for. In this mailing-list example, the obvious key is **last name,** and related fields are first name, street, city, state, and zip code. Each field keeps the same relative position in the entry.

One way to build the table is to use an array. Each element of the array will hold one entry, and the entire array will comprise the table. The array may be "initialized" to the standard length of 72 bytes per entry (element) by a loop that sets up each element with dummy characters.

```
90   CLEAR 8000
100  DIM A$(99)                '100 entries
110  FOR I=0 TO 99             ┌ ' set up loop
120  A$(I) = STRING$(72,"*")   │ ' fill with dummy characters
130  NEXT I                    └ ' loop
```

Now we can use the string operators (LEFT$, MID$, etc.) to access the fields within each entry. If, for example, we wanted to change the street for the 13th entry in the table, we could perform the following code

```
1000   A$(12) = LEFT$ (A$(12), 24) + "NEW STREET ******" + MID$ (A$(12),41,32)
```

Note that every field must be padded out so that the entry remains at a length of 72 bytes to simplify access of fields in the general case.

Tables may be **fixed length** or **variable length.** Fixed-length tables have a constant number of entries, while variable-length tables have an open-ended number of entries. To find the start of any entry, we compute the entry number times the length of each entry to find a **displacement,** which is then used as a starting point to access the fields. Suppose that we have a fixed entry length of 72 characters per entry, and that 16 characters have been allocated to the last-name field, as shown in Figure 6-7. To find the location of the first name of the 51st entry, we would find the displacement of the entry by

$$50 \times 72 = 3600$$

and then add 16 to point to the first name.

Cumbersome? Yes, and it's more difficult to work with tables in BASIC than other software levels such as assembly level since it's hard to keep things a fixed length. Bear in mind, though, that this type of data structure can be used when each entry can be made to be a fixed length and may prove to be useful some cold, dark night when you're bored with arrays and DATA lists.

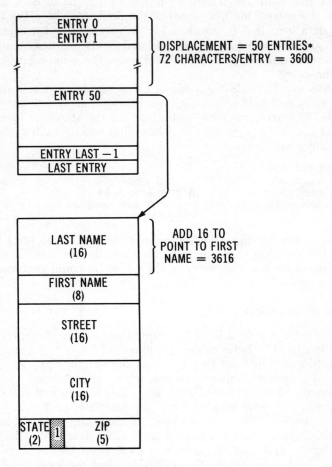

Figure 6-7. Table use.

Two Dimensions and Beyond

One-dimensional arrays are pretty easy to visualize. So are two-dimensional arrays such as a chess or checkerboard, as Alice found out in *Through the Looking Glass* (Figure 6-8):

> "... *and a most curious country it was. There were a number of tiny brooks running straight across it from side to side, and the ground between was divided up into squares by a number of little green hedges, that reached from brook to brook.* ..."

Figure 6-8. A two-dimensional array.

Two-dimensional arrays can be used to represent any two-dimensional condition, such as chessboards, a matrix of a screen or printer display, or a point on a graph.

Taking the case of a chessboard, for example, we have a square configuration of 8 by 8 positions, for a total of 64 squares. We *could* use a one-dimensional array of 64 elements, numbered 0 through 63, each one corresponding to one of the 64 squares. However, in this case it is much simpler to relate a two-dimensional array to the chessboard as shown in Figure 6-9.

Each of the squares is referenced by two values, representing the row and column, as shown in the figure. As the first element of the array is always numbered "0," the first square of the chessboard will be row 0 and column 0. We could use an order of "row, column" or "column, row"; the choice is completely arbitrary. Whichever one we use, of course, must be maintained for any reference to the array. We will use a row, column orientation so that the upper left square is designated row 0, column 0, the next square (knight) is row 0, column 1, and so forth.

Any time we want to refer to a particular position on the chessboard, we can find its row, column notation and then use the two values to reference a two-dimensional array.

The array in this case is defined by

100 DIM A$(7,7)

Don't forget that in defining the array the value in the parentheses represents the *maximum* value of the array and not the number of

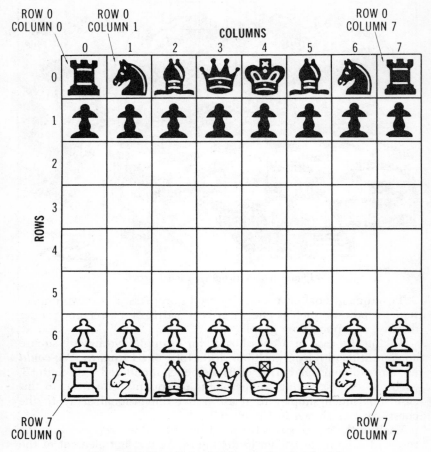

ROW 0 COLUMN 0   ROW 0 COLUMN 1

COLUMNS

ROW 0 COLUMN 7

ROWS

ROW 7 COLUMN 0

ROW 7 COLUMN 7

Figure 6-9. Two-dimensional array for chessboard.

elements. In this case, the array is 8 by 8, but the "last" element is referenced by (7,7).

Having defined the chessboard array, we can now reference any position by two values, row and column. To "initialize" the array to starting chess positions, we can use chess notation.

```
200   DIM A$(0,0)="BQR"        'black queen's rook
210   DIM A$(0,1)="BQKT"       'black queen's knight
220   DIM A$(0,2)="BQB"        'black queen's bishop
```

etc.

112

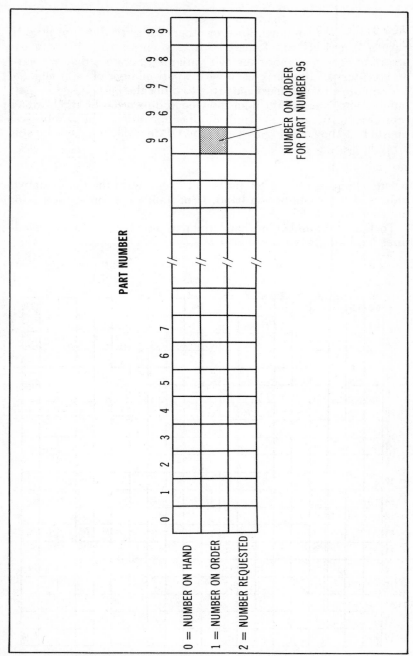

Figure 6-10. Two-dimensional array for inventory.

Of course, a two-dimensional or other size array does not need to have a "physical" counterpart such as a chessboard. We can use arrays to represent more abstract variables. Suppose that we have an inventory of 100 parts, each with a part number of 0 through 99. We can use a two-dimensional array to order the parts based on part number and "status." We'll let the second dimension be three values representing number on hand, number on order, and number requested, as shown in Figure 6-10. The **DIM**ension statement for this array is

```
100   DIM A(99,2)
```

where 99 represents the 100 parts and 2 represents the three "status" indices of 0 for number on hand, 1 for number on order, and 2 for number requested.

To find the number on hand for part number 55 (a left-hand-threaded blidgit), we'd use

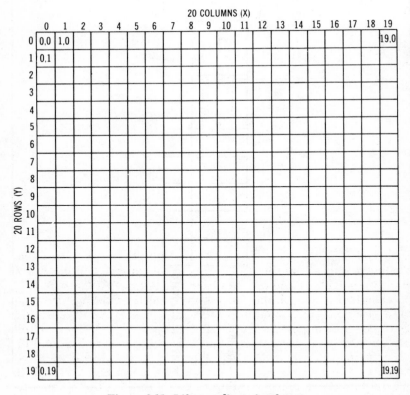

Figure 6-11. Life two-dimensional array.

```
200   B=A(55,0)     'find number on hand
```
while
```
210   B=A(55,1)     'find number on order
```
would find the number on order, and
```
220   B=A(55,2)     'find number requested
```
would find the number requested.

One of the more fascinating numerical games to appear in recent years is the game of Life. Life is very simple in concept but (as they say, ominously) has far-reaching implications. Life is played on an infinite two-dimensional array checkerboard. Since it's rather hard to fit an infinite array into a finite space (even in 48K), we'll limit it to an array about 20 by 20. Each cell of the array can be defined by a row and a column, as shown in Figure 6-11.

The rules of the game of Life are: We start off with some arbitrary pattern on the array, such as the one shown in Figure 6-12.

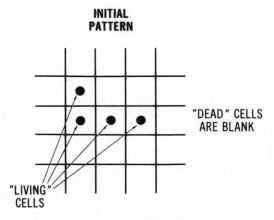

Figure 6-12. Life example.

Each cell is living (on) or dead (off). On the next generation, whether a cell lives or dies depends on its neighbors. If it has fewer than two neighbors, the cell dies from loneliness. If it has 4, 5, 6, 7, or 8 neighbors, the cell dies from overcrowded conditions. If a cell has 2 or 3 neighbors, it survives to the next generation. In addition, if any cell is dead and the number of neighbors is 3, then a new cell is born on the next generation. These rules are shown in Figure 6-13.

The game proceeds from generation to generation, and it's fascinating to watch whole colonies appear, die, spawn new patterns—in general to watch a process analogous to ... well ... life! (Based on its interest, since 1975 Life has probably burned up hundreds of

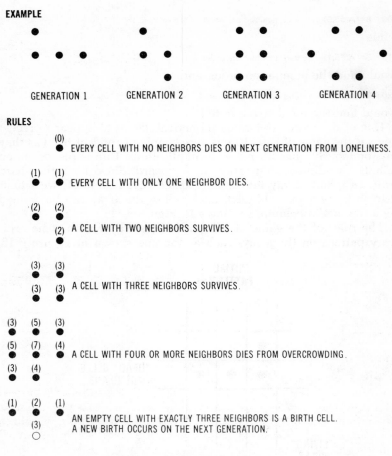

Figure 6-13. Life rules.

millions of dollars worth of computer time on expensive computers.) If you're interested in finding out more about Life (and there are many subtleties), you can find material in hobbyist computer magazines and back issues of *Scientific American*.

To set up our Life game, we'll use two arrays, one for the current generation, and one for the next. This is a slow way to implement the game, but it will allow us to do some manipulation of two-dimensional arrays. The program is shown in Figure 6-14. (How 'bout an exercise for you: Speed up the operation 100-fold.)

The arrays are called A and B and are defined by the DIMension statements DIM A(21,21) and DIM B(19,19). A is an array of 484 elements, 22 on a side, while B is an array of 400 elements, 20 on a

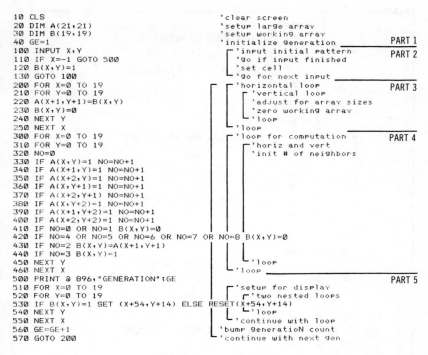

```
10 CLS                                    'clear screen
20 DIM A(21,21)                           'setup large array
30 DIM B(19,19)                           'setup working array
40 GE=1                                   'initialize generation _____  PART 1
100 INPUT X,Y                            ⌐'input initial pattern           PART 2
110 IF X=-1 GOTO 500                      |'go if input finished
120 B(X,Y)=1                              |'set cell
130 GOTO 100                             ⌐┘'go for next input _____
200 FOR X=0 TO 19                        | ⌐'horizontal loop                PART 3
210 FOR Y=0 TO 19                        | |⌐'vertical loop
220 A(X+1,Y+1)=B(X,Y)                     | || 'adjust for array sizes
230 B(X,Y)=0                             | ||_'zero working array
240 NEXT Y                               | | ┘'loop
250 NEXT X                               |⌐┘ 'loop _____
300 FOR X=0 TO 19                        | ⌐'loop for computation           PART 4
310 FOR Y=0 TO 19                        | |⌐'horiz and vert
320 NO=0                                 | ||'init # of neighbors
330 IF A(X,Y)=1 NO=NO+1                   | ||
340 IF A(X+1,Y)=1 NO=NO+1                 | ||
350 IF A(X+2,Y)=1 NO=NO+1                 | ||
360 IF A(X,Y+1)=1 NO=NO+1                 | ||
370 IF A(X+2,Y+1)=1 NO=NO+1               | ||
380 IF A(X,Y+2)=1 NO=NO+1                 | ||
390 IF A(X+1,Y+2)=1 NO=NO+1               | ||
400 IF A(X+2,Y+2)=1 NO=NO+1               | ||
410 IF NO=0 OR NO=1 B(X,Y)=0              | ||
420 IF NO=4 OR NO=5 OR NO=6 OR NO=7 OR NO=8 B(X,Y)=0
430 IF NO=2 B(X,Y)=A(X+1,Y+1)             | ||
440 IF NO=3 B(X,Y)=1                      | ||
450 NEXT Y                               | ||_'loop
460 NEXT X                               |⌐┘ 'loop _____
500 PRINT @ 896,"GENERATION";GE          |   'setup for display            PART 5
510 FOR X=0 TO 19                        | ⌐'two nested loops
520 FOR Y=0 TO 19                        | |⌐
530 IF B(X,Y)=1 SET (X+54,Y+14) ELSE RESET(X+54,Y+14)
540 NEXT Y                               | ||_'loop
550 NEXT X                               |⌐┘ 'continue with loop
560 GE=GE+1                              |   'bump generatioN count
570 GOTO 200                            ┘   'continue with next gen
```

Figure 6-14. Life program.

side. The periphery of A is never used and always contains zeroes. A always contains the current generation, while B contains the next generation. The program is made up of five parts. Part 1 initializes the two arrays and sets variable GE to 1. GE is the "generation" counter and increments by 1 for each generation.

Part 2 allows the user to input an initial pattern. A good one to try is the "R pentomino" pattern of 10,11; 11,10; 11,11; 11,12; 12,10. The form of the input is x,y, where x is the horizontal coordinate for the array of 0 to 19, and y is the vertical coordinate of 0 to 19. Inputting a −1,0 terminates the input. After inputting the initial data, array B has been set to a one for every cell specified. A GOTO part 5 prints array B by displaying it in the center of the screen. As the screen center is at x=64 and y=24, the upper left-hand corner of the array area will be at x=54, y=14. The cells in the B array are converted to screen coordinates by the SET and RESET commands which look at every element of the B array and either set or reset a screen point.

Normally, the flow is part 3, part 4, part 5, and back to part 3 again. Part 3 transfers the last generation in the B array to the A

117

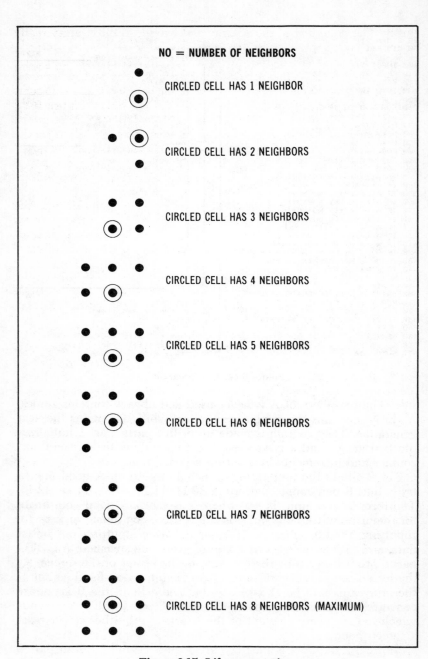

Figure 6-15. Life computation.

array. The boundary of the A array is not used, so the A array really starts at x=1, y=1.

Part 4 is the heart of the program that computes the next generation. Every cell in the A array now contains the last generation. The program looks at every cell in the active area of A and computes the number of neighboring cells (NO), as shown in Figure 6-15. Each cell in B is set according to the number of neighbors in the corresponding A cell, according to the Life rules. If NO is 2, the B cell is set to the same value as the A cell. If NO is 3, a "birth" occurs in the B cell. At the end of the computation in part 4, part 5 is entered so that the B array can be printed. Parts 3 through 5 are then repeated for the next generation.

The Life program is a good exercise in array manipulations. We actually translated one array (B) to a new position in the A array. In addition, we converted the B array to a third two-dimensional array, the screen. Note that the screen display is really a "hardware" array of 128 by 48 points when we are in the graphics mode.

This version of Life could be speeded up considerably by using only one array and by scanning for empty "horizontal" and "vertical" lines. (*Oops—didn't mean to give away any secrets for your exercise. . . .*)

We've seen one-dimensional arrays and two-dimensional arrays, but how about three dimensions and above? Level II BASIC permits any dimension of array, and in fact multi-dimensional arrays can easily be used for mathematical problems such as computing three-dimensional vectors. For non-mathematical processing, however, it does get rather hard to visualize arrays above three dimensions. The physical appearance of one-, two-, and three-dimensional arrays is shown in Figure 6-16, along with their corresponding DIMension statements.

About the only restriction on the use of arrays is their size. Large areas will gobble up a great deal of memory in a very short time, especially if the array variables are types that occupy a large number of bytes. A three-dimensional array that is 20 by 20 by 20 and uses integer variables DIM A% (19, 19, 19), for example, will use 20*20* 20*2 or 16000 bytes for the body of the array plus 12 more for parameters to describe the array. The same array using single-precision variables (the default variable type) would be twice as large—32,012 bytes! You might want to investigate the storage requirements of arrays by changing the DIMension statement in the program below and RUNning the program with various DIMensions.

```
100   A=MEM
110   DIM A%(19,19,19)
120   PRINT "ARRAY USED ";A-MEM;" BYTES"
```

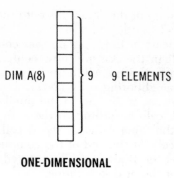

ONE-DIMENSIONAL

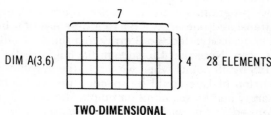

TWO-DIMENSIONAL

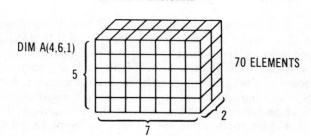

THREE-DIMENSIONAL

Figure 6-16. Three common array models.

Initializing Arrays

Early in this chapter, we mentioned that arrays could be initialized by using data from DATA lists. This is an excellent usage of both DATA statements and arrays and is quite common. The DATA statements are used to hold all of the initial data for program arrays in any convenient order. One massive READ operation at the beginning of the program goes through the DATA list and initializes all arrays in the program that require a starting set of values. Since this is done only at the beginning of the program, the initialization process may be as complicated as required; thereafter, the arrays hold the proper data and may be accessed in their normal "random-access" fashion. Many programs from this point on will illustrate this procedure.

CHAPTER 7

The Search for Better Data
and Sorting It All Out

In this chapter, we'll continue the saga of the "Data Structure Conspiracy." When we last left Ernie List (mild-mannered programmer known only to a select few as ★DATAMAN★), he was fighting his way out of a diabolical matrix constructed by his arch enemy, Dr. Dimension.

In today's episode we'll follow the adventures of Dataman as he searches for the missing data and then attempts to sort it all out . . .

Although sometimes one wishes there was a *real* Dataman to organize and search for data, the techniques discussed in this chapter should help define the ways in which data is organized and accessed.

Unordered Data—No Order At All

One way to order data, of course, is to not order it at all. The data is simply dumped into an array as it comes in. There are certain advantages to this if the number of data elements is small or if the data is actually ordered on the basis of appearance. If the number of data elements is large, however, it takes quite a length of time to find a particular data element. To illustrate data ordering, searching, sorting, and merging (sounds like a stock brokerage, eh?), we'll use the "Standard" data list shown in Table 7-1. This is simply a typical list of data that must be processed. Because much of the processing of this type involves alphanumeric data, we've made the

121

data string data, although numeric data could just as easily have been used.

The order in Table 7-1 appears to be *unordered,* but there is a definite order—that of size. If we were working with a list according to size, then this indeed would be an ordered list. From the standpoint of an alphabetical list, however, the standard list is unordered.

Table 7-1. "Standard" Data List Unordered

```
ELECTRON (PART OF OUTPUT TO CASSETTE)
LA SMOG (PARTICULATE MATTER)
DIAMOND (20 POINTS)
PEA (FROM 1971 POLITICAL FUND RAISING DINNER)
MARBLE (SHOOTER)
#3 BALL BEARING (FROM SANTE FE REEFER CAR)
FABERGE EGG (FROM HERMITAGE)
BASEBALL (PETE ROSE AUTOGRAPH)
ORANGE (ONE OF THREE)
BOWLING BALL (USED FOR PERFECT 150 GAME)
BALLOON (WITH THE WORDS "THE TRS-80 IS A GAS")
BALL OF STRING (IN BEDROOM)
747 TIRE (SOUVENIR OF HAWAII TRIP)
DOUGHNUT (SIGN AT DRIVE-IN)
GOODYEAR BLIMP (WITH ANIMATED SIGN)
PERISPHERE (AT 1939 WORLD'S FAIR)
RAMA (IN CLARKE ORBIT)
PHOBOS (ONE OF TWO)
MARS (A PLUG FOR FUNDING)
EARTH (IS THERE INTELLIGENT LIFE HERE?)
```

Much of the time, we will be working with alphabetically ordered lists in data processing on the TRS-80, although, as we see from the example, the order may be based on parameters such as employee number, zip code, disk track and sector number, or others.

In this chapter, we'll be comparing some of the different techniques used to find data and to order it, so it will be convenient for us to have a "standard" way of timing the techniques. Another word for the techniques or approaches to a problem is **"Algorithm"** (*derived, believe it or not, from Al Khwarizm, a ninth century Arabic mathematician*). Searching and sorting are some of the slowest processes in BASIC and other types of programming since the amount of data to be searched is usually very large and the search involves time-consuming (string) comparisons. With a standard list of 20 items, however, the searches can't take *too* long. . . .

The code below slows down the search or sort by a one-second delay between comparisons and displays the current item in the list being investigated. It is in the form of a subroutine which we'll call for different searching algorithms.

```
100 CLS                        'clear screen
110 DIM A$(20)                 'array for data
120 FOR I=0 TO 19             ┌─'setup for data to array
130 READ B$                   │ 'read data item
140 A$(I)=B$                  │ 'move to array
150 NEXT I                    └─'continue til done
160 INPUT "ITEM FOR SEARCH";C$  'input item to be found
170 CLS                        'clear screen
180 FOR I=0 TO 9              ┌─'setup loop for display
190 PRINT TAB(5);I;A$(I);TAB(40);I+10;A$(I+10)
200 NEXT I                    └─'loop
210 FOR I=0 TO 19            ┌─'setup loop for search
220 GOSUB 20000              │ 'print action
230 IF C$=A$(I) GOTO 270     │ 'go if found
240 NEXT I                   └─'not found,continue
250 PRINT @896,"ITEM NOT FOUND    "
260 GOTO 260                   'loop here
270 PRINT @ 896,"ITEM FOUND AT ";I;"    "
280 GOTO 280                   'loop here after find
300 DATA "ELECTRON","LA SMOG","DIAMOND","PEA","MARBLE"
310 DATA "#3 BALL BEARING","FABERGE EGG","BASEBALL","ORANGE","BOWLING BALL"
320 DATA "BALLOON","BALL OF STRING","747 TIRE","DOUGHNUT","GOODYEAR BLIMP"
330 DATA "PERISPHERE","RAMA","PHOBOS","MARS","EARTH"
20000 PRINT @ 896,"TESTING ENTRY # ";I 'print test action
20010 FOR J=0 TO 100           'delay loop
20020 NEXT J                   'loop
20030 RETURN                   'return to calling program
```

Figure 7-1. Sequential search of unordered list.

```
20000   REM A HAS ENTRY #                      'for display
20010   PRINT @ 896,"TESTING ENTRY # ";A       'message
20020   FOR I=0 TO 100                       ┌ 'timing loop
20030   NEXT I                               └ 'continue
20040   RETURN                                 'return
```

The time required to search for a given entry in an unordered list varies. At best, the sought entry is the first entry; at worst, it is the last entry of the list. The average number of comparisons that must be made in an unordered list is ½ the number of entries in the list. In the case of our "standard" list, the average search would involve testing about ten entries.

The code in Figure 7-1 initializes a string array A$ with the twenty string items (without comments) and then illustrates the searching process for an unordered list.

The search time to find a particular data item is quite short for this; we even had to slow it down for a reasonable display. If the timing loop in the 20000 subroutine is taken out, however, you can see that about one second is required to search the entire unordered list for a data item that is not in the list. If the list is hundreds of items long, it is easy to extrapolate and calculate that a linear search of an unordered list may take several minutes. If we have a great deal of repetitive searching to be done, say searching for items in an inventory, the entire task could become very time-consuming.

Ordered Lists

It behooves us, then, to try to reduce the search time. The first step in doing this is to **order** the list we have to search. In the case of much data that we process in TRS-80 BASIC, this order will be alphanumeric. Well, that's easy enough—we'll just alphabetize everything. But what about the "#" character and digits such as "7"?

There *is* a definite order to all string data in Level II BASIC. Its order is defined by the ASCII character set used by Level II BASIC. The character set for character codes 32 through 127 is shown in Table 3-1. In an extraterrestial telephone directory ordered according to these codes, a plasma drive mechanic with the last name of %ZZK will appear before a Zarful-dog trainer by the name of &ANDER-SON. Names prefixed by lower-case letters such as an itinerant Welshman by the name of "apRoberts" appear after "ZZZ Tailors." Blanks or spaces, when used, will appear before just about anything else; ROBERTS ED will come before ROBERTS,ED. It's somewhat important to know the order of things so that there are no unpleasant surprises when the computer generates a list based on the **weights** of the ASCII codes used.

When data is according to lower-valued items first, it is ordered in **ascending** order. There is no reason that we cannot have other orders, such as **descending** order, but we'll use ascending order in all of the examples here. Table 7-2 gives our standard list in ascending order.

Table 7-2. "Standard" Data List Ordered

```
#3 BALL BEARING
747 TIRE
BALL OF STRING
BALLOON
BASEBALL
BOWLING BALL
DIAMOND
DOUGHNUT
EARTH
ELECTRON
FABERGE EGG
GOODYEAR BLIMP
LA SMOG
MARBLE
MARS
ORANGE
PEA
PERISPHERE
PHÓBOS
RAMA
```

Now that all is in order, how do we efficiently search an ordered list? Right away we're in better shape than with the unordered list when we're dealing with data items that are not in the list. In the case of the unordered list, we had to search the *entire* list to determine that a data item was not in the list. For a twenty-item list this meant twenty comparisons. When we have an ordered list, we only need to search forward in the list until we find an item whose weight is greater than the item for which we are searching! This amounts to comparing the input string with the string from the list and ending the search if the list string < input string.

The average search for an equal distribution of items in the list and items not in the list will be a search of about ten items. The average search through an unordered list will be about fifteen items. This linear search of an ordered list is shown in Figure 7-2.

```
100 CLS                               'clear screen
110 DIM A$(20)                        'array for data
120 FOR I=0 TO 19                    ┌'setup for data to array
130 READ B$                          │'read data item
140 A$(I)=B$                         │'move to array
150 NEXT I                           └'continue til done
160 INPUT "ITEM FOR SEARCH";C$        'input item to be found
170 CLS                               'clear screen
180 FOR I=0 TO 9                     ┌'setup loop for display
190 PRINT TAB(5);I;A$(I);TAB(40);I+10;A$(I+10)
200 NEXT I                           └'loop
210 FOR I=0 TO 19                    ┌'setup loop for search
220 GOSUB 20000                      │'print action
230 IF C$=A$(I) GOTO 270             │'go if found
235 IF C$<A$(I) GOTO 250             │'go if past logical point
240 NEXT I                           └'not found,continue
250 PRINT @896,"ITEM NOT FOUND        "
260 GOTO 260                          'loop here
270 PRINT @ 896,"ITEM FOUND AT ";I;"  "
280 GOTO 280                          'loop here after find
300 DATA "#3 BALL BEARING","747 TIRE","BALL OF STRING","BALLOON","BASEBALL"
310 DATA "BOWLING BALL","DIAMOND","DOUGHNUT","EARTH","ELECTRON"
320 DATA "FABERGE EGG","GOODYEAR BLIMP","LA SMOG","MARBLE","MARS"
330 DATA "ORANGE","PEA","PERISPHERE","PHOBOS","RAMA"
20000 PRINT @ 896,"TESTING ENTRY # ";I 'print test action
20010 FOR J=0 TO 100                  'delay loop
20020 NEXT J                          'loop
20030 RETURN                          'return to calling program
```

Figure 7-2. Sequential search of ordered list.

We could extend the idea of testing whether a list item is greater than the search item further by taking every, say, fifth item and doing a comparison on the list item and sought item. We could then find out in a series of four steps in which general area of the list it was. Then we could do a sequential search of that subgroup. This would save considerable time on a long list. What is the ultimate extension of this idea? Take off your shoes, light your pipe, and I'll recount a tale of adventure and intrigue I learned in the Mediterranean. . . .

The Binary Search Mystery

Do you remember the paradox of Zeno and the Tortoise . . . or was it Aristotle and the Hare? In any event, if you start off traveling toward your front stoop from the sidewalk, and once each second you go ½ the remaining distance, how long will it take you to arrive at the stoop? Well, to make a long story short, although each second the distance is decreased by one-half, you will never arrive, as you take shorter and shorter steps. With luck, our search does arrive, but the idea is somewhat the same. In the binary search, the range to be searched is halved for each step, or **iteration**, of the search.

Let's see how this works. Suppose that we take our "standard list" and search for "MARBLE" as shown in Figure 7-3. We know the

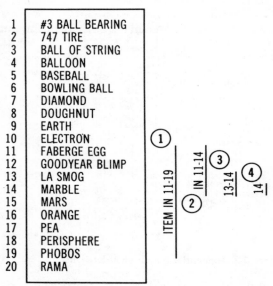

INPUT ITEM = "MARBLE"

1. FIRST COMPARISON AT ITEM 10.
   "ELECTRON" < "MARBLE," SO NEW RANGE IS 11-19.

2. SECOND COMPARISON AT ITEM $(19-11)/2 + 11 = 15$.
   "MARS" > "MARBLE," SO NEW RANGE IS 11-14.

3. THIRD COMPARISON AT ITEM $(14-11)/2 + 11 = 12$.
   "GOODYEAR BLIMP" < "MARBLE," SO NEW RANGE IS 13-14.

4. FOURTH COMPARISON AT ITEM $(14-13)/2 + 13 = 13$.
   "LA SMOG" < "MARBLE," SO ITEM MUST BE AT 14 (OR NOT IN LIST).

Figure 7-3. Binary search algorithm.

list is twenty items long. We'll search first midrange at item 10 and compare the input item with the list item. The list item is less than the input item, so we know that the item must be in the upper ½ of the list, items 11-19. We'll split that range at 15 and compare again. This time item 15 is greater than the input item, so we know that the sought item is in the ¼ of the list from 11-14. The next comparison is made at 12, where the list item is less than the input item, making the next range 13 to 14. At 13, the list item is still less than the input item. The list item is therefore at item 14 (or is not there at all!).

This search is called a **binary search** and is one of the most efficient searches for long lists of ordered data. The maximum number of comparisons (or iterations) that must be performed is represented by the power of 2 that results in a number greater than the number

```
100 CLS                                         'clear screen
110 DIM A$(20)                                  'array for data
120 FOR I=0 TO 19                           ┌─'setup for data to array
130 READ B$                                 │  'read data item
140 A$(I)=B$                                 │  'move to array
150 NEXT I                                  └─'continue til done
160 INPUT "ITEM FOR SEARCH";C$                  'input item to be found
170 CLS                                         'clear screen
180 FOR I=0 TO 9                            ┌─'setup loop for display
190 PRINT TAB(5);I;A$(I);TAB(40);I+10;A$(I+10)  │
200 NEXT I                                  └─'loop
202 HI=20                                       'initialize hi item
204 LO=0                                        'initialize lo item
206 I=10                                        'initialize middle item
208 FOR IC=0 TO 4                           ┌─'item must be fnd in 6
209 GOSUB 20000                             │  'display action
210 IF A$(I)=C$ GOTO 270                     │  'go if found
212 IF A$(I)<C$ THEN LO=I ELSE HI=I          │  'pick 1/2 remaining
214 I=INT((HI-LO)/2)+LO                       │  'find new midpoint
216 NEXT IC                                 └─'continue loop
250 PRINT @896,"ITEM NOT FOUND                  "
260 GOTO 260                                    'loop here
270 PRINT @ 896,"ITEM FOUND AT ";I;"           "
280 GOTO 280 .                                  'loop here after find
300 DATA "#3 BALL BEARING","747 TIRE","BALL OF STRING","BALLOON","BASEBALL"
310 DATA "BOWLING BALL","DIAMOND","DOUGHNUT","EARTH","ELECTRON"
320 DATA "FABERGE EGG","GOODYEAR BLIMP","LA SMOG","MARBLE","MARS"
330 DATA "ORANGE","PEA","PERISPHERE","PHOBOS","RAMA"
20000 PRINT @ 896,"TESTING ENTRY # ";I 'print test action
20010 FOR J=0 TO 100                            'delay loop
20020 NEXT J                                    'loop
20030 RETURN                                    'return to calling program
```

Figure 7-4. Binary search.

of items in the list. For example, if a list has 150 items, then 2^8 is the next power of 2 larger than 150 ($2^8 = 256$). The power of two is 8; therefore, a binary search will take 8 iterations to find out where the item is in the ordered list, compared to an average of 75 for a sequential search! The binary search is therefore quite powerful and very efficient.

Let's see how this works in a practical example. Figure 7-4 shows a binary search for our standard list. The number of iterations here is determined by 2^5, which is 32, the next power of two greater than the size of the list, 20. The number of iterations is therefore 5. We've set up a loop to go through 5 iterations at the end of which the input string has not been found in the list. If the string *is* found, then the loop is exited. Running the program in Figure 7-4 illustrates the approximate speed of the binary search. For small lists, the "overhead" of the additional string comparison is significant, but you will find that as lists become longer and longer, it becomes less and less of a factor.

There are other searching algorithms (as a matter of fact, there are literally books full of them), but the sequential search and binary search are two of the most common techniques employed in BASIC programming.

Algorithms of a Different Sort

In the previous discussion, we've assumed that our list of items to be searched was ordered. How do we order the list in the first place? In the next few pages, we'll compare the ways in which data can be **sorted.** Here, as in searching, there is enough descriptive material on sorting to fill the national archives, but we'll consider the most common techniques for BASIC.

Suppose that we go back to our standard unordered list from Table 7-1, and order it by several methods. The first method that comes to mind is to sort the list using two arrays. We could go through the first array (the list) and look for the smallest item. After scanning the entire list, we now have the smallest item, which can be put into the next element of the second array. Next, we would look for the second smallest item, and so forth, until all of the items from the unordered array have been moved to the sorted array. This process is shown in Figure 7-5.

The code for this sort is shown in Figure 7-6. This is a demonstration program that displays the data in both arrays as the sort occurs. The main loop in the program starts off with the first entry in the list array A$. This loop first looks for a "non-blanked" entry. (As each entry is moved from the first array to the second array, it is blanked by a string of "*****".) If it cannot find the next (0 to 19) non-blanked entry, the sort is done. If it does find a non-blank entry, then it scans the remainder of the array for a data item smaller than the current data item. If one is found, then the new item becomes the smallest. At the end of the scan, the smallest item remaining is transferred to the second array and then blanked in the first array. This process continues until all items have been transferred. This "two-buffer" sort is perhaps the slowest of all sorts, but it is direct and easy to code.

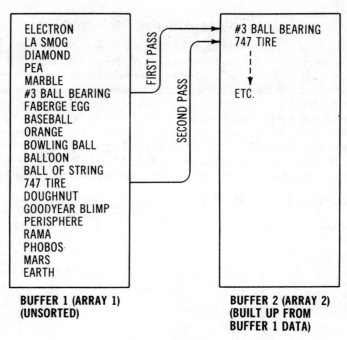

Figure 7-5. Two-buffer–sort algorithm.

```
90 CLEAR 1000                           'allocate string storageE
100 DIM A$(19)                          'allocate unsorted array
200 DIM B$(19)                          'allocate working array
300 FOR I=0 TO 19                      ┌─'setup loop for initialization
400 READ C$                            │ 'read data item
500 A$(I)=C$                           │ 'store in array
600 B$(I)="****"                       │ 'mark b$ array entry unused
700 NEXT I                             └─'loop
1000 K=0                                 'initialize b$ index
1100 FOR I=0 TO 19                     ┌─'outer loop for nxt entry
1700 IF A$(I)="****" GOTO 2500         │ 'go if unused
1800 FOR J=I TO 19                     │┌─'loop for smallest
1900 IF A$(J)="****" GOTO 2100         ││ 'go if unused
2000 IF A$(J)<A$(I) THEN I=J           ││ 'new smallest
2100 NEXT J                            │└─'loop
2200 B$(K)=A$(I)                       │ 'make entry in b$
2300 A$(I)="****"                      │ 'mark unused
2400 K=K+1                             │ 'bump b$ index
2405 CLS                               │ 'clear screen
2410 PRINT TAB(5),"A$ ARRAY",TAB(40),"B$ ARRAY"
2415 FOR L=0 TO 19                     │┌─'loop for display
2420 PRINT TAB(5),A$(L),TAB(40),B$(L)  ││ 'print contents of arrays
2425 NEXT L                            │└─'loop
2430 I=-1                              │ 'start from beginning
2500 NEXT I                            └─'go for next entry
2600 PRINT "SORT DONE"                   'end message
3000 DATA "ELECTRON","LA SMOG","DIAMOND","PEA","MARBLE"
3100 DATA "#3 BALL BEARING","FABERGE EGG","BASEBALL","ORANGE","BOWLING BALL"
3200 DATA "BALLOON","BALL OF STRING","747 TIRE","DOUGHNUT","GOODYEAR BLIMP"
3300 DATA "PERISPHERE","RAMA","PHOBOS","MARS","EARTH"
```

Figure 7-6. Two-buffer sort.

129

Rising With the Tide

Another of the disadvantages of the two-buffer sort is that a great deal of memory is required—twice that of the unsorted list. The sort we'll talk about here—the **bubble** sort—requires only the memory for the unsorted list itself. The separate elements of the list are moved around within the list until they are ordered from beginning to end. Because the lower-weighted or "lighter" elements "bubble" to the top, the name "bubble-sort" is very descriptive. The algorithm works as shown in Figure 7-7. Starting from the beginning of the list, each item (I) is compared with the next item (I+1). If the next item is of lower weight, the two items are swapped so that the lower-

One Pass Through a Bubble Sort of 9 Data Items

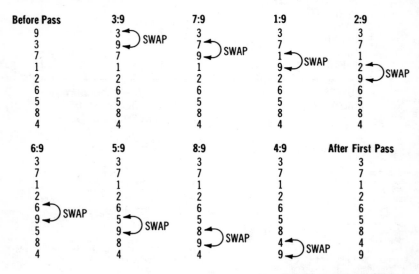

Figure 7-7. Bubble-sort algorithm.

weighted item rises to the top. This process continues until the end of the list is reached. The program then goes back to the beginning of the list and repeats the process. All items in the list have been sorted when a complete pass is made through the list without *any* swap of items having occurred.

Figure 7-8 shows a bubble sort implemented in our usual grandstand display mode. (People tend to watch anything on a screen in these days of multiple-tv households.) This program shows the actual bubble sort, with, of course, a built-in display. (There is enough "overhead" to dispense with a timing loop.) The sort routine itself first resets the "swap flag" SW. If a pass is made through the list without SW being set, then the list is sorted.

Next, the first element of the array is compared to the next. If A$(I) > A$(I+1), then the two elements are swapped and SW is set to 1. Otherwise, no swap is made. At the end of the loop, SW is tested. If it equals one, at least one swap was made in the pass, and the process is repeated once more; otherwise, the sort has been completed.

```
100 CLS                                    'clear screen
110 DIM A$(20)                             'array for data
120 FOR I=0 TO 19                      ┌─'setup for data to array
130 READ B$                            │ 'read data item
140 A$(I)=B$                           │ 'move to array
150 NEXT I                             └─'continue til done
155 FOR I=0 TO 18 STEP 2               ┌─'loop for array display
160 GOSUB 20000                        │ 'display array
165 NEXT I                             └─'loop
170 SW=0                                  'set change flag
175 P=P+1                                 'bump pass count
180 FOR I=0 TO 18                      ┌─'setup loop for sort
190 IF A$(I)<=A$(I+1) GOTO 240         │ 'go if sorted (2 items)
200 B$=A$(I)                           │ 'temporary storage
210 A$(I)=A$(I+1)                      │ 'move item up
220 A$(I+1)=B$                         │ 'move item down
230 SW=1                               │ 'set change flag
235 GOSUB 20000                        │ 'display change
240 NEXT I                             └─'continue with loop
245 PRINT @896,"PASS";P;                  'print pass count
250 IF SW=1 GOTO 170                      'go again if change
260 PRINT @ 896, "SORT DONE"              'done
270 GOTO 270
300 DATA "ELECTRON","LA SMOG","DIAMOND","PEA","MARBLE"
310 DATA "#3 BALL BEARING","FABERGE EGG","BASEBALL","ORANGE","BOWLING BALL"
320 DATA "BALLOON","BALL OF STRING","747 TIRE","DOUGHNUT","GOODYEAR BLIMP"
330 DATA "PERISPHERE","RAMA","PHOBOS","MARS","EARTH"
20000 C$="          "
20010 IF I<10 PRINT @(I*64+5),A$(I);C$;ELSE PRINT @(I-10)*64+35,A$(I);C$;
20020 I=I+1
20030 IF I<10 PRINT @(I*64+5),A$(I);C$;ELSE PRINT @(I-10)*64+35,A$(I);C$;
20040 I=I-1
20050 RETURN
```

Figure 7-8. Bubble sort.

The worst-case time for this type of sort occurs when the list is ordered in reverse order. Then a swap must be made for each set of elements except for those not ordered at the bottom from previous passes. For a twenty-item list, this worst case is 19+18+17+ . . . +2+1=190 swaps and nineteen passes, quite time consuming for a sort! (You may want to reorder the list in worst-case fashion and note the increased time.) The bubble sort becomes increasingly longer as the list grows in size. One list twice as long as another may take ten or twenty times the time to sort. Clearly, what we need is a faster sort than the bubble sort, if we are ever going to get our mailing list sorted and printed out.

The (New) Shell Game

One sort that is quite a bit faster than the bubble or double-buffer sort is the **Shell-Metzner sort,** named after the originator, Shell, and a modifier, Metzner. The Shell-Metzner sort divides up the sorting task into several internal sorts as shown in Figure 7-9. The 16 elements shown in this example are divided first into eight groups of two. The items for each set are sorted. Next the list is divided into

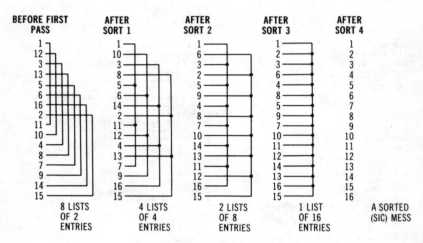

BEFORE FIRST PASS	AFTER SORT 1	AFTER SORT 2	AFTER SORT 3	AFTER SORT 4
1	1	1	1	1
12	10	6	2	2
3	3	3	3	3
13	8	2	6	4
5	5	5	4	5
6	6	9	8	6
16	14	4	5	7
2	2	8	9	8
11	11	7	7	9
10	12	10	10	10
4	4	14	11	11
8	13	13	12	12
7	7	11	14	13
9	9	12	13	14
14	16	16	16	15
15	15	15	15	16
8 LISTS OF 2 ENTRIES	4 LISTS OF 4 ENTRIES	2 LISTS OF 8 ENTRIES	1 LIST OF 16 ENTRIES	A SORTED (SIC) MESS

Figure 7-9. Shell-Metzner sort algorithm.

four groups of four, and these elements are sorted in a manner reminiscent of the bubble sort. Then the list is divided into two groups of eight with another bubble-like sort occurring. Finally, a sort of one group of 16 is performed to end the sort. The entire sort has been implemented in a maximum of $8+12+14+16=50$ swaps in four passes, whereas the maximum for the bubble sort would have been $15+14+13+ \ldots +2+1=120$ swaps and 15 passes.

The Shell-Metzner sort for our standard list is shown in Figure 7-10. It displays in similar fashion to the bubble sort discussed earlier. The Shell-Metzner sort executes quite a bit more rapidly than the bubble sort even for such a small list, and it will operate at speeds hundreds of times faster for longer lists.

Toward a *Faster* Sort

Is the Shell-Metzner sort the ultimate sort? There are faster sorts, such as Hoare's Quicksort, but the Shell-Metzner is a good solid

```
100 CLS                              'clear screen
110 DIM A$(20)                       'array for data
120 FOR I=0 TO 19                  ┌─'setup for data to array
130 READ B$                        │ 'read data item
140 A$(I)=B$                        │ 'move to array
150 NEXT I                         └─'continue til done
155 FOR I=0 TO 18 STEP 2           ┌─'loop for array display
157 J=I+1                          │
160 GOSUB 20000                    │ 'display array
165 NEXT I                         └─'loop
166 P=0                              'set pass count to 0
170 M=20                             'set # of lists to array sz
175 M=INT(M/2)                   ┌───'processing loop one
180 IF M=0 GOTO 270              │    'go if done
182 P=P+1                        │
184 PRINT @896,"PASS=";P         │
185 FOR ST=0 TO M-1              │ ┌──'processing loop two
190 I=ST                         │ │  'start of a list
195 J=ST+M                       │ │
200 SW=0                         │ │  'set change switch to 0
205 IF A$(I)<A$(J) GOTO 235      │ │┌─'if ordered,continue
210 SW=1                         │ ││ 'not ordered,swap
215 B$=A$(I)                     │ ││ 'temporary storage
220 A$(I)=A$(J)                  │ ││ 'move up
225 A$(J)=B$                     │ ││ 'move down
230 GOSUB 20000                  │ ││ 'print change
235 I=J                          │ ││ 'look for next two
240 J=J+M                        │ ││ 'entries
245 IF J<20 GOTO 205             │ │└─'go if still this list
250 IF SW=0 GOTO 260             │ │  'go if this list sorted
255 GOTO 190                     │ │  'this list still unordered
260 NEXT ST                      │ └──'go for next list
265 GOTO 175                     └────'go for next set of lists
270 PRINT @ 896,"SORT DONE"           'dont that beat all
280 GOTO 280                          'loop here for appearance
300 DATA "ELECTRON","LA SMOG","DIAMOND","PEA","MARBLE"
310 DATA "#3 BALL BEARING","FABERGE EGG","BASEBALL","ORANGE","BOWLING BALL"
320 DATA "BALLOON","BALL OF STRING","747 TIRE","DOUGHNUT","GOODYEAR BLIMP"
330 DATA "PERISPHERE","RAMA","PHOBOS","MARS","EARTH"
20000 C$="          "
20010 IF I<10 PRINT @(I*64+5),A$(I);C$;ELSE PRINT @(I-10)*64+35,A$(I);C$;
20030 IF J<10 PRINT @(J*64+5),A$(J);C$;ELSE PRINT @(J-10)*64+35,A$(J);C$;
20050 RETURN
```

Figure 7-10. Shell-Metzner sort.

sort that is still understandable to the BASIC user (and the author) and can therefore be adapted to a variety of data structures.

How about another exercise? Find faster and faster sorts until (in a relative way) you are able to sort your data even prior to loading it into the machine!

Mergers Are Big Business

We've now talked about searches and sorts. Are you ready for merges? (Wait! Come back!) Merges are another common operation in data processing. A merge takes (generally) sorted data from one list and merges it into sorted data in a second list. Business data processors call this creating a new master file from an old master file and a transaction file. The transaction file contains the current data, while the old master contains the previously ordered data base.

Merging, in the case of BASIC lists, involves obtaining a data item to be merged and then searching a list for the point at which the

133

data item should be inserted, as shown in Figure 7-11. The data *after* the insertion point is then moved down, and the data item is inserted in the "gap." The search technique can be any of the search types we have discussed in this chapter.

Commonly, we would like to be able not only to search for and insert data, but also to delete items from lists and modify existing items in lists. These operations have a wide variety of uses from updating inventories to maintaining directories of disk files.

OPERATION: MERGE "MACKEREL" INTO LIST

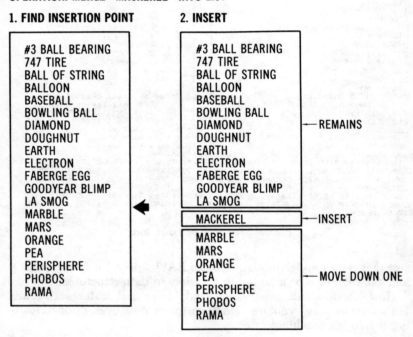

Figure 7-11. Merging algorithm.

The deletion is the reverse of the insert, as shown in Figure 7-12. The item to be deleted is located by a binary or other type of search and then deleted by moving the remainder of the data in the list up over the item to delete it. The last data item is then zeroed or blanked to create a new "gap" at the end of the list. The process of moving data in both the insert and delete functions can be very time consuming, as shown in this code that moves 200 elements of an array up one block to simulate a deletion.

OPERATION: DELETE "EARTH" FROM LIST

1. FIND ITEM

2. DELETE

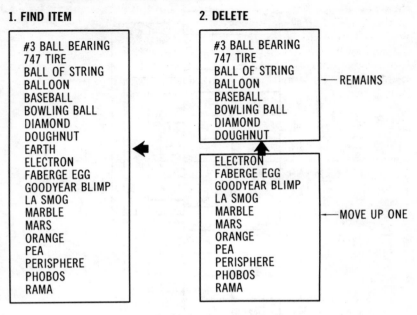

Figure 7-12. Deletion algorithm.

```
100   DIM A(2000)          'establish array
110   For I=0 TO 1998      ⌈'start of loop
120   A(I)=A(I+1)          |  'move up
130   NEXT I               ⌊'loop
```

The above code takes about 26 seconds. If many block moves are to be done for merge operations, might not there be a faster way to maintain ordered lists? Ah yes, my friends . . . I have here a little gem-dandy device called the . . .

Cures slow-speed merges, dandruff, loss of weight. . . . The price, you ask? . . . Well, my friend, only a little more complex data structure. . . .

Linked lists are worth mentioning here because they are an efficient data structure. The expense *is* a more complicated data struc-

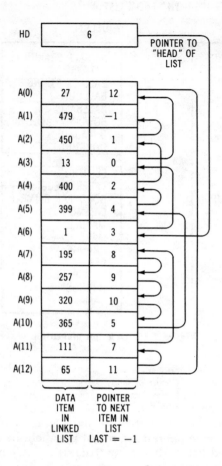

Figure 7-13. Linked-list structure.

ture, together with larger storage requirements for data. A linked list is shown in Figure 7-13.

The linked list is made up of data items which are linked to each other by pointers. Because each element points to the next, the data elements do not have to physically follow one another, as shown in the figure. What is the advantage of this? Because a link may be broken at any spot, a data item may easily be inserted or deleted. Figure 7-14 shows an insert operation, for example. The item 345 is to be inserted in its proper place in the list. Starting from the *head* of the list, a search is made for the insertion point, which is after

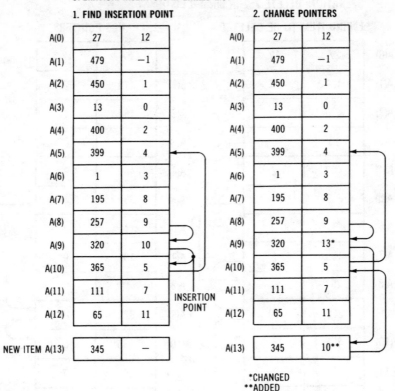

Figure 7-14. Insertion using linked list.

320 and before 365. The pointer at item 320 points to 365. This pointer is changed to point to 13 (the number of the new item), and the pointer associated with the new item is initialized to point to item 10. The new item has been inserted in the list without moving a large block of data.

Deletion of an item in a linked list is shown in Figure 7-15. Item 257 is to be deleted from the list. Item 195 points to item 257, which points to item 320. Item 257 is removed by changing the pointer in item 195 to point to 320. The storage associated with item 257 is released back to a storage pool by blanking item 257 in some fashion such as putting in an invalid item number.

Insertions and deletions of linked-list items can be done very rapidly once the insertion or deletion point is found. Because of the pointer structure, however, the search to find the insertion or deletion point is essentially a sequential search that starts from the head

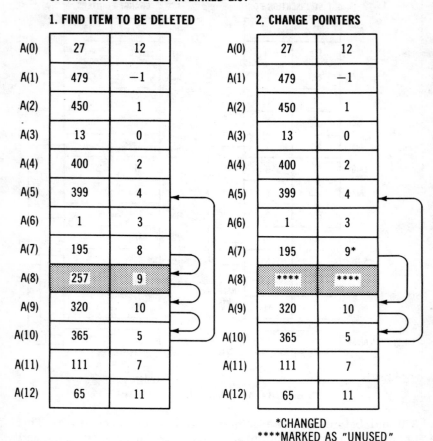

OPERATION: DELETE 257 IN LINKED LIST

1. FIND ITEM TO BE DELETED

A(0)	27	12
A(1)	479	−1
A(2)	450	1
A(3)	13	0
A(4)	400	2
A(5)	399	4
A(6)	1	3
A(7)	195	8
A(8)	257	9
A(9)	320	10
A(10)	365	5
A(11)	111	7
A(12)	65	11

2. CHANGE POINTERS

A(0)	27	12
A(1)	479	−1
A(2)	450	1
A(3)	13	0
A(4)	400	2
A(5)	399	4
A(6)	1	3
A(7)	195	9*
A(8)	****	****
A(9)	320	10
A(10)	365	5
A(11)	111	7
A(12)	65	11

*CHANGED
****MARKED AS "UNUSED"

Figure 7-15. Deletion using linked list.

of the list; like all sequential searches, it is rather time consuming.

Let's take a look at a practical example of the linked list concept in BASIC. Figure 7-16 shows a linked-list structure for a list of alphabetic data, our standard Chapter 7 list of odds and ends. The structure has two arrays. Array A contains the pointers, while array A$ contains the items of the list. The pointers are actually the indices to the elements of array A$. The last pointer is a −1 to signify that there are no more items in the linked list.

Initially, the items in the linked list are ordered by initializing the pointer array as shown in Figure 7-16. In this case, the items are ordered *physically* as well as ordered in the linked list.

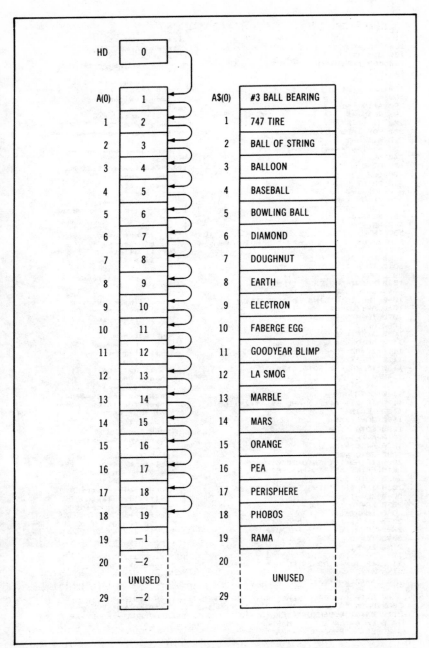

Figure 7-16. Example of linked list.

```
100 CLS                                          'clear screen
110 CLEAR 1000                                   'clear string storage
120 DIM A(29)                                    'pointer array
130 DIM A$(29)                                   'item array
140 FOR I=0 TO 18                              ┌─'loop for first 19
150 A(I)=I+1                                    │ 'setup pntrs
160 READ B$                                     │ 'read from data list
170 A$(I)=B$                                    │ 'and store in array
180 NEXT I                                     └─'loop til done
190 A(19)=-1                                      'last pntr = -1
195 READ B$                                       'get last data item
200 A$(I)=B$                                      'and put in array
210 FOR I=20 TO 29                             ┌─'loop for unused entries
220 A(I)=-2                                     │ 'mark pntr unused
230 A$(I)="****"                                │ 'mark item unused for disp
240 NEXT I                                     └─'loop
250 HD=0                                          'set head to first item
400 CLS                                           'clear screen
410 PRINT "HD=";HD                                'head title
420 FOR I=0 TO 29                               ┌───'loop for items
430 PRINT TAB(5);I,A(I),A$(I)                   │   'print items
440 FOR J=0 TO 10                               │ ┌ 'timing for disp
450 NEXT J                                      │ └ 'loop
460 NEXT I                                      └───'loop for print
500 INPUT "DELETE (D) OR INSERT (I)";B$           'prompt user
510 IF B$<>"D" AND B$<>"I" GOTO 500               'test response
520 IF B$="D" GOTO 2000                           'go if delete
1000 FOR ZC=0 TO 29                             ┌─'loop for unused item
1010 IF A(ZC)=-2 GOTO 1050                      │ 'go if unused
1020 NEXT ZC                                    └─'no unused found yet
1030 PRINT "NO FREE ITEMS"                         'no free items
1040 GOTO 500                                      'back to command mode
1050 INPUT "STRING TO INSERT";B$                   'input insert string
1060 A$(ZC)=B$                                      'fill into array
1070 IF HD<>-1 GOTO 1110                            'go if items in list
1080 HD=ZC                                          'head now current
1090 A(ZC)=-1                                       'current now last
1100 GOTO 400                                       'back to command
1110 ZL=HD                                          'last item
1120 ZN=A(ZL)                                       'next item
1130 IF ZN<>-1 GOTO 1170                            'go if not end of list
1140 A(ZL)=ZC                                       'change pointer
1150 A(ZC)=-1                                       'new end of list
1160 GOTO 400                                       'back for new command
1170 IF B$>=A$(ZL) AND B$<A$(ZN) GOTO 1210          'check for insert point
1180 ZL=ZN                                          'not fnd-continue
1190 ZN=A(ZN)                                       'new next
1200 GOTO 1130                                      'keep looking
1210 A(ZL)=ZC                                       'found-change pntr
1220 A(ZC)=ZN                                       'current to next
1230 GOTO 400                                       'back for next command
2000 IF HD<>-1 GOTO 2030                            'delete here-go if items
2010 PRINT "STRING NOT FOUND"                       'no items in list
2020 GOTO 500                                       'back to command
2030 INPUT "STRING TO DELETE";B$                    'input delete string
2040 ZL=-1                                          'initialize last
2050 ZC=HD                                          'initialize current
2060 ZN=A(ZC)                                       'next
2070 IF A$(ZC)=B$ GOTO 2120                         'go if found
2080 IF A(ZC)=-1 GOTO 2010                          'go if end of list
2090 ZL=ZC                                          'not this entry
2100 ZC=A(ZC)                                       'get next
2110 GOTO 2060                                      'keep searching
2120 IF ZL=-1 HD=ZN ELSE A(ZL)=ZN                   'found-change pntrs
2130 A(ZC)=-2                                       'mark unused
2135 A$(ZC)="****"                                  'mark entry for display
2140 GOTO 400                                       'back to command input
3000 DATA "#3 BALL BEARING","747 TIRE","BALL OF STRING"
3005 DATA "BALLOON","BASEBALL","BOWLING BALL","DIAMOND"
3010 DATA "DOUGHNUT","EARTH","ELECTRON","FABERGE EGG","GOODYEAR BLIMP"
3020 DATA "LA SMOG","MARBLE","MARS","ORANGE","PEA","PERISPHERE"
3030 DATA "PHOBOS","RAMA"
```

Figure 7-17. Linked-list code.

The code shown in Figure 7-17 allows us to delete or insert items in the linked list. The contents of the list are displayed on the screen in the form

POINTER	ITEM

so that you can see what is actually happening in the insertions and deletions. Each deletion is handled by searching the A$ array by using the pointers, starting with HD, a variable which points to the first item of the linked list. When the item to be deleted is found, the previous pointer is changed to the pointer value for the deleted item, and the pointer element in A is marked as unused by setting it to −2. Each insertion finds an unused position by searching the A array for −2 and then searches the A$ array for the insertion point. When it is found, the previous pointer is changed to the new location, and the pointer for the new location is changed to the value found in the previous location.

Naturally, we have provisions for deleting all items in the list and for **overflow** of the size of the arrays. (A favorite trick for computer science students is trying to "crash" the time-sharing system; it's human nature to look for loopholes, but we must warn you that all programs in this book are perfect and that any such attempts will result in confiscation of your TRS-80 monitor!)

That completes our discussion of data structures, sorting, searching, and merging. We hope that this chapter will provide some alternatives in the way you arrange your data and maintain it in an orderly fashion. There is no optimum data arrangement or sorting technique that will work for all cases. The "correct" techniques must be related to the type, size, and speed requirements of the program and data involved.

CHAPTER 8

The TRS-80 Functions Perfectly

In this chapter, we'll cover the built-in TRS-80 **functions.** Functions are "built-in" operations to process specific things, rather than general-purpose statements. Naturally, the specific things that the functions process are commonly used operations, such as finding the sine of an angle or generating a random number. Functions in Level II BASIC can be divided into four different types—precision functions, numeric functions, random-number functions, and trigonometric functions. We'll discuss all four and the applications of each.

What? *More* Precision Operations?

We know, we covered precision in Chapter 2. The statements in Chapter 2, however, defined a variable as an integer, single-precision, or double-precision variable. The variables defined by the precision statements and suffixes remained that precision for the entire program. The two functions presented here, CDBL and CSNG, allow the user to force a double-precision or single-precision operation without having to define the variables as double or single precision. CSNG forces a single-precision result. If, for instance, we have two double-precision variables, A# and B#, the results of any operations would normally be carried out to 17 digits as in the code

```
100 CLS                        'clear screen
200 INPUT "A#=";A#            ┌ 'input 1st dp value
300 INPUT "B#=";B#            │ 'input 2nd dp value
400 PRINT "A#*B#=";A#*B#      └ 'print product
500 GOTO 200                    'go for next set
```

Inputting A# = 1.22222222222222 and B# = 2.33333333333333 would result in an answer of 2.851851851851843. However, if we

forced the answer to single precision, using the CSNG function, the
answer would be 2.85185, a single-precision number.

```
1000 CLS                              'clear screen
1100 INPUT "A#=";A#              ┌─'input 1st dp value
1200 INPUT "B#=";B#              │ 'input 2nd dp value
1300 PRINT "A#*B#=";CSNG(A#*B#)  └─'print product sp
1400 GOTO 1100                      '90 for next set
```

The CSNG function is a means of limiting results to single-precision accuracy without having to introduce a single-precision variable
as in

```
2000 CLS                'clear screen
2100 INPUT "A#=";A#  ┌─'input 1st dp value
2200 INPUT "B#=";B#  │ 'input 2nd dp value
2300 C=A#*B#         │ 'convert product to sp
2400 PRINT "A#*B#=";C └─'print sp product
2500 GOTO 2100          '90 for next set
```

which would give the same result as the CSNG function above.
When the CSNG function converts a double-precision function to
single precision, it **rounds off**, rather than **truncating**, the least significant digits.

The CDBL function operates in similar fashion to CSNG, except
that it forces a double-precision operation. CDBL performs the same
operation as the generation of the double-precision value C# from
A and B

```
3000 CLS                                      'clear screen
3100 INPUT "A=";A                         ┌─'input 1st sp number
3200 INPUT "B=";B                         │ 'input 2nd sp number
3300 C#=A*B                               │ 'convert to dp
3400 PRINT "C#=";C#,"CDBL(A*B)=";CDBL(A*B) └─'90 for next set
3500 GOTO 3100
```

Converting to the double-precision format, by the way, cannot
"restore" accuracy to a number. If operations have been performed
in single precision in a program, then only seven digits of precision
are maintained (six are printed). Double-precision format must be
used continuously to guarantee 17 digits of accuracy!

Converting from single to double precision also has its pitfalls.
Converting the single-precision number 1.999995 should result in
1.9999950000000000, shouldn't it? In fact, converting this number,
as in

100   PRINT CDBL(1.999995)

results in "1.999994874000549"! Similar conversions also produce
extraneous digits at the end.

A better method of converting from single to double precision is
to use the approach

143

which converts the single-precision value of A! into a string value and then converts the string into a double-precision numeric value. (See Chapter 3 for a discussion of STR$ and VAL.) When this method is used with 1.999995, a "rounded-off" value of "2" results, without extraneous digits. We'll say more about truncation and roundoff shortly.

Are You Good at Fractions?

There are several numerical functions in Level II BASIC that help us in dealing with integers. They are CINT, INT, and FIX.

CINT returns an integer value in the range −32768 through +32767. This is a comparable function to the CSNG and CDBL functions we have just discussed. The CINT function is equivalent to creating an integer value such as A% rather than forcing a conversion to integer form with a function.

```
100 CLS                                'clear screen
200 INPUT "A=";A                      'input 1st sp number
300 INPUT "B=";B                      'input 2nd sp number
400 C%=A*B                            'find integer value
500 PRINT "C%=";C%,"CINT(A*B)=";CINT(A*B)
600 GOTO 200                          'go for next set
```

Because of the way negative numbers are held in two's complement form (see Chapter 2) and the truncation method of conversion, CINT converts a negative fractional number to the next lowest integer value. CINT will convert the following values as shown

Before CINT	After CINT
−1.1	−2
−1.9	−2
−12.001	−13
−32767.1	−32768

Positive fractions are converted to the integer portion of the number. The fractional part is truncated, or chopped off.

Before CINT	After CINT
1.1	1
1.9	1
12.001	12
32767.1	32767

CINT is very similar to another integer function, "INT." CINT is a high-speed version of the more general INT. INT will work with numbers greater than +32767 and less than −32768. Because INT is more general, it is almost always used in BASIC programming in preference to CINT.

CINT is commonly used in operations to find the remainders of numbers. This type of operation comes up frequently in number conversions and rounding operations. Decimal numbers can be converted to binary or hexadecimal numbers by a common method known as "divide and save remainders." It's a good application to show the use of CINT.

Before we look at the code, let's see the "pencil and paper" operation. Suppose we have a decimal number that we want to convert to binary. We start by dividing by 2 and save the remainder at each division, as shown in Figure 8-1. The remainders in reverse order are the binary-number equivalent of the decimal number we started with. This method works for any number base—binary, octal (8), or hexadecimal (16).

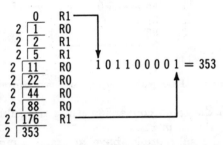

Figure 8-1. Decimal-to-binary conversion.

For those of you interested in assembly-language coding and for anyone interested in binary representation, we present the following subroutine to convert any given decimal number from 0 to 255 into binary form. The number is in variable ZN, and the result is put in array ZZ defined by a previous DIM ZZ(7).

```
10000 FOR ZI=7 TO 0 STEP −1      ┌─ 'setup 8 time loop
10010 ZZ(ZI)=ZN−INT(ZN/2)*2      │  'find remainder
10020 ZN=INT(ZN/2)               │  'find quotient
10030 NEXT ZI                    └─ 'continue
10040 RETURN                        'return to calling prog
```

The subroutine does not check for a number outside the proper range of 0 through 255. If a number greater than 255 is to be converted, you'll get an incorrect answer. (Eight divisions will only resolve numbers that are 255 or less. You might like to try 16 divisions with a 16-element array for use with numbers of 65535 or less.) The number to be converted is in variable ZN. A one-dimensional array,

145

ZZ, must have been defined previously. (Defining it in the subroutine would result in a DD error for subsequent calls.) For eight iterations through the loop, the number is divided by two to give some quotient. This quotient will probably be a fractional number. To find the integer portion of the quotient, INT is used. INT(ZN/2) will give the integer quotient value. If this quotient is multiplied by 2, and the result subtracted from the original number, we can find the remainder. The remainder is calculated this way and stored in the array in reverse order. An example might make this more lucid (*I'm even confused at this point*).

Suppose we want to convert 213 to binary form. If we did it with paper and pencil, we would have the calculation shown in Figure 8-2.

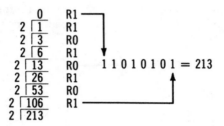

Figure 8-2. Example of decimal-to-binary conversion.

When we do the same conversion using the subroutine, we get the calculations shown in Figure 8-3.

We can use the subroutine above to practice our binary operations (don't forget those ANDs and ORs) or to PEEK at memory lo-

I	ZN	ZN/2	INT(ZN/2)	INT(ZN/2)*2 (ZN)	ZN−INT(ZN/2)*2 (ZZ)
7	213	106.5	106	212	1
6	106	53	53	106	0
5	53	26.5	26	52	1
4	26	13	13	26	0
3	13	6.5	6	12	1
2	6	3	3	6	0
1	3	1.5	1	2	1
0	1	0.5	0	0	1

Figure 8-3. Decimal-to-binary conversion algorithm.

cations for assembly-language work. To convert any number from 0 to 255, use the following code.

```
1000 DIM ZZ(7)                                'allocate 8 dim array
1100 PRINT                                   ┌'new line
1200 INPUT "DECIMAL # TO BE CONVERTED"; ZN
1300 IF ZN>255 OR ZN<0 GOTO 1200              'check for range 0-255
1400 GOSUB 10000                              'convert
1500 PRINT "BINARY EQUIV IS ";                'print result msg
1600 FOR I=0 TO 7                            ┌'loop for digits
1700 PRINT ZZ(I);                            │'print digit
1800 NEXT                                    └'continue
1900 GOTO 1100                                'go for next number
```

To convert a given range of ROM or RAM memory locations, use this code.

```
2000 DIM ZZ(7)                                'allocate 8 dim array
2100 INPUT "START LOCATION";A                 'input starting location
2200 INPUT "END LOCATION";B                   'input ending location
2300 FOR I=A TO B                            ┌'outer loop for locns
2400 ZN=PEEK(I)                              │'get next location
2500 GOSUB 10000                             │'convert byte
2600 PRINT "LOCATION=";I;"CONTENTS=";        │'location msg
2700 FOR J=0 TO 7                            │┌'inner loop for digits
2800 PRINT ZZ(J);                            ││'print digits
2900 NEXT J                                  │└'continue for 8
3000 PRINT                                   │'new line
3100 NEXT I                                  └'get next location
3200 END
```

A second use of INT is to test whether a number is divisible by another number. Many times, it's convenient to test whether this is the seventh or tenth time through a loop, for example. If we are displaying 16 lines of characters on the video display, we can pause while the user scans the current page by keeping a count of the number of lines and testing for multiples of 16. This code is not a working program, but illustrates how the test may be integrated in a program. A$ represents the ENTER response to the pause at the 16th line. GOTO 800 is the branch to "other" processing.

```
1000 PRINT A,B
1010 CT=CT+1
1020 IF INT(CT/16)=CT/16 THEN INPUT A$
1030 GOTO 800
```

Another use of INT is to test whether a number is an integer value (not a fraction). A convenient way to do this uses INT:

```
100 INPUT A                                  ┌'input test number
200 IF INT(A)=A PRINT "A IS INTEGER" ELSE PRINT "A NOT INTEGER"
300 GOTO 100                                 └'continue for next
```

The fractional portion of any positive number can be found by

```
100 FR=A-INT(A)
```

Since INT converts to the next lowest negative integer for negative numbers, $A - INT(A)$ will not give the correct result for $A < 0$.

However, still another function, FIX, will give the fractional portion of a negative number or positive number correctly.

FIX truncates all fractional digits. Some examples are

Before FIX	After FIX
1.2	1
13.1	13
13.99	13
128.123	128
−1.1	−1
−3.3	−3
−128.99	−128
−99999.9	−99999

Why are there so many ways to derive similar things? What is truth? What is beauty? Some of the functions described above are very similar, and it's hard to know when to use one or the other, but please don't complain—the alternative might be a BASIC stripped of all these niceties. It's better to have too much than too little (*Guard—take down the name of that reader threatening to go back to his hand calculator!*).

A word should be said here about **truncation** and **roundoff**. We have seen how INT and FIX truncate values. For small numbers such as 1.9 or 2.7, the error resulting from truncation is quite large. A roundoff scheme may be used to reduce this error for individual numbers. In roundoff, we make some arbitrary judgment as to whether the number should be rounded "up" to the next larger integer or rounded "down" to the next smaller integer. (This scheme can also be used for fractional numbers.) The following code rounds up if the fraction is 0.5 or greater and rounds down if the fraction is less than 0.5.

```
100  INPUT A          ⌐'input test number
200  B=FIX(A)         |  'truncate fraction
300  IF ABS(A−B)>=.5 B=B+1
400  PRINT A,B        |  'print input and result
500  GOTO 100         ⌐'continue for next
```

A Sign Function—Absolutely!

The SGN function is used to test for a negative, zero, or positive result. Here again, we could do this by other means such as

```
100  IF A<0 GOTO 1000 ELSE IF A=0 GOTO 2000 ELSE GOTO 3000
```

The SGN function makes the job somewhat easier, however,

```
100  ON SGN(A)+2 GOTO 1000,2000,3000
```

The SGN returns −1 if the argument is less than 0, 0 if the number is equal to 0, and 1 if the argument is greater than 0. In the state-

148

ment above, the result of −1, 0, or 1 is converted to 1, 2, or 3 by the SGN(A) + 2 to cause a "computed" GOTO, transferring control to 1000 for negative numbers, 2000 for numbers equal to 0, and 3000 for positive numbers.

Another simple-minded function is the absolute value. (*Sorry, we didn't mean to shun the absolute value—we mean it's easy to understand.*) The absolute value, as we know from Algebra One, returns A if A is positive or zero, and returns −A if A is negative. All this says is that the magnitude of the number is returned. A = ABS(−32) returns 32 for A, A = ABS(+32) returns 32 for A, and A = ABS(0) returns 0 for 0. A zero value, by the way, is treated as a positive number in the TRS-80 hardware and software (and in virtually all other computing systems). The absolute value function is used extensively in many mathematical calculations, as, for example, to find the displacement along the X axis for two points on a graph

```
100   DX=ABS(X2−X1)
```

Another mathematical function that is built into Level II BASIC is the square root function, SQR. We know that we can find the power of any number by using the exponentiation operator ↑. SQR simply duplicates the exponentiation function for A ↑ .5 and is somewhat faster. Of course, square roots are common operations in mathematical routines, and it's convenient to have a built-in SQR function.

We won't say much more about the EXP and LOG functions except that EXP(A) is the exponential function e^A and that LOG(A) returns the natural logarithm of A. Natural logarithms are used extensively in higher mathematics.

Pick a Number, Any Number

Chances are the number you pick won't be a random number, especially if you keep selecting numbers for some time. The computer can be used (and has been used) for a number of years for **simulation** of various real-world events. One of the powerful uses a computer can be put to is to produce "pseudo-random" numbers for use in simulations.

What are pseudo-random numbers and how do they differ from random numbers? Truly random numbers can be produced by flipping a coin. We cannot predict whether the next flip will be heads or tails (assuming the coin is perfectly balanced and we are not introducing any "tricks" in the flip). If we recorded the heads and tails and equated them to ones and zeroes, we would have a long list of binary numbers which could be broken up into bytes (see Figure 8-4). The bytes would now represent a list of 8-bit binary numbers ranging in value from 0 through 255. The **distribution** of

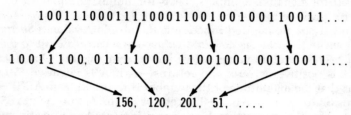

HEADS = 1
TAILS = 0

100111000111100011001001001100 11...

1 0 0 1 1 1 0 0, 0 1 1 1 1 0 0 0, 1 1 0 0 1 0 0 1, 0 0 1 1 0 0 1 1, . . .

156, 120, 201, 51, ...

Figure 8-4. Random binary numbers.

the numbers would tend to be uniform the longer the list was made. That is, if we had millions of numbers, the number of 0 values would be about 1/256 of the total number, the number of 1 values about 1/256 of the total, and so forth.

The problem of generating random numbers is not a trivial one, and many articles (and books) have been written about the subject. As a matter of fact, there *are books* of random numbers, used as lists of **good** random numbers without bias. It's not only important to have unpredictability in Las Vegas, but in computer simulation as well. We can generate random numbers in the TRS-80 by manual methods. If we increment a count fast enough and then stop the count, we have a fairly random number. The following routine does this by examining the shift key and stopping the count when it is pressed. A count of 0 to 127 is generated. (The USR call here is intended only for Level II and not Disk BASIC.)

```
100 A$=CHR$(58)+CHR$(128)+CHR$(56)+CHR$(183)+CHR$(40)+CHR$(250)+CHR$(237)+
    CHR$(95)+CHR$(111)+CHR$(38)+CHR$(0)+CHR$(195)+CHR$(154)+CHR$(10)
500 B=VARPTR(A$)
600 POKE 16526,PEEK(B+1)        'get block location
700 POKE 16527,PEEK(B+2)        'setup usr call
800 A=USR(0)                    'second byte of address
900 PRINT A                     'call machine language
1000 FOR I=0 TO 50              'print value
1100 NEXT I                     'delay for bounce
1200 GOTO 800                   'loop
                                'go for next value
```

The "R" register in the CPU Z-80 microprocessor is continually being updated by adding one. An instantaneous value from R will be 0–127. (The character string at A$ constitutes an assembly-language routine embedded in a "dummy string." We'll discuss this technique in a later chapter.)

Isn't there a more convenient method to generate random numbers? I'm glad you asked, son. Step over here and let me show you this little gadget called the RND number generator. . . .

RND does not generate **random** numbers, but *pseudo*-**random** numbers. Pseudo-random numbers are predictable in that if one starts with the same **seed** number, the same sequence of numbers will be generated each time. The numbers generated still have a good distribution of values. Generating numbers from 0 to 255 would result in about 1/256th of numbers equal to 0, 1/256th equal to 1, and so forth, if done over long periods of time. The fact that the series is predictable is not necessarily bad. We would like to be able to repeat experiments and simulations from the same point, after all, and working with truly random numbers does not provide that capability.

Let's look at a sequence of random numbers generated by the RND function. The code below prints random numbers from 1 to 255. The format of the RND function is RND(A). If A is 0, a single-precision value between 0 and 1 is generated. If A is 1 to 32767, a pseudo-random value between 1 and the argument is printed. In this case, the argument is 255 to generate a value from 1 to 255.

```
100   CLS
200   PRINT RND(255);" ";
300   GOTO 200
```

Did you see any repeats? (*Well, it is somewhat fast.*) The RANDOM function reseeds the random-number generator. If RANDOM is not used, then turning off the computer, turning it on, and executing

```
100   PRINT RND(10000)      'or other range
```

will produce the same number for each power-up. RANDOM ensures that a new sequence will be started more than 99 times out of 100. Power down again, power up, and execute

```
100   RANDOM              'randomize
200   PRINT RND(10000)    'print starting number
```

several times. You will see different starting values essentially generated by the same process of taking a count from a register as we performed with our *random* program.

What is the provision for starting over from the same seed? Since we cannot specify a starting seed value in RANDOM, we must do some POKEing in memory. If we have a seed from 0 through 65535 in variable SD, we can reinitialize the seed by

```
100 FOR J=1 TO 5              ┌─ 'setup for 5 lines
200 SD=12345                  │   'seed
300 POKE 16554,0              │   '0 to first seed byte
400 POKE 16556,INT(SD/256)    │   'ms byte to third seed byte
500 POKE 16555,SD-INT(SD/256)*256 │ '1s byte to second seed byte
600 FOR I=1 TO 8              │  ┌─ 'setup for 8 values
700 PRINT RND(10000),         │  │  'random # from 1-10000
800 NEXT I                    │  └─ 'get next number
900 PRINT                     │   'skip line
1000 NEXT J                   └─ 'get next set of 8
1100 GOTO 1100                   'loop for comparison
```

The seed for any random generation is contained in the three bytes of 16554 through 16556. We have arbitrarily zeroed the first byte and put the value of SD into the next two. Any scheme such as this could be used as long as the three bytes are always initialized to the same value for the start of each new pseudo-random number cycle.

RND can be used as a simulation tool for any number of real-world events. Suppose, for example, that we want to simulate a dice roll. Each die has a face value of one through six, and there are two dice. We can easily simulate the roll of each die by using RND(6), which will generate pseudo-random values of 1 through 6.

```
2000 CLS                       'clear screen
2100 R=0                       '0 total # of rolls
2200 DIM NO(12)                'setup array for totals
2300 FOR I=0 TO 50            ┌─ 'roll the dice
2400 PRINT @530,RND(6)        │   'get value of 1-6
2500 PRINT @550,RND(6)        │   'get value f 1-6
2600 NEXT I                   └─ 'keep on rolling
2700 R=R+1                      'bump # of rolls
2800 A=PEEK(15360+531)-48       'get current die value
2900 B=PEEK(15360+551)-48       'from screen positions
3000 NO(A+B)=NO(A+B)+1          'increment total for point
3100 PRINT @ 850,"total # of rolls=";R
3200 PRINT @ 908,"  2  3  4  5  6  7  8  9 10 11 12"
3300 PRINT @972,"";
3400 FOR I=2 TO 12            ┌─ 'loop for totals
3500 PRINT USING "###";NO(I); │  'print totals
3600 NEXT                     └─ 'loop
3700 FOR I=0 TO 50            ┌─ 'pause before next roll
3800 NEXT I                   └─ 'loop
3900 GOTO 2300                 'go to roll again
```

The program continuously rolls the dice and prints out the totals for each of the points 2 through 12. Let the program run for a while to see how the totals compare to the odds of "making" 2 through 12. The odds are given below in percentage of times a point will come up.

Point			Point	
2	2.8%		9	11.1%
3	5.6%		10	8.3%
4	8.3%		11	5.6%
5	11.1%		12	2.8%
6	13.9%			
7	16.7%			
8	13.9%			

Another example of how RND may be used is in a simulation of a fortune teller. In the program below, YES/NO questions are answered by the MYSTIFYING ORACLE program. RND is used to generate a value of 1 through 10. This value is then used to obtain one of ten strings from string array A$ to answer the question. This concept can be used in many similar cases to obtain random answers, events, or conditions.

```
140 DIM A$(10)                        'string array
150 A$(1)="NO"
160 A$(2)="YES"
170 A$(3)="MAYBE"
180 A$(4)="YOU GOTTA BE KIDDING"
190 A$(5)="PLEASE REPHRASE"
200 A$(6)="POSSIBLY"
210 A$(7)="EXCUSE ME, I HAVE ANOTHER CALL."
220 A$(8)="NOPE"
230 A$(9)="NEGATORY, GOOD BUDDY"
240 A$(10)="SURE, WHY NOT"
250 CLS                               'clear screen
260 PRINT "MYSTIFYING ORACLE"         'title message
270 INPUT "YES";A$                   ⌐'input question
280 PRINT A$(RND(10));" - NEXT QUESTION"
290 GOTO 270                         ⌐'continue
```

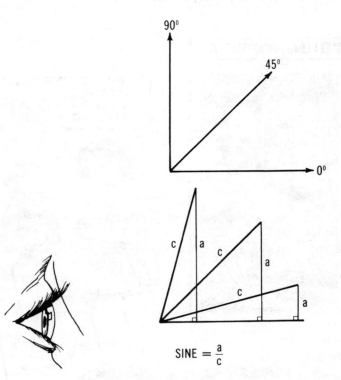

$$SINE = \frac{a}{c}$$

Figure 8-5. Sine function.

The **distribution** of answers in this program will be spread quite evenly among A$(1) through A$(10) if a very large number of cases are tried. If we want to "load" the program to bias it toward certain responses, the same response could be used as many times as desired.

Another technique used quite often in game programs is to generate that "random" catastrophic effect—the plague that strikes during Hammurabi or the loss of photo torpedoes during Space War. This can be accomplished "n times out of 100" by using a code such as

```
1000   IF RND(100)=100 THEN ....
```

or

```
1000   IF RND(100)>96 THEN ....
```

The first example would be true one time out of 100 when RND (100)=100, and the second example would be true four times out of 100 when RND(100)=97, 98, 99, or 100.

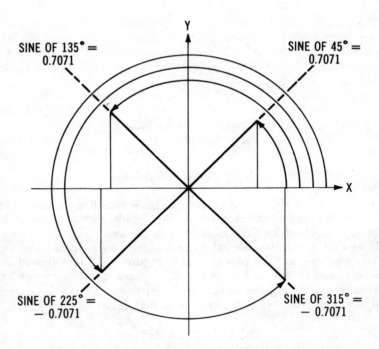

Figure 8-6. Sine function through 360°.

Trigonometric (Say What?) Functions

The last group of functions we'll talk about are the trigonometric functions, pronounced "Trig-oh-no-*met*-ric" if you are a purist. The trigonometric functions, as you might guess, are those arch enemies of high school and college students—sines, cosines, and tangents.

We'll present a short review here, but feel free to peruse other material, too, if you feel you need a better understanding of these mathematical functions. (*If you don't feel that ambitious, just stick around here.*)

For any right triangle (a triangle with one right angle), the ratio of the **opposite side** over the **hypotenuse** is called the **sine,** as shown in Figure 8-5. Opposite to what? To a large eye that we've included in the figure. When this angle is very small, the ratio a/c is very small. If side c is kept at a constant size, as the angle increases, side a increases in size. Close to 90 degrees, the sides are about equal, and at 90 degrees, the sides are equal.

If we continue through 90 degrees to 180 degrees, the ratio of side a to c decreases down to 0 again. We can carry this through 360 degrees, as shown in Figure 8-6. Notice that for angles greater

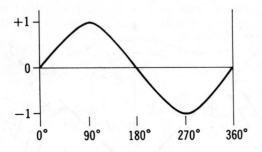

Figure 8-7. Plotted sine function.

than 180 degrees, the sine is negative. This is true if we assume that the triangles are constructed on an x-y graph with the points located by standard x-y "rectangular" coordinates.

If we now graph the sine values for various angles from 0 through 360 degrees, we get the plot shown in Figure 8-7. The value of the sine increases from 0 to 1 from 0 to 90 degrees, decreases from 1 to 0 from 90 to 180 degrees, decreases to −1 from 180 to 270 degrees, and increases from −1 to 0 from 270 to 360 degrees.

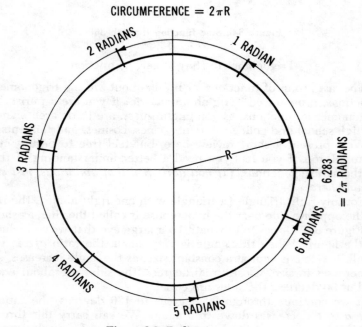

Figure 8-8. Radian measure.

The sine function, expressed by the graph, is used extensively in mathematics and physics. Many physical events operate on a periodic basis that follows the sine function.

Does everyone know the formula for the circumference of a circle? (*Let's see, I have it here somewhere. . . .*) It's 2 times pi times the radius of the circle, as shown in Figure 8-8. The circumference of a circle with radius of three feet is 2 * 3.14159 * 3, or 18.8496. Because the circumference is $2\pi r$, a convenient unit known as a **radian** was invented. A radian represents an angle of $360/2\pi$, or about 57.296 degrees. It's the angle represented by laying the radius of a circle along the circumference as shown in the figure.

Trigonometric functions are often expressed in terms of radians because they easily express critical angles around the circle, such as 45 ($\pi/4$ radians), 90 ($\pi/2$ radians), 180 (π radians), 270 ($3\pi/4$ radians), and 360 degrees (2π radians). If you would rather not worry about radians, simply divide the angle you're using by 57.29578 to convert from degrees to radians and forget about any mystery involved.

Let's display various values for the sine function from 0 to 360 degrees.

```
100 CLS                          'clear that screen
200 FOR I=1 TO 360              ┌'avoid /0 error
300 SET ((I/360)*127,(24-23*(SIN(I/57.29578))))
400 NEXT I                      └'continue for 360 degrees
500 GOTO 500                     'loop here for display
```

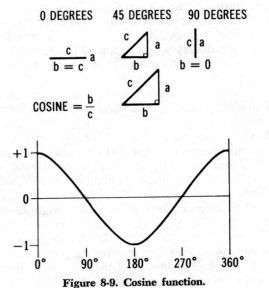

Figure 8-9. Cosine function.

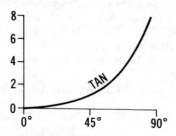

Figure 8-10. Tangent function.

This plot uses the TRS-80 x coordinates from 0 to 127 and the y coordinates from 1 to 23 to avoid problems with going over the y=0 and x=127 boundaries. (We could also have explicitly checked for y<0 or x>=128.) The plot shows the sine values from 1 to 360 degrees (0 to 2π radians) with the top of the screen representing 1 and the bottom representing -1, identical to the plot shown in Figure 8-7.

The cosine function is similar to the sine function. It expresses the ratio of side b divided by side c. As we can see from Figure 8-9, the cosine graph starts off at 1 for an angle of 0 degrees, goes to 0 for an angle of 90 degrees, goes to -1 for 180 degrees, goes to 0 for 270 degrees, and returns to 1 for 360 degrees. The cosine function also figures in a great many physical and mathematical relationships. The format of the cosine function is identical to SIN, with the argument in radians.

The tangent function is the third common trigonometric function represented in the TRS-80. It expresses the ratio of side a to b, as shown in Figure 8-10. It's easy to see that for angles near 90 degrees, the tangent increases to infinity, and for this reason it's hard (if not impossible) to graph. The format of the tangent is identical to SIN, using radians for the argument. Whereas TAN(A) gives the tangent ratio for a known angle, ATN(A) does the inverse. ATN(A) gives the angle from the ratio. Both are used often in higher mathematics. (*That's what tall math profs play with.*)

```
1000 FOR I=0 TO 89          ┌─'for 0 to 89 degrees
1100 A=TAN(I/57.29578)      │ 'find tangent
1200 B=ATN(A)               │ 'find angle from tangent
1300 PRINT I/57.29578,B     └─'print radians,arctan(rad)
1400 NEXT I                    'continue for 89 degrees
```

CHAPTER 9

How to Get It All on Tape

Cassette tape is a fairly recent innovation for computer systems. Previous systems used much more complicated **digital magnetic tape recorders** that were (and are) very expensive. In this chapter, we'll discuss the CSAVE, CLOAD, CLOAD?, INPUT#, and PRINT# commands, tape data formats and speeds, blocking of records, files, error recovery, and tape backups.

Tape Commands

There are three cassette tape commands in Level II BASIC—CSAVE, CLOAD, and CLOAD?. The use of these is very straight-forward. To save a BASIC program, set the cassette recorder level to the proper setting, rewind the tape to the beginning (or a known point using the cassette counter), set the tape recorder controls to Record, and type in CSAVE *"name"*. The BASIC program will be written out to cassette tape in roughly the same fashion that it is stored in memory.

To reload the program or any other program stored on cassette, reposition the recorder to the beginning of tape (or the counter position), set the recorder control to Playback, and type in CLOAD or CLOAD *"name"*. The BASIC program will be read into RAM.

Simple and foolproof . . . What could go wrong? Well, a couple of things. First of all, make certain that you are past the leader (the non-magnetic material at the beginning of the tape) on the cassette. Many tape recorders have trouble recording data on the leader (*that's a joke, son!*). Secondly, make certain that the level setting on the tape recorder is at the recommended value for the type of recorder you're using. It may take some experimentation to find the optimum level for consistently good writes and reads. Thirdly, not only must you be clear of the leader on the tape, but it's a good idea to erase a portion of the tape to "bracket" the starting point, as shown in Figure 9-1. The reason for this third point is to be found in the general tape format that's used for Level II tape operations.

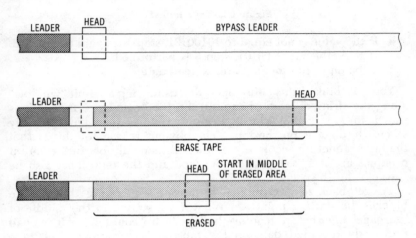

Figure 9-1. "Bracketing" tape writes.

Follow the Leader

All tape operations write data to the cassette by first writing 255 bytes of zeroes and by then writing a single byte of a value of 165, as shown in Figure 9-2. The remainder of the write contains the BASIC program or data to be written. On a subsequent read (CLOAD), the tape read routine expects to find zeroes initially, followed by the 165 value. As a matter of fact, it uses the 165 byte as a "synchronization byte" or "sync byte" so that it knows where the data starts.

Data is written on the cassette **serially** as a long string of binary data. (*There's that darn binary again!*) The 255 bytes of zeroes and the one byte of 165 result in 2048 bits of "leader," as shown in Figure 9-2. When the CLOAD is performed (or when any tape read is performed), the read goes something like this:

1. A bit is read.
2. The tape input routine moves this bit left into an 8-bit value.
3. The value is compared to 10100101 (165).

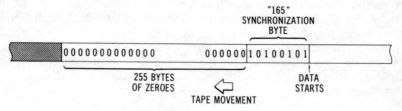

0 0 0 0 0 0 0 0 0 0 0 0   0 0 0 0 0 0 | 1 0 1 0 0 1 0 1

255 BYTES
OF ZEROES

TAPE MOVEMENT

DATA
STARTS

Figure 9-2. Tape format.

4. If the value is not equal to 10100101, step 1 is again performed. If the value is 10100101, step 5 is performed.
5. Tape input routine prepares to read data.

You can think of this entire operation as moving an 8-bit "window" along the string of leader bits until the 165 "sync byte" is found, as shown in Figure 9-3. The tape input routines then know exactly where the data is on the tape. The obvious reason for this is that the tape cannot be accurately positioned manually because each bit occupies about 1/250 inch on the tape and the tape must also be "brought up to speed."

To get back to our original discussion on erasing the tape to bracket the starting point . . . What if we started in the middle of "garbage" data before reading the tape? This could occur if we had previously recorded data on the tape and repositioned the tape sometime before the actual start of the new leader, as shown in Figure 9-4. Now, if the data included *any* 8 bits of data in the series 10100101, the tape input routine would be fooled into thinking that this was a legitimate sync byte and would then start reading data, which would be garbage. The chances of this happening are about one in 1 inch of tape. So . . . please follow our advice about bracketing the starting point on writes, or at least reposition the counter slightly past the point at which writing started. (*We'll be*

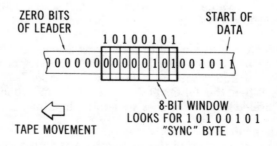

ZERO BITS
OF LEADER

1 0 1 0 0 1 0 1

START OF
DATA

0 0 0 0 0 | 0 0 0 0 0 1 0 1 | 0 0 1 0 1 1

8-BIT WINDOW
LOOKS FOR 1 0 1 0 0 1 0 1
"SYNC" BYTE

TAPE MOVEMENT

Figure 9-3. Synchronization operation.

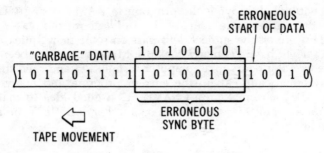

Figure 9-4. Synchronization problems.

sending around our armed guard soon to RND (users) to remind you . . .)

Returning to the CSAVE and CLOAD commands, let's write out a short program. The shortest program I know of is

`100  REM`

CSAVE this under "SHORT" and then CLOAD it in. Time the operation. The entire operation took about 5 seconds. Most of the time in this case is devoted to writing out the 255 bytes of zeroes. It's easy to figure out the time involved in writing out any known length of data. We know from diligent study of our Radio Shack manuals that Level II records at 500 baud and that 500 baud (in this case) is about 500 bits per second. The amount of data per second, then, is roughly 500/8 bytes, or 62.5 bytes per second. The leader of 255 bytes would therefore take about 255/62.5 or about 4 seconds to write. We'll be using the 62.5 bytes per second in later discussion, so it might behoove you to take this constant and have it engraved on a wall plaque for reference in later reading . . . (*we'll wait while you do . . .*).

Why Is There a Question Mark After CLOAD??

We'll be discussing this subject shortly, after we give a definitive statement about truth and beauty. The question mark marks this CLOAD as a "check" CLOAD. As you know from some late-hour CLOADS, one of the things that always seems to occur (especially at the end of the day) is to finish debugging a BASIC program, CSAVE it on tape, CLOAD it in again, and have it give an error part way through the load.

Unfortunately, at this point the program cannot be recovered, and you don't have an old copy. Ah yes, the trials of a programmer. . . . The CLOAD? is a well-thought-out command to enable you to compare what you have CSAVED with the program currently in

RAM (without destroying the program in RAM). Using CLOAD? will result in many extra hours of sleep (*I'll go for that!*).

While we're on the subject, let's pass on some more quick advice. One can never have *too* many backups. Many times, I've been working late evening hours in a computer installation and seen the computer systematically eat up the current program and many of the backups. If you're making a CSAVE, it's a good idea to make two copies on the same cassette or even on another cassette. Your TRS-80 may be hungry.

What's That (Blinking) Asterisk?

On a CLOAD or CLOAD? (and on other inputs), two asterisks are used. One of them blinks on and off for every line of BASIC program read. If you have excellent reflexes, you may be able to verify that the number of program lines read in is correct during a CLOAD operation.

Using PRINT# and INPUT#

CSAVE and the CLOAD commands are fairly easy to use and understand. The cassette data is made up of the BASIC program lines; all data is of about the same format on tape.

The PRINT# and INPUT# statements, though, are more general-purpose. They are used to output variable-length data **records** to the cassette and to input the records into the BASIC interpreter for processing. Try the following:

```
100 INPUT "READY TAPE";A$      'wait for position
200 PRINT #-1,"this is a test" 'output one record
300 INPUT "ready tape";A$      'wait for tape positioning
400 INPUT #-1,B$               'input one record
500 CLS                        'clear screen
600 PRINT @ 530,B$             'print input record
700 GOTO 700                     'for display
```

This code shows the basic format for outputting and inputting cassette data from a BASIC program. The "#" marks the PRINT statement as cassette output and the INPUT statement as cassette input. The −1 is used to refer to cassette tape unit number 1. (If you have an Expansion Interface, it is possible to write to either of *two* cassettes, and allowable numbers in the PRINT and INPUT statements are −1 and −2.)

The operation above writes one **record,** made up of the string "THIS IS A TEST" and the usual leader of 255 bytes of zeroes and a sync byte, to the cassette. The record appears as shown in Figure 9-6. As you can see, most of the space in the record is made up of leader and very little of data.

Rewind the tape and run the following program.

```
1000 INPUT "READY TAPE";A$          'wait for tape positioning
1100 PRINT #-1,111.33,737,"THIS IS A TEST",1E-05
1200 GOTO 1100                      'continually output record
```

Let the program run for several minutes. After accumulating several minutes worth of data on the tape, key in the following program, and run it after first rewinding the tape.

```
2000 DATA 175,205,18,2,205,150,2,205,53,2,183,32,7
2100 DATA 62,10,205,51,0,24,240,205,51,0,24,238
2200 A$="THIS IS A DUMMY FOR FILL!"
2300 A=VARPTR(A$)                   'get address of block
2400 B=PEEK(A+1)+PEEK(A+2)*256      'get address of string
2500 FOR I=B TO B+24             ┌─ 'setup loop for poke
2600 READ C                      │  'read value
2700 POKE I,C                    │  'poke into string
2800 NEXT I                      └─ 'loop for 25
2900 POKE 16526,(PEEK(A+1))         'store ls byte of address
3000 POKE 16527,(PEEK(A+2))         'store ms byte of address
3100 CLS                            'that ol clear screen
3200 A=USR(0)                       'call to never return
```

The program above reads data files on cassette and displays the data on the screen by using a short machine-language program filled into the dummy string A$. (We'll learn more about this technique in the next chapter.) Every new record is displayed on a new line. This program can be used for any data tape. As we can see from the data on the display, the format of the data on the tape is as shown in Figure 9-5. Each numeric value in the string for the PRINT#—1 was written onto the tape in ASCII with one leading and one trailing blank, and a comma between data items. The string value was written out without a leading or trailing blank.

The PRINT#, therefore, is really very similar to a print on the display or line printer in that it writes out ASCII data rather than binary values. This makes the data easy to read for a routine such as the one above, but it makes the data storage somewhat inefficient. (A binary value of 32767 would take 2 bytes instead of 5 bytes in ASCII, for example.)

PRINT# will output any number of variables or constants that can be contained within a line in the above format. Each list of variables for the PRINT will be contained within one record, with 255 leading zeroes and the sync byte. A record is simply a somewhat arbitrary collection of variables, logically grouped into a single area. A file of data consists of a number of records of related data. If your TRS-80 was used to record time and temperature in each record, for example, the Tuesday, September 25, 1979 temperature file might contain 48 records, one for every ½ hour temperature reading.

The INPUT# statement is similar in action to a normal INPUT statement. It reads the next record from cassette after first discard-

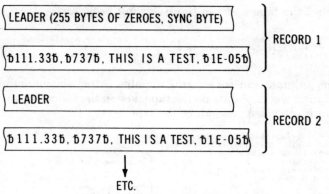

Figure 9-5. Tape data formats.

ing the zeroes and detecting the sync byte. It separates the ASCII data items by looking for commas. **It expects to find exactly the same number of data items as there are on the INPUT# line and in the same format.** If the number of data items in the record does not match the number specified on the INPUT# line, an OD (Out of Data) error may result. If the types of data items do not match, an FD (bad File Data) error results. The input routines in the BASIC interpreter convert the ASCII data found in the record to the variable types listed in the INPUT# line.

Now that we know something about the data format used by Level II BASIC, we can accurately predict how long it will take to read and write data from cassette. This is very important, since the cassette is a relatively slow-speed device, operating at **data transfer** rates 500 times slower than a TRS-80 floppy disk. It will benefit us to spend some time discussing some thoughts about cassette space, speed, and packing. (*Sorry, I couldn't find another "s" word for alliteration.*)

Space, Speed, and (S)Packing

First of all, let's consider how *much* data can be stored on a cassette. If we write 62.5 bytes per second to a cassette, then we have the following absolute storage capacities for *one side* of a C30 cassette and a C60 cassette.

$$C30 = 15 \text{ minutes} \times 60 \frac{\text{seconds}}{\text{minute}} \times 62.5 \frac{\text{bytes}}{\text{second}} = 56250 \text{ bytes}$$
$$C60 = 2 \times C30 = 112500 \text{ bytes}$$

We say **absolute** because this would be the storage capacity if the cassette were used to read or write one huge record of this size without inter-record **gaps** of zeroes and a sync byte. If we want to find out how much **record** data can be put on the cassette, that's another story. We must really figure that out for each individual program that writes to cassette. Let's see how we do it in a sample case.

Suppose, to use the weather analogy again (it's always fair weather when good data gets together) . . . Let's say that we have the following PRINT# statement for weather data

100 PRINT # – 1,MO,DA,YR,TM,WS,BP,WD

The variables are MO for month, DA for day, YR for year, TM for temperature, WS for wind speed, BP for barometric pressure, and WD for wind direction. If we assume 2 digits for month, day, and year, and four digits plus decimal point for TM, WS, BP, and

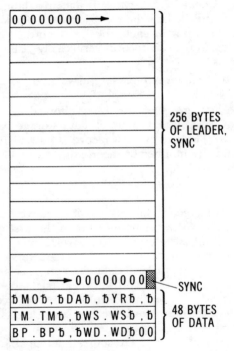

Figure 9-6. Example of record format.

WD, then we have records that look like Figure 9-6. Each record will contain about 48 ASCII bytes of data plus 256 bytes of leader (zeroes and sync byte) for a grand total of 304 bytes. Now, how many of these records can we get on a single side of a C60 cassette? Easy . . .

$$\frac{112500}{304} = 370 \text{ records}$$

Of course, in actual practice the number of ASCII characters per variable may vary, trailing zeroes will be discarded, and so forth. Still, we can get a pretty good idea of the number of records the tape will actually hold by doing this type of analysis. Another approximate way to calculate the number of records is to assume that each record is about $5\frac{1}{4}$ seconds long. Using this approximation and knowing that there are $30 \times 60 = 1800$ seconds per side of a C60 cassette, we can approximate 340 records. This is not *too* far off; the smaller the number of variables in the record, the more accurate this method is, of course.

Now, just for fun, let's try **packing** data. Packie Data . . . wasn't he Roy Autrey's sidekick? No, we said **packing** data, another data-processing buzzword. When data is packed or **blocked,** more than one logical record is put in each physical record. We can put two weather readings into each record very easily using arrays, by a statement such as

```
100   PRINT  # − 1,MO(I),DA(I),YR(I),TM(I),WS(I),BP(I),WD(I),MO(I + 1),DA(I + 1),YR(I + 1),
              TM(I + 1),WS(I + 1),BP(I + 1),WD(I + 1)
```

This writes the first group of variables followed immediately by a second group of variables. How much data storage have we gained by this approach? The size of each record is now 256+48+48 bytes, or 352 bytes, and the number of records is

$$\frac{112500}{352} = 320 \text{ records}$$

However, since each record holds 2 sets of data, we have the equivalent of 640 records, 170% of the number in the first case!

The practical limit is determined by two factors. The first is the maximum size of the statement line (240 characters); the second is the maximum record length (240 data characters or 596 total bytes). The equivalent number of records for various blocking factors is shown in Table 9-1. For example, in the case of records blocked 6 sets of variables to one record, we can squeeze 1242 sets of variables onto one side of a C60 cassette. Quite an improvement over 370 for an unblocked record! Of course, the smaller the size and number of variables, the greater the blocking factor can be, up to the limit of the statement line length or maximum record length.

We can say some interesting things about speed when records are blocked. There is a direct relation between the blocking factor and speed of access of any record; the more blocking employed, the faster we will be able to read in the data. Using a blocking factor of 6, for example, the 370th set of variables is about 30% "down

Table 9-1. Blocking Factor Versus Data, Sample Case

Blocking Factor	Number of Bytes/Record	Maximum Number of Records, One Side of C60	Number of Records Times Blocking Factor (Equivalent Number of Variable Sets)
1	304	370	370
2	352	320	640
3	400	281	843
4	448	251	1004
5	496	227	1135
6	544	207	1242

the tape" or about 9 minutes, while it is at the end (30 minutes) of an unblocked tape.

Sequential Cassette Files

Is it practical to use cassette tape to hold data files for processing? It all depends on the type of data file. If we want to process the weather data we were discussing previously and have to find records at **random,** then it is impractical to store the records on cassette tape, because each time we require a new record we have to intervene manually and rewind the tape to the beginning of the cassette before the search. An example of this **access** of **random** records would be a user requesting the weather data for July 27 at 12:30 pm, then the data for June 10 at 10:00 am, then the data for March 11 at 5:00 am. The records are ordered on the tape in sequential fashion based on the date and time. Each search for a random record takes between no time and 30 minutes, with an average of 15 minutes (assuming one side of a cassette completely filled with data). Fifteen minutes to access a record is intolerable, even for patient TRS-80 programmers, and the manual intervention is also a nuisance.

If, however, we want to compile a list of all times when the temperature was below −30 degrees and a second list of all times when the wind speed was above 20 miles per hour, this is a relatively easy and practical problem. One pass through the cassette could yield two lists with the required data in about 30 minutes, not an unreasonable time, especially when the manual intervention of rewinding is not required.

The second type of processing is **sequential** in nature. Cassette data files lend themselves fairly well to sequential processes, but not at all to random processes. Cassette data files can efficiently hold any data that can be ordered and processed sequentially.

It's easy to see how sequential files can be generated. An initial set of records is input into memory, blocked, and then output to the cassette in ordered fashion. How are new records merged or old records modified or deleted?

If your system has only one cassette recorder, then the size of the file is limited by the amount of data that can be held in memory and processed. Assuming that about half of the record is data and half is leader (512-byte record), then we have about 45,000 bytes maximum that we could put on one side of a C60 cassette. That would stretch the limits of a 48K Level II BASIC system, since we have about 48,340 bytes initially *without* a program to process the data, but it gives some clue as to the maximum amount of data we can handle with one cassette. In this case, all of the data records on the cassette would have to be read into memory, the data processed by adding new records, modifying old records, and deleting old records, and a new cassette rewritten after the processing was done.

I hear a strident voice protesting (*Guard! Confiscate his C60 cassettes—leave only the C½s!*). No, data cannot be rewritten *over* records on the tape, for two reasons. First of all, there is that manual intervention again to reposition the cassette to the start of the record to be modified by rewriting. Secondly, although there are expensive **incremental** tape recorders for computer use, an audio cassette cannot be repositioned accurately enough to guarantee that a new record *exactly* overwrites the old. (Remember the possible erroneous sync byte problem we discussed earlier?) The only way to update an old file with new data is to rewrite all of the records after they've been modified.

Two Cassettes Are Better Than One

Having two cassettes simplifies the file update problem considerably. Of course, an Expansion Interface is necessary for operation of the second cassette. One cassette is cassette number −1, and the second is cassette number −2. The current transactions, whether they are deletions, modifications, or additions, are input to the system from the keyboard (or from a third cassette). Now the records from the *old master* file (−1) are read one at a time and rewritten to the new master file (−2). If a record is to be modified, it is modified after it is read into memory, and rewritten to the new master file. If a record is to be deleted, it is not written to the new master. If a record is to be added, it is added between the two records of the old master file.

The time involved to update an old master file into a new master file on the second cassette is twice that of working with one cassette, but the entire operation can go very smoothly and is fairly efficient for sequential files.

CHAPTER 10

To Err Is Human

We're certain you, like the author, hardly ever make mistakes. . . . In spite of that, we'll be discussing some of the common errors in Level II BASIC programs in this chapter. We'll also talk about some very handy features in BASIC that allow the computer to handle errors automatically. Why is this important? Suppose you've developed a sophisticated BASIC program that does everything but tuck you in at night. You have self-prompting messages, menus, and a number of other things. In the course of running the program, however, let's say you enter some invalid data which results in total sales being divided by a number-of-months variable that is equal to 0. Suddenly the program spits out "/0 ERROR IN 1088," and you sit there dumbfounded. (Or at least sit there for about 20 milliseconds before starting to scream.)

BASIC has a built-in automatic error-handling provision that can avoid problems such as this. It also provides the ability to **simulate** the errors to check out the error logic itself.

We'll also give you some homespun advice in this chapter on general debugging philosophy, and we'll talk about some of the built-in aids to debugging—such as the trace capability.

Unprintable Errors and Other Types

Our favorite error type is "unprintable error"; that's exactly the way we feel about all errors! The unprintable error and all of the other types are listed in Table 10-1. Let's discuss each of them and see how they are generated.

Table 10-1. Level II BASIC Error Codes

Error Code		Error Description
1	NF	NEXT without FOR
2	SN	Syntax error
3	RG	Return without GOSUB
4	OD	Out of data
5	FC	Illegal function call
6	OV	Overflow
7	OM	Out of memory
8	UL	Undefined line
9	BS	Subscript out of range (bad subscript)
10	DD	Redimensioned array
11	/0	Division by zero
12	ID	Illegal direct
13	TM	Type mismatch
14	OS	Out of string space
15	LS	String too long
16	ST	String formula too complex
17	CN	Can't continue
18	NR	No RESUME
19	RW	RESUME without error
20	UE	Unprintable error
21	MO	Missing operand
22	FD	Bad file data
23	L3	Disk BASIC only

One of the most straightforward errors is the UL, or "undefined line" error. This occurs when a statement line reference is made to a line that doesn't exist anywhere in the program.

```
1000   GOTO 2000            'go to 2000
1010   A=2*3.2+ZZ           'get total
3000   PRINT "TOTAL=";A     'print it
```

The code above, for example, would result in "UL ERROR IN 1000."

The SN, or syntax error, is another easy type of error to understand. A syntax error occurs when the format of a statement line is incorrect. Many times this occurs if the number and type of parentheses are incorrect. This ranges from simple statements such as

```
100   X=A(5/B
```

to complex giants such as

```
100   ZZ=(RIGHT(2B$,(A-2)*3))
```

The number of right parentheses must always match the number of left parentheses. It's a good idea to get into the habit of counting and comparing parentheses in long, complex statement lines. It's easy to miss an internal parenthesis. Syntax errors are also caused by other errors in format such as

```
100   A=B//C
```
or
```
100   A$=LEFT$(B$)
```

Syntax errors are a kind of catchall for every type of statement format error.

The NEXT without FOR error, NF, and RETURN without GOSUB, RG, are two program-format errors that are also obvious. NF occurs when a loop is improperly set up without a FOR statement, or the program branches *to* a point where a NEXT is to be executed without being currently in a loop. An example of this is

```
100   GOTO 300           'goto 300
200   FOR I=1 TO 300  ┌ 'start of loop
300   PRINT I         │ 'print index
400   NEXT            └ 'continue
```

The RG is similar; a RETURN is to be executed without currently having called a subroutine.

OD, out of data, occurs when READ statements have read data values until the end of all data has been reached. As you know from previous chapters, all DATA statements anywhere in the program constitute one table of DATA values. When a RESTORE is done, a pointer is set back to the beginning of the DATA. Subsequent reads read one data value for every item in the read list. An easy error to make is to have a dummy terminating value to mark the end of the DATA values and then not put in enough "dummies" to complete the READS for multiple items. For example, suppose we are reading three DATA values at a time and using a −1 to mark the end of the values.

```
100  READ A,B,C                       ┌ 'read 3 data values
150  IF A=-1 END                      │ 'terminator is -1
200  PRINT "A=";A,"B=";B,"C=";C        │ 'print values
250  GOTO 100                         └ 'go for next set
300  DATA 1,2,3,4,5,6,7,8,9,-1
```

The logic of the above program is flawed, since the last READ attempts to read the next three values and can find only one. An OD error results.

An illegal function call error, FC, occurs when you're using the BASIC functions and specifying invalid arguments. For example, what is the square root of a negative number? The code

```
100   A=SQR(-23)
```

will produce an FC error. Another type of invalid argument producing the same results is a graphics related

```
100   SET(223,5)
```

or a matrix related

```
100   B=A(-1,0)
```

The OV error, overflow, results when a data value is too large for the variable involved. As we saw in an earlier chapter, all variable types have their limits, beyond which they will not be pushed. Trying to INPUT a value greater than +32767 or less than −32768 will result in an OV error for

100 INPUT A%

as will attempting to input 1.1E127 for A or A#.

Choose one from the following: "OM, out of memory" occurs when

A. The RAM chips are pulled from their sockets.
B. Bornstein takes a vacation.
C. The stack builds down into the text/variable/array area.
D. The program expands and the text/variable/array area moves into the stack.
E. A new simple variable expands the text/variable/array area into the stack.
F. An array is dimensioned and the text/variable/array area expands into the stack.
G. A CLEAR is performed that expands the string/stack space into the text/variable/array area.
H. I forgot the question.

If you chose any of the above, you are probably right. Any time the free memory between the text/variable/array area and the stack/string area is small, the action of running the program may dimension arrays, clear string space, add new variables, or perform other actions to use up the last available memory (see Figure 10-1).

Anticipating that some users might be prolific coders, the designers of Level II BASIC were faced with two alternatives:

1. Let the program gobble itself up, or
2. Print an OM error.

They chose the latter. To see how much memory is still left under various conditions, you may include a "PRINT MEM" at any point in the program. Doing a rough estimate on the amount of storage required by arrays also is a help. If you *do* run out of memory, possible alternatives are:

Reduce the program size by deleting REMarks and blanks, and building multiple statement lines.
Make single-precision variables into integer variables when possible, especially for arrays.
Reduce the string area defined by CLEAR.
Segment the program into two or more sections.

174

An OS (out of string space) error related to OM occurs when the string space allocated by a CLEAR statement is too small to handle string manipulations. The string area may be made as large as re-

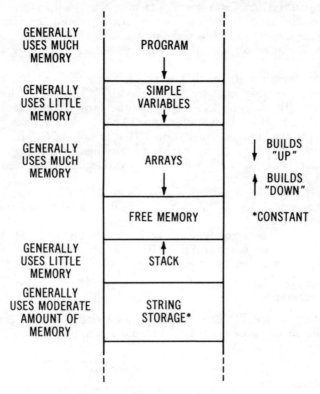

Figure 10-1. Free memory area.

quired, subject to other storage, so don't hesitate to throw caution to the winds and say

```
100   CLEAR 20000
```

if required. This also eliminates or reduces dynamic string allocation in the middle of execution. (You know, the interminable pauses that make you think that it's time to visit the repair center.)

The BS, or subscript out of range, error occurs when an array subscript is greater than the dimension value specified in the DIM statement or is otherwise incompatible. Arrays are specified by DIM values that represent the *maximum* value for the dimension. For example, the statement DIM A(5,5,5) specifies an array that is six by six by six with values for each dimension of from 0 through 5.

Another array-related error is DD, a redimensioned array. Arrays can be dimensioned once and once only, and cannot be redimensioned. A DIM statement at the beginning of the program sets up the array in the array storage area of memory by allocating memory space for the array based on the variable type and the size of the array. It is not permitted to redefine the array later in the program, and, as a matter of fact, that's just gosh-darn bad programming practice.

We've probably all heard our math instructor say that division by 0 is not possible or at least "undefined." When the computer attempts to divide by 0, the answer is the largest possible number that can be held in the variable type. This is clearly wrong as the answer for the integer calculation 333/0 is not 32767! Just as our math instructor did not know what to do when he attempted to divide a number by 0, neither does the BASIC interpreter, and it produces a /0 error.

The ID, or illegal direct, occurs when INPUT is entered as a direct command. INPUT A,B is meaningless if not associated with a statement line.

There are three error types associated with strings, TM, LS, and ST. TM, type mismatch, occurs when the program attempts to define a string variable, a numeric value, or vice versa.

```
100   A$=12.34
200   A="STRING"
```

will both produce TM errors. The LS, or string too long, error will occur if a string value exceeds 255 characters in length as in

```
1000  CLEAR 1000           'clear string storage
1100  A$="14 CHARACTERS!"   '14 char string
1200  B$=B$+A$             'concatenate
1300  PRINT B$             'print concatenated string
1400  GOTO 1200            'keep on slogging
```

The ST error, or string formula too complex, occurs when the BASIC interpreter just cannot handle the machinations of the programmer. I have never experienced the ST error (which may say something about the sophistication of my coding!). We'll leave it up to you to produce samples of string statements that produce this error.

The CN error, can't continue, occurs when the program has reached a logical end and a CONTinue statement is meaningless. It is the interpreter's way of saying "THINK AGAIN, HAMMU-RABI!"

The NR, RW, and UE errors will be discussed shortly when we discuss the error functions.

The MO, or missing operand, error occurs for cases where an operation is specified but no operand exists. The code

176

will produce an MO error.

Bad file data, FD, occurs when a cassette read operation is taking place and invalid data is read in as a result of bad data on the tape, or "glitches" in reading the cassette. Errors such as this are classed as recoverable or non-recoverable. A recoverable error means that the same data may be reread and recovered. Unrecoverable generally means that three (or more) retries were unsuccessful in recovering the data.

The last error code, L3, is displayed when a Disk BASIC command is attempted without disk. An example of this would be an attempt to execute a KILL command to kill a file or a non-existent disk. An L3 error would result.

Trapping the Wild Error

As we're all aware, the BASIC interpreter stops program execution after encountering an error, prints the two-letter error type, and returns to a READY condition. This is a reasonable action to take in the general case. If you can anticipate the errors that may occur, however, you can utilize the Level II Error functions to process the errors and either correct the condition or prompt yourself into correcting the condition. The error functions that you have at your disposal are the "ON ERROR GOTO" trap (which transfers to a given statement number for any error), a RESUME statement (which acts as a type of CONTinue after the error), the ERL and ERR/2+1 (which return an error line number and error code number, respectively), and an error simulate, the ERROR function. Before we discuss how we can trap errors, let's talk briefly about what errors we *want* to trap.

We could conceivably set up a program to trap (process) all errors. However, some errors, such as SN, NF, and RG, are clearly program logic errors. *In other words, the program has not been sufficiently debugged when these errors occur!* It does not make sense to process such errors that are involved with program logic. It *does* make sense to process errors that are a result of incorrect data input by the user, overflow conditions on input, division by 0, type mismatch on input, or bad file data. The error trapping ability is meant primarily as a means to make a program "idiot-proof" in the kindest sense of the word—to anticipate the normal types of errors that occur primarily as a result of operator errors in inputting data.

Now that we know *what* errors we want to trap, let's see *how* we go about processing them. First, we'd better take a close look at the "ON ERROR GOTO" statement. This statement defines an error-processing routine for the interpreter. Henceforth, any error condition will result not in a printout of the error type, but a transfer to the line that begins the error processing routine.

```
100   ON ERROR GOTO 10000
```

informs the interpreter that the error processing routine is at line 10000 and that any errors that occur should cause an automatic transfer to that line.

The ON ERROR GOTO function may be disabled by executing an ON ERROR GOTO 0 statement at any time. By alternating between ON ERROR GOTO *n* and ON ERROR GOTO 0 statements, error trapping may be turned on and off depending upon the section of the program that is currently being executed. If, for example, the program only handles error processing for bad cassette data, then any time cassette data is *not* being INPUT an ON ERROR GOTO 0 may be executed to disable the trap.

The RESUME statement is used to resume normal operation after error processing has taken place. There are three formats for the RESUME.

1. RESUME or RESUME 0 causes a return to the statement where the error occurred.
2. RESUME *n* causes a transfer of control to a specified line number *n*.
3. RESUME NEXT causes a transfer of control to the line immediately after the line at which the error occurred.

We'll show examples for all three using the infamous /0 error type. First, the RESUME case.

```
2000 ON ERROR GOTO 2500          'setup error trap locn
2100 A=2/0                       'cant divide by 0!
2200 PRINT "LINE 2200"           'print line #
2300 PRINT "LINE 2300"           'print line #
2400 END                         'this is the end
2500 PRINT "error trap"          'error trap location
2600 RESUME                      'resume processing @ 2200
```

Execution of this program causes the error-processing routine line number to be stored by the interpreter as "2500." A divide by 0 error results at line 2100, causing the interpreter to transfer control to the error-processing routine at line 2500. This routine prints "ERROR TRAP" and then executes a RESUME, which transfers control back to line 2100, which causes a divide-by-0 error, which transfers control to the error-processing routine at line 2500 which, ... Well, anyway, you get the idea.

```
3000 ON ERROR GOTO 3500          'setup error trap locn
3100 A=2/0                       'cant divide by 0!
3200 PRINT "LINE 3200"           'print line #
3300 PRINT "LINE 3300"           'print line #
3400 END                         'this is the end
3500 PRINT "ERROR TRAP"          'error trap location
3600 RESUME 3300                 'resume processing @ 3300
```

Execution of this version causes an error trap to line 3500, print-out of "ERROR TRAP", and a transfer of control to line 3300 with termination of the error condition.

```
4000 ON ERROR GOTO 4500        'setup error trap locn
4100 A=2/0                     'cant divide by 0!
4200 PRINT "LINE 4200"         'print line #
4300 PRINT "LINE 4300"         'print line #
4400 END                       'this is the end
4500 PRINT "ERROR TRAP"        'error trap location
4600 RESUME NEXT               'resume next line
```

Execution of this version causes an error trap to line 4500, printout of "ERROR TRAP", and a transfer of control to the line immediately following the line causing the error condition, line 4200.

Error Processing

Error processing involves three steps: identifying the error, correcting the error, and RESUMEing at a logical point. We'll talk about the first two, since the third is dependent upon the success in solving the error condition.

There are two statements that we can use to identify the error, ERL and ERR/2+1. ERR/2+1 provides the error code (see Table 10-1), while ERL provides the line number. The code below prints out the error code and line number on which the error occurred. Try running this code not only with the /0 error, but with other erroneous code at statement 200.

```
100 ON ERROR GOTO 500          'setup error trap locn
200 A=2/0                      'naughty,naughty!
300 PRINT "LINE 300"           'print line #
400 END                        'end program
500 PRINT "ERROR#=";ERR/2+1,"ERROR LINE=";ERL
600 RESUME NEXT                'resume at next line
```

If we only wish to process certain types of errors in our error processing routine, we can easily eliminate the catastrophic errors such as NEXT without FOR, syntax, and others by comparison of the error type.

```
1000 ON ERROR GOTO 1400        'setup error trap locn
1100 A=2/0                     'again?!
1200 PRINT "LINE 1200"         'print line #
1300 END                       'end program
1400 A=ERR/2+1                  'get error code
1500 IF A<>11 AND A<>13 AND A<>22 GOTO 1800
1600 PRINT "/0 OR TM OR FD ERROR"   'was one of the three
1700 RESUME NEXT               'resume at next line
1800 ON ERROR GOTO 0           'reset error trap
1900 RESUME                    'resume at error line
```

The above code processes only a /0, type mismatch, or bad data error by testing the error code ERR/2+1. If one of these three errors occurs, a message is printed, and the program resumes at the next line following the error. If none of these errors occurs, the error trapping is reset by ON ERROR GOTO 0, and a RESUME causes line 1100 to be re-executed resulting in the "normal" error type print-out and the READY prompt by BASIC.

Having identified the errors we wish to process, how can we correct the conditions causing the error? This is really an unanswerable question, since it depends so much upon the type of program. If the error occurred because of overflow or type mismatch during data entry, then it is relatively simple to output an error message that prompts the user to re-enter the data. In word-processing applications, an out-of-memory error could result, and suitable action, such as "flushing" the text onto cassette, could be taken. Divide-by-zero problems may be solved by re-entering the data, also. (Truthfully, though, many divide-by-zero problems should be handled earlier by checking the data for validity and proper range.)

An FD error, bad file data, may be hard to handle for cassette. A floppy-disk may be easily reread, but cassette file errors call for repositioning. A step-by-step procedure may be implemented to help the operator reposition the tape for a new try at reading. After three tries or so, some other action must be taken to replace the lost data, or the program may have to be terminated.

Simulating Errors

The last error function is the ERROR statement, which simulates an error code. This is a handy feature for debugging the error trapping functions. (The question, "What do we use to debug the debug of the error trapping functions?" arises, but since we see an endless loop appearing, we'll continue.) ERROR n produces a **simulated** error. In the code above, we could have made line 1100

```
1100   ERROR 11
```

which would have the same effect as a /0 error.

The code below causes simulated errors for error codes 1 through 23. Each code is printed, and the error trap routine then causes execution at the NEXT line following the error line.

```
2000 ON ERROR GOTO 2400          'setup error trap
2100 FOR I=1 TO 23             ┌ 'loop for error codes
2200 ERROR I                   │ 'simulate error
2300 NEXT                      └ 'continue
2350 END
2400 PRINT ERR/2+1,              'error processing print
2500 RESUME NEXT                 'resume next line
```

Now for those three missing error codes, RW, NR, and UE. All three are associated with error trapping or simulation. RW is

RESUME without error and occurs when a RESUME is encoun-
tered without a previous ON ERROR GOTO statement. NR is NO
RESUME and occurs when program end is reached while still in
an error trapping mode. The last, that !!!$#*!! unprintable error,
UE, is caused by attempting to simulate an error with an invalid
error code, as in

```
100   ERROR 87      '!!!$#*!!
```

Debugging

In the old computer days ten years or so ago when computer time
was at a premium, the process of debugging a program was completely different than it is now on the TRS-80. The procedure then
(and now at larger computer installations) was to do a great deal
of "desk checking" of programs before "getting on" the machine.
Getting on amounted to submitting the program as one of fifty "jobs"
to be run on the computer installation. When its turn came, the
program would run, exercise some test data, and "blow up." The
programmer would then retrieve the new listing and test data and
try to piece together what had happened in the program. The luxury
of having a computer to oneself was only infrequently possible, and
programmers were forced to adapt to this type of debugging.

In the

however, and in most personal computer systems, the debugging is
interactive. A programmer can monopolize the whole system (and
why not!) and debug his program until his program runs perfectly.
Some programmers, ingrained with the procedures of the computer
dark ages, may sneer at this method of debugging, but it is extremely efficient, fast, and with the tools in Level II BASIC, very
powerful.

The first step in efficient debugging, however, is **good design.**
The program does not have to be written, but flowcharting or listing the steps may help in the on-line program editing. Breaking up
the program into separate modules performing well-defined functions also helps for long programs. Generally, the more thought
given to good design, the less trouble there will be in debugging.

The next step, of course, is entering the program via the edit
mode. The AUTO feature of the editor may be used to sequence
line numbers automatically with increments of 10 to allow additions of statement lines during debugging. Give some thought also

to segmenting the functions of the program. A mailing-list program, for example, that has add, delete, modify, read from cassette, and write to cassette may be conveniently segmented into

Command Interpreter and Menus	Lines 10-999
ADD	Lines 1000-1999
DELETE	Lines 2000-2999
MODIFY	Lines 3000-3999
READ	Lines 4000-4999
WRITE	Lines 5000-5999

As sections of code are entered, there is no reason not to debug on the spot with a RUN after setting up the proper values. If the code segment at 1000-1999 is the add function, for instance, perform a RUN 1000 to execute and debug the add function as a separate entity. Breaking down the program into small portions for debugging purposes will speed up the overall debugging process.

When the program blows up at a line and an error message of "BS ERROR AT LINE 3250" is displayed, don't scratch your head and look at the listing. *Don't forget that the data causing the blowup is still in RAM.* Enter a series of PRINT statements in the command mode to print out the current values of the variables causing the blow-up.

>PRINT I,J,(A*2+17)

This method of dumping the variables at the occurrence of the bug may be done as much as required.

If the bug is still present, put a STOP statement anywhere in the program before the line at which the error occurs, and repeat the process of displaying the variables to see where the error is introduced. A type of "binary search" may be used to converge on the statements causing the error; if things are all right up to a certain point, halve the portion of the program remaining, STOP, and display the variables. CONTinue until the bug is found and squished.

The Trace option may also be used to help in debugging. Trace may be turned on by TRON and off by TROFF. A trace on any computer system traces the flow of the program by printing locations or line numbers that the program follows. The trace capability on the TRS-80 is very fast because line numbers are displayed on the screen, which is an efficient input/output device. TRON/TROFF may be temporarily embedded in the program to trace only at the point at which problems arise. It may also be used to flag the programmer that a certain section of the program has been erroneously entered.

A "snapshot" capability may also be used in TRS-80 debugging. Snapshots differ from traces in that they selectively display loca-

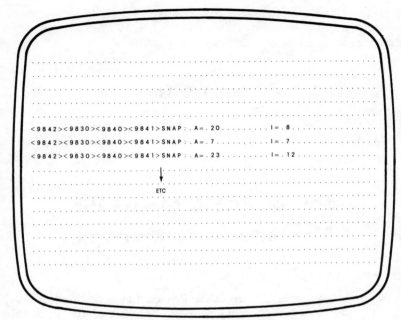

```
<9842><9830><9840><9841>SNAP: . A=. 20.........I=.8.........
<9842><9830><9840><9841>SNAP: . A=. 7...........I=.7.........
<9842><9830><9840><9841>SNAP: . A=. 23.........I=.12........

                          ↓
                         ETC
```

Figure 10-2. Example of snapshot.

tions or variables at different parts of the program. Suppose that
you are having problems with a section of code at line 9830. You
may invoke the Trace mode to print out the line and PRINT out
the troublesome variables directly after, and then turn off the trace.
Every time the program sequences through that portion of the program, you will get a snapshot of the variables at that point, as shown
in Figure 10-2.

```
9825 TRON
9830 A=A+1
9840 I=LEN(A$)
9841 PRINT "SNAP: A=";A,"I=";I
9842 TROFF
```

After you have found the *last error* in your program, it's time to
start debugging in earnest! Not exactly debugging, but exercising,
actually. Run the program, and try as many combinations of inputs
and data as possible. Be like playful computer-science students at
time-sharing terminals who try to "crash" the system! If the program is to be sold or even supplied free to friends, the users won't
appreciate unexpected crashes of a "completely debugged" program!

CHAPTER 11

Son of BASIC Meets the Machine Code Monster

Machine language, like English or French, has gone through many changes since its inception. During the building of the pyramids, machine language consisted mainly of groans and sighs. Later, during the industrial revolution, clicks and whirs replaced the earlier grunts. Still later, machine language made a transition to a silent stream of ones and zeroes fed into a computer. The term **machine language** is somewhat confusing to many BASIC programmers. What is it? How can I use it? Why are we asking so many rhetorical questions? These and other aspects of machine language will be revealed in this chapter as we present

SON OF BASIC MEETS THE MACHINE CODE MONSTER

• • • • • • • • • • •

Alan Load as Dr. Binary
Sylvia Compari as Gretchen
Knute Exchange as Bret Wonderguy

• • •

A Tandy Production — Filmed in BASICvision

What we'll attempt in this chapter is to present the *very rudiments* of machine-language or assembly-language programming and how to interface to assembly-language code using BASIC. For a more thorough treatment, see Radio Shack's TRS-80 *Assembly-Language Programming* (62-2006).

Hello, Mr. Chips

The TRS-80 is constructed around a microprocessor called the Z-80. The Z-80 semiconductor chip is almost a complete microcomputer in a piece of silicon material measuring a fraction of an inch on each side. The semiconductor material is etched and processed to contain miniature electronic components—tens of thousands of them.

The Z-80, like its predecessors, has a built-in **instruction set** or **instruction repertoire.** In the early days of computing when electronics were expensive, the amount of circuitry was limited and in turn limited the number of instructions that could be implemented. The actual instructions that the computer understood were such simple primitives as add two 16-bit numbers, subtract two numbers, compare two numbers, jump to a new location, and the like. Later, as circuitry became less and less expensive, more instructions were added. However, the number and types of instructions had a practical limit dictated by their generality. After all, specific instructions such as "If this number is 512 or greater, subtract 23" have limited application.

The instruction set in the Z-80 consists of hundreds of instructions. At first, the sheer number of instructions seems overpowering, but the instructions can be grouped into several dozen different categories. Within each category, the instructions are very similar in many cases.

Within the Z-80 are a set of internal **registers.** The registers may be thought of as additional memory locations similar to RAM memory. The registers accessible to the programmer are shown in Figure 11-1. Instructions within the Z-80 operate between the Z-80 registers or between registers and memory. Typical instructions would be ones such as

```
LD  A,(1234)    Load register A with the contents of memory location 1234.
LD  (17000),A   Store the contents of register A into memory location 17000.
ADD A,B         Add register A and B and put results in A.
JP  1700        Jump to memory location 1700.
```

The instruction length varies from one byte for an instruction such as ADD A,B to four bytes for an instruction such as LD A,(IX), which loads the A register with the memory location pointed to by the IX register. The average instruction is about two bytes long.

Each instruction is represented by an operation code (**opcode**) and operands within the instruction. For example, the 8-bit code

185

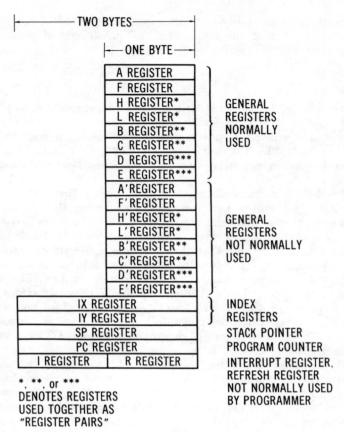

Figure 11-1. Z-80 registers.

10000001 represents the instruction "Add the A register and C register and put the result in the A register." To make instructions such as this easier to write down, every instruction has a mnemonic form, such as "ADD A,C." The number of **bits** for each instruction, then, varies from 8 for a one-byte instruction to 32 for a four-byte instruction. The binary code for each instruction is called the **machine-language** version of the instruction.

One could code a program in machine language. The stream of ones and zeroes could then be fed into TRS-80 RAM by POKEs and would execute as a machine-language program if properly called by BASIC or by a SYSTEM command.

You can always recognize programmers who worked in the 1950s by their eyeglass or contact-lens prescriptions. Coding in ones and zeroes is somewhat tedious, to say the least. Machine-language

"WILSON IS THE LAST OF THE ORIGINAL 1950's PROGRAMMERS."

coding was quickly replaced by a form of coding called **assembly-language** coding. In this scheme, instructions are still coded from a table, but the table is referenced by an assembler program rather than a programmer. The programmer supplies text mnemonics such as "ADD A,B," and the assembler program automatically assembles them into the proper machine-language form.

The TRS-80, being a sophisticated computer, has quite a nice interactive Assembler/Editor which can be used to assemble machine-language programs of several instructions to thousands. The resulting machine-language code can then be manually POKEd into RAM or be input by means of a SYSTEM or T-BUG tape. We'll be discussing both the use of SYSTEM tapes and the POKE method in this chapter. But first . . .

TRS-80 Memory Layout

Before we use any machine-language routines, we must get an idea of the memory layout of the TRS-80. That way we will not be (to use a technical term) **clobbering** any machine-language program with which we are interfacing. Figure 11-2 shows the BASIC memory layout.

The first 12K bytes of the 64K bytes (remember, K=1024) of memory locations available to the TRS-80 are dedicated to the ROM

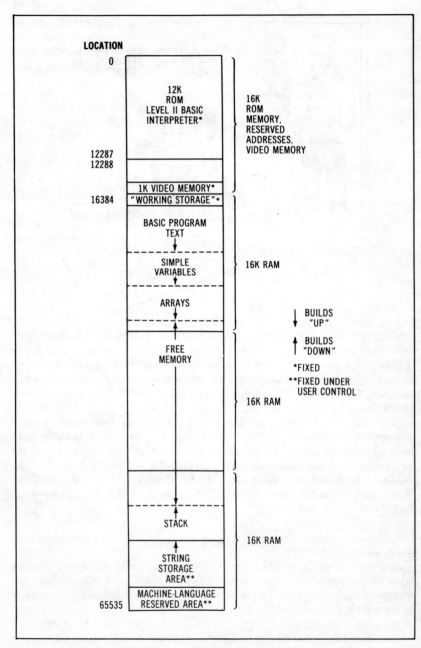

Figure 11-2. BASIC memory layout.

containing the Level II BASIC interpreter. ROM, of course, is Read-Only Memory and can't be changed. The next 4K is a mixture of video display memory, which is 1K bytes long and located at the end of the 4K segment, and dedicated memory addresses. The dedicated memory addresses do not exist as memory but are detected by such system devices as printer logic and the RS-232 interface.

The next 4K to 48K of memory is RAM, or Random Access Memory. RAM can be read from and written into (*Editor's Note: Never use a preposition to end a sentence with!*). It can be loaded with programs or data or can be altered by POKEs. Depending upon the size of your system, you may have 4K, 16K, 32K, or 48K of RAM. The memory location of RAM starts at 16384 and continues to 65535 for a 48K (RAM) system.

During the use of Level II BASIC, certain areas of the RAM are used by the interpreter, as shown in Figure 11-2. The first portion of RAM contains "Working Storage," followed by BASIC program text, simple variables, and arrays. As a BASIC program is created, this area expands as new variables and statements are added; it is not static, but "grows" toward high memory addresses.

At the same time the text, variables, and arrays are using up low RAM, the string space and stack are using high memory. A CLEAR statement clears a fixed area at the top of RAM for use as string working storage. Immediately below the string space is the **stack** area. The stack area is expanding and contracting as the BASIC interpreter is run, but uses only several dozen bytes of memory or so at any given time.

The area between the stack and arrays is free memory. The figure is somewhat misleading, as free memory usually constitutes a major portion of available memory, dependent upon the system memory and program size.

The area of memory immediately at the end of RAM may be reserved for use of machine-language code or any other use. When the Level II interpreter asks (in its inimitable fashion)

MEMORY SIZE?

and patiently waits for your answer, it takes the value specified and reserves the RAM area from "top of memory" to the specified value. Specifying 63000 in a 48K system, for example, would reserve RAM locations 63000-65535. These locations would never be used for string or stack storage, or for any other interpreter use. If no value is entered, no area is reserved.

How much memory can be reserved by the use of MEMORY SIZE?—any reasonable amount. The BASIC interpreter must have some memory available for program storage, variables, arrays, stack,

189

and string space, but as long as it has enough to cover every condition during BASIC program execution, the reserved area may be as large as necessary.

SYSTEM Tapes

Now that we have a little knowledge about the TRS-80 memory layout and machine code, let's disregard the homily and do a dangerous thing . . . create and use our first **system** tape. For this exercise, we'll create a short assembly-language program to white out the screen (do you have those stop watches ready?).

Our first step is to hand assemble the program using a table of opcodes or to use the Radio Shack Editor/Assembler to create the desired program.

The process of designing, coding, and debugging in assembly language may be quite involved, and we can't explain how to do it in this one chapter. The *end result* of the designing, coding, and debugging effort is shown in Figure 11-3. It is an assembly-language **listing** representing the assembly-language program to perform the screen white-out.

We will explain this one program fully to help you understand assembly language a little better; we'll bypass complete explanations of other assembly-language programs presented in the chapter. You may ignore the actual assembly-language code and concentrate on the techniques of **interfacing** to assembly-language subroutines, if you wish.

The left-hand column of Figure 11-3 represents the memory locations where the program resides. These hexadecimal values are the ·locations for the **machine-language** code found in the next column.

```
MEMORY LOCATIONS
FOR INSTRUCTIONS
       │     MACHINE-LANGUAGE
       │        INSTRUCTIONS
       │           │         LINE NUMBERS                        SOURCE CODE
       │           │            │
       ▼           ▼            ▼
  4A00             00100               ORG    18944
  4A00  21003C     00110  WHITE  LD     HL,15360          ;START OF SCREEN
  4A03  110004     00120         LD     DE,1024           ;1024 CHARACTER POSITIONS
  4A06  3EBF       00130  LOOP   LD     A,191             ;ALL ON
  4A08  77         00140         LD     (HL),A            ;STORE ALL ON
  4A09  23         00150         INC    HL                ;INCREMENT DISPLAY ADDRESS
  4A0A  1B         00160         DEC    DE                ;DECREMENT # OF BYTES
  4A0B  7A         00170         LD     A,D               ;GET MOST SIGNIFICANT
  4A0C  B3         00180         OR     E                 ;MERGE LEAST SIGNIFICANT
  4A0D  20F7       00190         JR     NZ,LOOP           ;LOOP IF NOT 1024
  4A0F  C9         00200         RET                      ;RETURN IF DONE
  0000             00210         END
  00000 TOTAL ERRORS
                                LABELS   MNEMONICS  OPERANDS             REMARKS
  LOOP    4A06                  COLUMN   COLUMN     COLUMN               COLUMN
  WHITE   4A00
```

Figure 11-3. Assembly-language screen white-out.

The machine-language code consists of two, four, six, or eight hexa-decimal digits representing one to four bytes of a machine-language instruction. The next (third) column is a line number, identical to BASIC line numbers. The remainder of the listing in the figure represents the **source code** of the program.

The assembly-language source code consists of four parts. The fourth (extreme right) column has the **comments** of the program. This column is optional. The second column of the source code has the actual Z-80 mnemonic form of the instruction. This is a shorthand representation of the instruction just as in BASIC statement types. An instruction may have several operands, and these are contained in the next column. The left-hand column of the source code holds optional **labels** which are used in place of line numbers for jumps (equivalent to GOTOs).

Now for the actual program to white out the screen . . .

Line 100 loads a CPU register (HL) with 15360, the address of the video display start. A second CPU register (DE) is then loaded with 1024, the number of characters on the screen. HL will be used as a pointer to 15360–16383 throughout the program loop just as a BASIC variable HL might be used for a POKE HL value. DE will be used as a count of the number of screen positions actually whitened, just as in the BASIC statement "FOR DE = 1024 TO 0 STEP −1".

Lines 120 through 180 constitute a program loop. The loop is performed 1024 times. Each time through the loop, the following actions occur.

1. The CPU A register is loaded with 191, a value representing a graphics "all ON" (line 120).
2. The contents of A (191) are stored into the video memory location pointed to by HL (line 130).
3. The pointer in HL is incremented by 1 to point to the next video memory location (line 140).
4. The count in DE is decremented by 1 (line 150). (When it reaches 0, the loop will terminate.)
5. The count in DE is tested for 0 (lines 160 and 170).
6. If the count in DE is not zero, another loop is made back to label LOOP. If the count is zero, the next instruction at line 190 is executed. (Line 180.)
7. When the count is zero after 1024 times through a loop, a RETurn instruction is executed to return to the BASIC program.

Where do we want this program to reside in RAM? To handle the case of every reader (unless someone out there has one of the early 3.3K TRS-80 systems), we'll plan on putting this program at

RAM location 20300, which is close to the top of a 4K RAM system. The starting location for machine-language routines is important, because the codes for the instruction operands vary according to where the instructions are placed in memory. Unlike BASIC, machine language references are to **absolute** memory locations, rather than line numbers of statements. As an interesting point, though, it just so happens that this particular assembly-language routine is **relocatable** to any part of RAM; it does not have to be reassembled. All of the machine-language routines in this book are relocatable in this fashion.

There are two alternatives to using an assembly-language program after it has been properly assembled, loading a SYSTEM tape created by the Radio Shack Editor/Assembler or using the listing values after assembly by POKEing them into memory. These two alternatives will hold true for all programs in this chapter. We'll explain how to use both methods for this program to white out the screen.

The first alternative is assembling and loading a SYSTEM tape. If we take the source program from Figure 11-3 and key it into the Radio Shack Editor/Assembler, not only will we get the listing of Figure 11-3, but the Editor/Assembler will generate a file on cassette called the SYSTEM (object) file that can be loaded by a SYSTEM command. To load the SYSTEM tape, type the following after initializing BASIC:

MEMORY SIZE? 18944
RADIO SHACK LEVEL II BASIC
READY
>SYSTEM
*?(Name of tape)

The SYSTEM tape created by the Editor/Assembler will now load under the name specified to the Editor/Assembler (or "NONAME" if none was specified). To get back to BASIC, hit BREAK after the tape has loaded.

The second alternative is to POKE the machine-language values from the assembly listing. After the assemble, we have two columns on the assembly listing that represent the locations for the machine-language code (starting at 18944) and the machine-language code itself.

In this program, the following machine-language code was generated by assembly:

Location	Hexadecimal (From Fig. 11-3)	Decimal
4A00 (18944)	21	33
4A01	00	0

4A02	3C	60
4A03	11	17
4A04	00	0
4A05	04	4
4A06	3E	62
4A07	BF	191
4A08	77	119
4A09	23	35
4A0A	1B	27
4A0B	7A	122
4A0C	B3	179
4A0D	20	32
4A0E	F7	247
4A0F	C9	201

We have converted the hexadecimal code to decimal for POKEing, as Level II BASIC will only accept decimal values. The hexadecimal values may be converted by reference to a hexadecimal-decimal conversion table such as the one that can be found in the Editor/Assembler manual.

The 16 locations may be loaded by POKEing by simply performing a POKE 18944,xx in the command mode or by using the short program below to input the starting address and the POKE values.

```
100 INPUT "START ADDRESS";A      'start address for pokes
200 INPUT "VALUE" ;B            ['input value 0-255
300 IF B=-1 STOP                ['terminate on -1
400 POKE A,B                    ['poke to next address
500 A=A+1                       ['increment next address
600 GOTO 200                    ['go for next value
```

Using the USR(0) Call

The 16 bytes of data comprising the short machine-language sub-routine are now in RAM from 18944 to 18959. How do we get to the subroutine from BASIC? A relevant question . . .

The USR(x) function causes a transfer to an address somewhere in RAM (or ROM). The address to be used in the call must have been placed in locations 16526 and 16527 previous to the USR call. In our case, we're using a machine-language program starting at 18944. Using standard address format, we must POKE the two bytes of address value 18944 into locations 16526 and 16527. Standard address format, as you may recall, is least significant byte followed by most significant byte. The code for POKEing 18944 into 16526 and 16527 is

```
1000 MS=INT(18944/256)          'calculate ms byte of address
1100 LS=18944-MS*256            'calculate ls byte of address
1200 POKE 16526,LS              'setup ls byte for usr
1300 POKE 16527,MS              'setup ms byte for usr
```

The statement for MS finds the upper (most significant) 8 bits of the address, and the code for LS finds the lower (least significant) 8 bits of the address. This scheme can be performed for any address value.

The next step is actually to call the subroutine using a USR(0) call. If all goes well, we should call the machine-language code, white out the screen, and return to the next BASIC statement.

```
1000 MS=INT(18944/256)      'calculate ms byte of address
1100 LS=18944-MS*256        'calculate ls byte of address
1200 POKE 16526,LS          'setup ls byte for usr
1300 POKE 16527,MS          'setup ms byte for usr
1400 A=USR(0)               'call machine-language
1500 CLS                    'clear screen
1600 PRINT "HOORAY"         'cheers
```

Did it work? (*Guard, get the name of that reader who never runs these routines. Better use a larger pad of paper . . .*) If you specified a memory size of 18944, POKEd the data correctly (or loaded a SYSTEM tape), and then used the program above, you will have seen a rapid flash of white before your eyes similar to the one you saw after writing out a check for a TRS-80 system. Did you time it? The time to white out the screen in this case was about 1/25 of a second, about 20 times faster than the fastest string graphics method!

Any Arguments?

The format of the USR(0) call set a variable (A) equal to the USR call. The 0 within the function was a dummy argument. The USR call provides for use of a real argument if the user desires. The value or variable within the parentheses will then be passed to the machine-language subroutine. Upon return, an argument will be passed back by setting the specified variable (in this case, A) equal to the argument to be returned.

What is the purpose of passing arguments back and forth? The obvious answer is that machine-language subroutines may require operands just as BASIC subroutines require operands. Let's illustrate how an argument is passed to a machine-language subroutine. Suppose that we require a subroutine to delete a character on the screen for word processing, sometimes called "text editing." Word processing enables us to construct text representing form letters, book manuscripts, or other text-related material. The deletion will cause the remaining text to "snake up." The character position (0–1023) of the character to be deleted will be passed to the machine-language subroutine, which will delete the character and snake up the remaining text on the screen. The code for this machine-language function is shown below.

```
0000 CD7F0A    00100 DELETE  CALL    2687            ;GET CURSOR POSITION
0003 E5        00110         PUSH    HL              ;FOR TRANSFER
0004 D1        00120         POP     DE              ;NOW IN DE
0005 210004    00130         LD      HL,1024         ;FOR 1K SCREEN
0008 B7        00140         OR      A               ;CLEAR CARRY
0009 ED52      00150         SBC     HL,DE           ;1024-POSITION
000B E5        00160         PUSH    HL              ;TRANSFER
000C C1        00170         POP     BC              ;TO BC
000D 21003C    00180         LD      HL,15360        ;SCREEN START
0010 19        00190         ADD     HL,DE           ;FIND POSITION
0011 E5        00200         PUSH    HL              ;FOR TRANSFER
0012 D1        00210         POP     DE              ;NOW IN DE
0013 23        00220         INC     HL              ;FOR SOURCE
0014 EDB0      00230         LDIR                    ;BLOCK MOVE
0016 3E20      00240         LD      A,32            ;BLANK
0018 32FF3F    00250         LD      (16383),A       ;STORE IN LAST POSITION
001B C9        00260         RET                     ;RETURN TO BASIC
0000          00270         END
00000 TOTAL ERRORS
34754  TEXT AREA BYTES LEFT

DELETE 0000 00100
```

The code above first calls a subroutine at location 2687 in ROM. This subroutine loads the HL register with the argument. If we had said

100 A=USR(1011)

1011 would have been the argument passed to DELETE in HL after we had CALLed the 2687 subroutine. *Every time an argument is to be passed to a machine-language subroutine, the "CALL 2687" must be executed to load the argument into the HL registers.* This is simply the way chosen to pass an argument between BASIC and a machine-language subroutine in the TRS-80. There is nothing profound about it.

With the argument of 0–1023 representing the character position in HL, a PUSH and POP are performed to also transfer the argument to the DE registers. Next, the argument is subtracted from 1024 to give the number of bytes between the character position specified and the end of the screen. HL is then loaded with the actual address of the screen memory location by adding 15360, the start of the screen memory, to the character position. This value is transferred to DE. One is then added to HL. All of this manipulation was necessary to set up the HL, DE, and BC registers properly so that a "Move Block" LDIR instruction could be executed. The LDIR moves all memory locations in video memory from the character position *plus one* down one location to effectively delete the character at the specified character position and "snake up" the text. As the last location in the video memory had nothing to fill it, a blank is used for the last screen character. The machine-code data after assembly for this machine code is given below. It is also **relocatable** code that could be placed anywhere in memory.

Hexadecima'   CD,7F,0A,E5,D1,21,00,04,B7,ED,52,E5,C1,21,00,
                3C,19,E5,D1,23,ED,B0,3E,20,32,FF,3F,C9
Decimal   ┌→ 205,127,10,229,209,33,0,4,183,237,82,229,193,33,
        ┌ 0,60,25,229,209,35,237,176,62,32,50,255,63,201 ←┐
    18944   18971

POKE the machine code above from 18944 through 18971 using the POKE program shown previously. Of course, once again, MEMORY must have been set to 18944 before the POKEs. You can optionally assemble this code and load a SYSTEM tape. If you do, enter the following source line before assembly:

00090   ORG   18944

We now have the machine-language program in RAM ready to be called by a BASIC "driver." For the driver, we'll use a routine to fill the screen with simulated text. The routine will then ask for the character position to be deleted, and delete the indicated character.

```
2000 CLS                                  'clear screen
2010 INPUT "CHARACTER POSITION=";B         'input position for delete
2020 IF B<0 OR B>1023 GOTO 2010            'test for valid position
2030 FOR I=15360 TO 16383               ┌─'setup loop for screen memory
2040 A=RND(6)                            │ 'random# for space
2050 IF A<>1 GOTO 2080                   │ 'go if not space
2060 A=32                                │ 'put word space every 6th
2070 GOTO 2100                           │ 'go to fill screen
2080 A=RND(90)                           │ 'get alpha character
2090 IF A<65 GOTO 2080                   │ 'throw out less than a
2100 POKE I,A                            │ 'store in screen
2110 NEXT I                             └─'loop for 1k
2120 MS=INT(18944/256)                     'get ms address byte
2130 LS=18944-MS*256                       'get ls address byte
2140 POKE 16526,LS                         'store ls for usr call
2150 POKE 16527,MS                         'store ms for usr call
2160 A$=INKEY$                          ┌ ┌'test keyboard input
2170 IF A$="" GOTO 2160                  └'loop if none
2180 A=USR(B)                            │ 'pass delete position
2190 GOTO 2160                          └  'delete at same position
```

The driver first clears the screen and asks for the character position for the delete. After a valid character position is input, the screen memory is filled with random text characters including spaces to simulate actual text. (A space is generated every five characters or so by the $A = RND(6)$ logic.) After the screen is filled, the standard POKE of the machine-language subroutine is made at 16526 and 16527. At the next key depression, the machine-language subroutine at 18944 is called by $A = USR(B)$. B is the character position previously input (0–1023). For every subsequent key depression, another character at the same character position is deleted as the text snakes up. The important points in this example are:

1. An argument was passed to the machine-language subroutine by USR(B).
2. The machine-language subroutine picked up the argument by a "CALL 2687."

196

Before we get on to a clever way to embed machine code in BASIC statements, let's cover two more topics about argument passing—passing arguments from the machine-language subroutine back to the BASIC program and passing multiple arguments.

Getting an Argument Back

Suppose that we continue with our word-processing analogy and create a machine-language subroutine to count the number of words on the screen. If a word is defined as a string of characters bracketed by spaces, we can easily count the words by counting the number of spaces. The machine-language routine will scan video-display memory and count the spaces, returning the word count as a variable. The assembly-language code for this is below.

```
0000 11003C    00100 COUNT  LD   DE,15360      ;START OF SCREEN
0003 010004    00110        LD   BC,1024       ;1K CHARACTERS ON SCREEN
0006 210000    00120        LD   HL,0          ;INITIALIZE SPACE COUNT
0009 1A        00130 LOOP   LD   A,(DE)        ;GET CHARACTER
000A FE20      00140        CP   32            ;TEST FOR SPACE
000C 2001      00150        JR   NZ,CONT       ;GO IF NOT SPACE
000E 23        00160        INC  HL            ;BUMP SPACE COUNT
000F 0B        00170 CONT   DEC  BC            ;DECREMENT LOOP COUNTER
0010 13        00180        INC  DE            ;BUMP LOCATION POINTER
0011 79        00190        LD   A,C           ;GET LS OF LOOP COUNT
0012 B0        00200        OR   B             ;MERGE MS OF LOOP CNT
0013 20F4      00210        JR   NZ,LOOP       ;GO IF NOT 1K
0015 C39A0A    00220        JP   2714          ;DONE,RETURN TO BASIC PROG
0000           00230        END
00000 TOTAL ERRORS
34749 TEXT AREA BYTES LEFT


CONT     000F 00170    00150
COUNT    0000 00100
LOOP     0009 00130    00210
```

The code above first loads the DE register with the start of the screen memory and the BC register with 1024, the number of locations to scan. HL is initialized to zero for the count. The code loops through "LOOP" to "JR NZ,LOOP" comparing each video display memory character with a space, ASCII 32. If a space is found, the count in HL is bumped by one. Each time through the loop, the address of the next memory location is incremented by one (INC DE), and the number of locations left is decremented by one (DEC BC). If the number of locations left in BC is not zero, another pass through the loop is made. At the end of the loop, HL contains the count of the number of spaces or words. *The last action is to execute a jump (JP) to location 2714. This transfers the count in HL to the variable in the USR call. This is the "standard" way to pass an argument back to a BASIC routine in the TRS-80.* Note that a "Return" (RET) instruction is not done in this case.

The machine code for this subroutine is shown below. POKE the values after first setting memory size to 18944. This code, as were the other two routines, is relocatable and can be placed anywhere in memory. Optionally, you can assemble this code with the Editor/Assembler and load the resulting SYSTEM tape. If you do, add the following source line before assembly:

00090   ORG   18944

Hexadecimal   11,00,3C,01,00,04,21,00,00,1A,FE,20,20,01,23,
               0B,13,79,B0,20,F4,C3,9A,0A
Decimal   ┌→17,0,60,1,0,4,33,0,0,26,254,32,32,1,35,11,19,
               │ 121,176,32,244,195,154,10
          18944 ┘

The BASIC driver for this subroutine fills the screen with simulated text characters as before, except that it ensures that only one space at a time is used. The number of spaces (words) is returned in variable A and printed.

```
3000 CLS                                'clear screen
3010 FOR I=15360 TO 16383             ┌─'setup loop for screen
3020 A=RND(6)                         │ 'get # for space
3030 IF A<>1 GOTO 3070                │ 'if not space continue
3040 POKE I,32                        │ 'poke space
3050 I=I+1                            │ 'bump character position
3060 IF I=16384 GOTO 3110             │ 'go if screen fill done
3070 A=RND(90)                        │ 'get non-space character
3080 IF A<65 GOTO 3070                │ 'ignore control codes
3090 POKE I,A                         │ 'poke alphabetic
3100 NEXT I                           └─'loop to fill screen
3110 MS=INT(18944/256)                  'get ms of address
3120 LS=18944-MS*256                     'get ls of address
3130 POKE 16526,LS                       'poke for usr call
3140 POKE 16527,MS                       'poke for usr call
3150 A=USR(0)                            'call word count routine
3160 CLS                                 'clear screen
3170 PRINT "NUMBER OF WORDS IS ";A       'print number
3180 IF INKEY$="" GOTO 3180 ELSE GOTO 3000
```

Handling Two-Way Passing and Multiple Arguments

The above example showed the mechanism for passing arguments back to the BASIC routine, and the example previous to that illustrated passing an argument to the machine-language routine. In some cases, it is necessary to both pass an argument to the machine-language routine and pass one back from the machine-language subroutine. An example of this might be a machine-language routine that scanned the display memory for a given character and then returned the character position of the character. In this case (we won't write the code), the call might be

100   A=USR(ASC(A$))

where A$ was the one-character string variable and A was the returned character position 0–1023, or −1 if the character was not found. In the corresponding machine-language code, the first in-

198

struction would "CALL 2687" to load the HL register with ASC(A$), and the last instruction would be a "JP 2714" to take the character position in HL and store it in variable A.

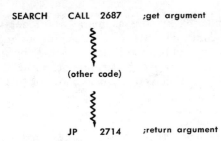

We know from the above examples how *single* arguments can be passed between a BASIC program and a machine-language subroutine, but how about multiple arguments? The HL register in the Z-80 is 16 bits wide and can therefore hold an *integer* variable. All arguments passed between BASIC and a machine-language subroutine must be integer variables of 16 bits or less. (We used single-precision arguments above that were converted by the 2687 routine to integer values. We also took the integer argument from the subroutine and converted it to a single-precision form. As long as the argument is between −32768 and +32767, this technique is valid, although it is probably wise to use integer variables such as A% or B% when setting up USR calls.)

If multiple arguments are required, it is possible to **pack** them into a 16-bit integer variable. An example of this would be use of a machine-language subroutine that drew a line from a given x,y point to another x,y point. The four arguments could be packed as shown in Figure 11-4.

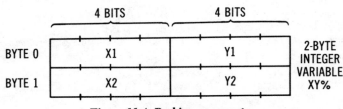

Figure 11-4. Packing arguments.

The subroutine, of course, would have to **unpack** them into four separate arguments. The packing code is shown below and assumes variables X1, Y1, X2, and Y2 are the appropriate x,y values. The packed result passed to the machine-language subroutine is in integer variable XY.

199

```
100   XY% = X1*4096 + Y1*256 + X2*16 + Y2
200   A = USR(XY%)
300   ⌇
```

Another method of passing as many arguments as required is simply to make multiple calls to the machine-language subroutine. On the first call, the subroutine starts counting the number of arguments and does not process the arguments until all the necessary arguments have been received. Typical code for this is shown below

```
100   A = USR(B%)      'first argument
200   A = USR(C%)      'second
300   A = USR(D%)      'third
400   A = USR(E%)      'fourth and go!
500   PRINT A          'done
```

A final method for passing a number of arguments is to store the arguments in a string. As in other examples we have seen, the string is a "dummy" string whose only purpose is to be filled with arguments for the machine-language subroutine. Suppose that we have four integer arguments to pass to the machine-language subroutine. We know that each integer argument requires two bytes and that we need, therefore, eight bytes to hold the arguments. The code below establishes a dummy string of eight bytes, finds the location of the string by VARPTR, fills in four arguments of 1000, 2000, 3000, and 4000, and then calls the machine-language subroutine with the address of the dummy string. Arguments can also be passed back to a BASIC program via the dummy string.

(LS, MS are precomputed address of subroutine.)

```
6000  A%=1000                        'first argument
6010  B%=2000                        'second argument
6020  C%=3000                        'third argument
6030  D%=4000                        'fourth argument
6040  A$="12345678"                  'dummy string
6050  B=VARPTR(A$)                   'address of parameter blk
6060  C=PEEK(B+2)*256+PEEK(B+1)      'address of string
6070  POKE C,A%                      'store first arg
6080  POKE C+2,B%                    'store second arg
6090  POKE C+4,C%                    'store third arg
6100  POKE C+6,D%                    'store fourth arg
6110  POKE 16526,LS                  'setup address
6120  POKE 16527,MS                  '   for call
6130  A=USR(C)                       'call machine language
```

Handling Multiple Machine-Language Subroutines

Is there any reason for not having multiple machine-language subroutines? None whatsoever. Just remember to POKE the address of the location of each new subroutine into 16526 and 16527 before the USR call is executed. If machine-language subroutine 1 was at 18900 and subroutine 2 was at 18950, for example, the code to call the two consecutively would be

```
100 POKE 16526,18900-INT(18900/256)*256
200 POKE 16527,INT(18900/256)
300 A=USR(0)
400 POKE 16526,18950-INT(18950/256)*256
500 POKE 16527,INT(18950/256)
600 B=USR(0)
```

Arguments to each subroutine could be handled by the same methods as we discussed above.

A Neat Method for Embedding Machine-Language Subroutines in BASIC Code

Now let's take a look at an extremely good method for using machine-language subroutines in BASIC programs. The idea is to construct a string variable by using the CHR$ function to embed machine-language values in the string. Then the location of the string is found by the VARPTR, the location is POKEd into locations 16526 and 16527, and a USR call is executed to perform the subroutine. The advantage of this method is that no separate set of POKEs or loading of a SYSTEM tape has to be done.

Let's use a fourth example of machine-language code to see how this technique works. First, we must assemble the subroutine as before. This particular subroutine contains *two* subroutines, one to write the contents of the video display to cassette tape and the second to read the cassette tape back and restore the display. The subroutines may be called from any BASIC program that contains them, so it is possible to save the appearance of the screen for game displays, business reports, or error conditions and restore the display at any later time. The subroutines use the machine-language cassette routines in Level II BASIC, so the entire process is very fast.

The machine-language code is presented below. The ROM routines CALLed are 212H (212 hexadecimal) (Define Cassette), 296H (Find Leader and Sync Byte), 235H (Read Byte), 1F8H (Turn Off Cassette), 287H (Write Leader and Sync Byte), and 264H (Write Byte). "IN" reads 1024 bytes from cassette to restore the display, while "OUT" writes out 1024 bytes from display memory. We can't go into detail on the cassette functions in this chapter, but we'll cover some of the code in the next chapter, "POKEing Around in Memory."

```
0000 AF        00100 IN     XOR    A          ;0 FOR CASSETTE 1
0001 CD1202    00110        CALL   212H       ;START CASSETTE
0004 CD9602    00120        CALL   296H       ;FIND LEADER, SYNC BYTE
0007 21003C    00130        LD     HL,3C00H   ;START OF SCREEN
000A 010004    00140        LD     BC,1024    ;1K BYTES IN SCREEN
000D CD3502    00150 IN10   CALL   235H       ;READ ONE BYTE
```

```
0010 77      00160        LD    (HL),A     ;STORE IN SCREEN MEMORY
0011 23      00170        INC   HL         ;POINT TO NEXT LOCATION
0012 0B      00180        DEC   BC         ;DECREMENT BYTE COUNT
0013 78      00190        LD    A,B        ;GET MS BYTE OF COUNT
0014 B1      00200        OR    C          ;MERGE LS BYTE
0015 20F6    00210        JR    NZ,IN10    ;GO IF NOT 1K
0017 CDF801  00220        CALL  1F8H       ;TURN OFF CASSETTE
001A C9      00230        RET              ;RETURN
001B AF      00240 OUT    XOR   A          ;0 TO A
001C CD1202  00250        CALL  212H       ;START CASSETTE
001F CD8702  00260        CALL  287H       ;WRITE LEADER ON TAPE
0022 21003C  00270        LD    HL,3C00H   ;START OF SCREEN MEMORY
0025 010004  00280        LD    BC,1024    ;BYTE CNT = 1K
0028 7E      00290 OUT10  LD    A,(HL)     ;GET BYTE
0029 CD6402  00300        CALL  264H       ;WRITE ONE BYTE
002C 23      00310        INC   HL         ;POINT TO NEXT
002D 0B      00320        DEC   BC         ;DECREMENT BYTE COUNT
002E 78      00330        LD    A,B        ;GET MS BYTE OF COUNT
002F B1      00340        OR    C          ;MERGE LS BYTE
0030 20F6    00350        JR    NZ,OUT10   ;GO IF NOT 1K
0032 CDF801  00360        CALL  1F8H       ;TURN OFF CASSETTE
0035 C9      00370        RET              ;RETURN
0000         00380        END
00000 TOTAL ERRORS
34334 TEXT AREA BYTES LEFT


IN      0000 00100
IN10    000D 00150    00210
OUT     001B 00240
OUT10   0028 00290    00350
```

The machine code for the subroutines is presented below in decimal form. It's relocatable and can be used anywhere in RAM memory. The "IN" portion starts at the first byte, and the OUT portion starts at the 28th byte.

```
175,205,18,2,205,150,2,33,0,60,1,0,4,
205,53,2,119,35,11,120,177,32,246,205,
248,1,201,175,205,18,2,205,135,2,33,0,
60,1,0,4,126,205,100,2,35,11,120,177,32,246,
205,248,1,201,255
```

The machine code above is converted to a string by one of two methods. The first uses CHR$ to assemble a string of the codes above.

```
100  ZA$=CHR$(175)+CHR$(18)+ ...
```

This method works fine, but there is a limit on the number of characters per statement line, and it's necessary to break up the string into several separate strings and then concatenate to get an entire **contiguous** string.

We'll use the second method, which assembles a string by moving DATA values into a dummy string, similar to the graphics method explored earlier in the book.

```
100 ZA$="THIS IS A DUMMY STRING THAT WILL BE FILLED WITH CHARACT"
200 ZA=VARPTR(ZA$)                        'find address of block
300 ZB=PEEK(ZA+1)+PEEK(ZA+2)*256          'find string address
400 ZC=ZB+27                              'find 2nd routine address
500 FOR ZI=ZB TO (ZB+LEN(ZA$)-1)        ┌─'setup loop for pokeing
600 READ ZZ                             │ 'get byte of ml
650 POKE ZI,ZZ                          │ 'poke ml byte
700 NEXT ZI                             └─'loop til done
```

```
800 DATA 175,205,18,2,205,150,2,33,0,60,1,0,4,205,53
900 DATA 2,119,35,11,120,177,32,246,205,248,1,201,175
1000 DATA 205,18,2,205,135,2,33,0,60,1,0,4,126,205,100
1100 DATA 2,35,11,120,177,32,246,205,248,1,201,255
```

The above code initializes the string to the machine-language values from the DATA statement. To call the OUT machine-language subroutine, use the following code

```
1900   POKE 16526,(ZC−(INT(ZC/256))+256
2000   POKE 16527,(INT(ZC/256))
2100   A=USR(0)
```

To call the IN machine-language subroutine, use the following code

```
2400   POKE 16526,ZB−(INT(ZB/256))*256
2500   POKE 16527,(INT(ZB/256))
2600   A=USR(0)
```

The complete "driver" is shown below. It fills the screen with random data, dumps the screen to cassette tape, clears the screen, and then restores the previous screen contents.

```
100  ZA$="THIS IS A DUMMY STRING THAT WILL BE FILLED WITH CHARACT"
200  ZA=VARPTR(ZA$)                        'find address of block
300  ZB=PEEK(ZA+1)+PEEK(ZA+2)*256          'find string address
400  ZC=ZB+27                              'find 2nd routine address
500  FOR ZI=ZB TO (ZB+LEN(ZA$)-1)      ⌐'setup loop for pokeing
600  READ ZZ                            │'get byte of ml
650  POKE ZI,ZZ                         │'poke ml byte
700  NEXT ZI                           └'loop til done
800  DATA 175,205,18,2,205,150,2,33,0,60,1,0,4,205,53
900  DATA 2,119,35,11,120,177,32,246,205,248,1,201,175
1000 DATA 205,18,2,205,135,2,33,0,60,1,0,4,126,205,100
1100 DATA 2,35,11,120,177,32,246,205,248,1,201,255
1200 CLS                                   'clear screen
1250 INPUT "READY CASSETTE, PRESS ENTER";A$
1300 FOR I=15360 TO 16383              ⌐'setup for screen fill
1400 A=RND(191)                         │'get character 1-191
1500 IF A<32 GOTO 1400                  │'ignore control codes
1600 POKE I,A                           │'fill screen
1700 NEXT I                            └'loop til done
1900 POKE 16526,ZC-(INT(ZC/256))*256       'setup address
2000 POKE 16527,(INT(ZC/256))              'second byte
2100 A=USR(0)                              'call routine to dump screen
2200 INPUT "READY CASSETTE, PRESS ENTER";A$
2300 CLS                                   'clear screen
2400 POKE 16526,ZB-(INT(ZB/256))*256       'setup address
2500 POKE 16527,(INT(ZB/256))              'second byte
2600 A=USR(0)                              'call routine to read screen
2700 INPUT "AGAIN";A$                       'continue if desired
2800 GOTO 1200                             'loop
```

This concludes our discussion of assembly and machine-language interfacing. We hope you haven't been frightened away, but rather that you see the potential for interfacing short machine-language routines in your BASIC programs for "time-critical" processing such as display work and cassette use. In the next chapter, we'll be looking at further machine-language topics when we discover some of the deep, dark secrets of Level II BASIC in ROM.

CHAPTER 12

POKEing Around in Memory

Are you one of those people who likes to find out how things work? Do you like to take apart grandfather clocks, threshing machines, and Boeing 747s? If so, you may be able to make BIG MONEY in Level II Computer Programming. Since we can't put this advertisement on a matchbook cover, we'll have to include it here, a logical place, since this chapter will reveal how (to a certain extent) Level II BASIC functions. Although we can't provide a complete theory of operation even in several pages, we can at least point out some of the high points, such as statement format, variable and string storage, device control blocks (DCBs), keyboard and cassette operation, and some ROM assembly-language calls. Some of these items may be used to great advantage in doing interesting things; others are

merely tutorial. We must caution you, however—if you tamper with the "internals" of a system such as Level II, you must be prepared to take the consequences if your experimentation doesn't turn out. Ready, Dr. Frankenstein? . . .

An Approach to PEEKing

First of all, we know that Level II BASIC is written in Z-80 ma- machine code and that it occupies roughly ROM locations 0 through 12287, the first 12K of the 16K addresses dedicated to ROM and system addresses (see Figure 11-2). If we know Z-80 assembly language, one way to decode how the interpreter works would be to PEEK at locations 0 on up and convert the data found there into the equivalent Z-80 instructions. We could then sit down at our leisure and follow these instructions to outline Level II BASIC operation. To do this, however, we must be fairly adept at "reading code." At times, even experienced programmers have trouble reading their own programs six months after they've written them.

The above approach is possible, however, and certainly has been performed. Rather than hand translating each value found, various Z-80 **disassemblers** are available that will automatically disassemble values into the corresponding Z-80 mnemonics. As a matter of fact, such a disassembler may be constructed using a BASIC program. The approach here is to get a value from memory, decode the "operation code" and operands, and print out the memory location, op code mnemonic, and operands. A typical printout of such a disassembler is shown in Figure 12-1.

We'll assume that you're not as conversant with Z-80 assembly language as you could be and take another approach. Interspersed with the assembly-language instructions in BASIC are sets of ASCII data. Error messages and other types of messages are in ASCII code, for example. Another ASCII-encoded set of data consists of the BASIC program statements themselves. If we PEEK and display in ASCII, we should be able to see all kinds of interesting things appear on the display as we scan through memory, ROM and RAM. Let's give it a try. The following program scans memory starting at a given location and continuing for 32K locations.

```
100 T=0                              'initialize flag
110 CLS                              'clear screen
120 INPUT "START ADDRESS";B          'input start address
130 INPUT "ASCII ONLY Y/N";C$        'give choice of data
140 FOR I=B TO 32767             ┌─'scan up to 32k
150 A=PEEK(I)                    │ 'peek current location
160 IF A<32 OR A>90 GOTO 210     │ 'go if not ascii
170 IF T=0 PRINT I;"/";CHR$(A);:ELSE PRINT CHR$(A);
180 T=1                          │ 'set location flag
190 NEXT I                       └─'get next location
200 STOP                             'stop at end of scan
210 IF T=1 PRINT                 │ 'if numeric, lf
220 T=0                          │ 'reset locn flag
230 IF C$="N" PRINT I;"/";A      │ 'print locn;data
240 NEXT I                       └─'get next location
```

```
0000 F3        DI
0001 AF        XOR  A
0002 C37406    JP   0674H
0005 C30040    JP   4000H
0008 C30040    JP   4000H
000B E1        POP  HL
000C E9        JP   (HL)
000D C39F06    JP   069FH
0010 C30340    JP   4003H
0013 C5        PUSH BC
0014 0601      LD   B,01H
0016 182E      JR   0046H
0018 C30640    JP   4006H
001B C5        PUSH BC
001C 0602      LD   B,02H
001E 1826      JR   0046H
0020 C30940    JP   4009H
0023 C5        PUSH BC
0024 0604      LD   B,04H
0026 181E      JR   0046H
0028 C30C40    JP   400CH
002B 111540    LD   DE,4015H
002E 18E3      JR   0013H
0030 C30F40    JP   400FH
0033 111D40    LD   DE,401DH
0036 18E3      JR   001BH
0038 C31240    JP   4012H
003B 112540    LD   DE,4025H
003E 18DB      JR   001BH
0040 C3D905    JP   05D9H
0043 C9        RET
0044 00        NOP
0045 00        NOP
0046 C3C203    JP   03C2H
0049 CD2B00    CALL 002BH
004C B7        OR   A
004D C0        RET  NZ
004E 18F9      JR   0049H
0050 0D        DEC  C
0051 0D        DEC  C
0052 1F        RRA
0053 1F        RRA
0054 01015B    LD   BC,5B01H
0057 1B        DEC  DE
0058 0A        LD   A,(BC)
0059 1A        LD   A,(DE)
005A 08        EX   AF,AF'
005B 1809      JR   0066H
005D 19        ADD  HL,DE
005E 2020      JR   NZ,0080H
0060 0B        DEC  BC
0061 78        LD   A,B
0062 B1        OR   C
0063 20FB      JR   NZ,0060H
0065 C9        RET
0066 310006    LD   SP,0600H
0069 3AEC37    LD   A,(37ECH)
006C 3C        INC  A
006D FE02      CP   02H
006F D20000    JP   NC,0000H
```

Figure 12-1. Typical disassembly of a BASIC interpreter.

The code on page 205 displays numeric and ASCII data or only ASCII data as requested by the user. Let's use it to display ASCII data only, starting at location 0. Use the "SHIFT @" keys to stop the display at any time; continue by hitting any key.

Some of the first ASCII data displayed consists of single "@" and other characters. This simply means that some of the values stored in ROM as instructions are also valid ASCII characters. Location 102, for example, is an ASCII "1" (49) which is also the operation code for an "LD SP" assembly-language instruction. The point is that even though data displays as an ASCII character, we can't be certain that it doesn't represent other data. We can be (fairly) certain, however, that the string of ASCII at locations 261, "MEMORY SIZE", and 273, "RADIO SHACK LEVEL II BASIC" are the messages printed out at the start of Level II BASIC. Let's continue . . .

The next interesting display starts at location 5713. The ASCII data here is shown in Figure 12-2 and looks suspiciously like BASIC statement words without the first letter. Let's record that location as an interesting spot and continue.

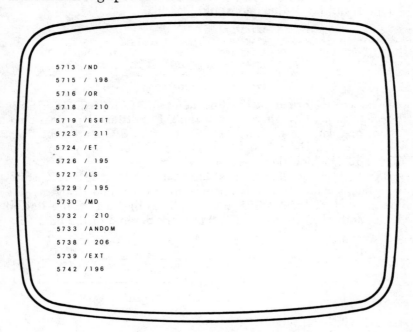

Figure 12-2. ASCII data in memory.

The next group of meaningful data is at location 6345. The string is "NFSNRGODFCOVO . . . DL3". These are the Level II error codes arranged in order of their code numbers. Continuing, location 6441 has the "READY" message, and 8568 has the "?REDO" message among others. The area from 12288 to 16383 may be skipped, as this is the area dedicated to device addresses (no memory) or video-display memory.

From 16384, we start to get very interesting displays. They seem to contain portions of our program statements, but are not intact. For example, " "INPUT START ADDRESS";B" is stored as " "START

ADDRESS";B." Other lines are stored in similar fashion. Let's stop at this point and investigate what's happening to our nice text input.

BASIC Statement Format

Let's take a look at the statement "120 INPUT"START AD-DRESS";B." First, find the start of " "START ADDRESS";B." It should be close to 17129. Having found it, run the program starting from about 5 locations before, listing both ASCII and numeric data. For example, if " "START ADDRESS";B" was at 17148, list 17143 on. A typical display of this line would look like

```
17143/21
17144/C
17145/120
17146/0
17147/137
17148/"START ADDRESS";B
```

What is the format of the line here? " "START ADDRESS";B" is recognizable, but where is the "INPUT" portion? By experimentation, one could soon find the format of BASIC statement lines. We'll save you the midnight hours, though, and let you refer to Figure 12-3, which shows the format.

BASIC statement lines start at location 17129. Each BASIC statement line is made up of a line pointer to the *next* line (2 bytes), the line number of the BASIC statement line, the text of the line in ASCII and **token** format, and a 0 to mark the end of the line. (For

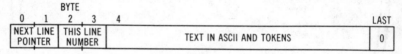

Figure 12-3. BASIC line format.

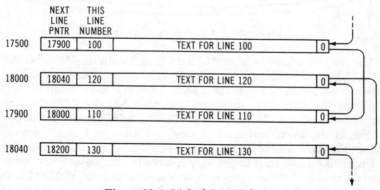

Figure 12-4. Linked BASIC lines.

208

those who read Chapter 7, this format is known as a "single-ended linked list.") This means that a BASIC program may consist of lines that are not in physical order, as shown in Figure 12-4. This arrangement permits easy editing of BASIC programs.

To see how a BASIC program is stored, we'll use a BASIC program to track itself. The program below lists the line formats of itself by following the "thread" of the linked lines starting with the line at location 17129.

```
1000 CLS                                     'clear screen
1100 NL=17129                                'set to first BASIC line
1200 PRINT:PRINT                             'skip two lines
1300 PRINT "LINE AT ";NL;":"                 'print location
1400 PRINT "NL POINTER=";PEEK(NL)+PEEK(NL+1)*256
1500 IF PEEK(NL)+PEEK(NL+1)*256=0 GOTO 2400
1600 PRINT "LINE #=";PEEK(NL+2)+PEEK(NL+3)*256
1700 PRINT "TEXT FOLLOWS"
1800 FOR I=NL+4 TO NL+255            ┌'setup loop for chars
1900 IF PEEK(I)=0 GOTO 2200          │'go if line end
2000 IF PEEK(I)<32 OR PEEK(I)>90 PRINT "/";PEEK(I);"/";ELSE PRINT CHR$(PEEK(I));
2100 NEXT I                          └'loop
2200 NL=PEEK(NL)+PEEK(NL+1)*256              'get next line address
2300 IF INKEY$="" GOTO 2300 ELSE GOTO 1200
2400 PRINT "END OF PROGRAM"                  'end
```

Run the above program, and observe how the lines are linked and the content of each of the lines. Numeric data is bracketed by slashes ("/"), while ASCII data is simply printed out. The last line of any program is a dummy line whose next line pointer is equal to 0.

Within the text of every line are numeric values called **tokens** that represent statement types. Why is this done? Using tokens drastically shortens the storage of program lines. Storing a 178 value in place of a "PRINT," for example, saves four bytes. Since many lines have multiple statements, it is easy to see how a 25% reduction or more in storage requirements could result.

The token codes may be listed easily if we recall that one of the mysterious areas that we saw earlier in our ASCII display was at 5713. The area from 5712 on is a table of tokens that can be listed by the following code.

```
100 CLS                                      'clear screen
200 N=128                                    'initialize token #
300 FOR I=5712 TO 6175              ┌'setup loop for table
400 A=PEEK(I)                       │'get value from table
500 IF A>127 PRINT CHR$(10);N;" ";CHR$(A AND 127); ELSE PRINT CHR$(A);
600 IF A>127 THEN N=N+1             └'bump # if start
700 NEXT I                          └'loop for next token
```

For your convenience, the tokens are also listed in Table 12-1. The first character of every token in the table has the most significant bit set to **delimit** each statement character string from the next, since they are "variable length." This table also includes Disk BASIC tokens that are not accessible in Level II BASIC. The token table

Table 12-1. Level II BASIC Tokens

128	END	169	NAME	210	AND
129	FOR	170	KILL	211	OR
130	RESET	171	LSET	212	>
131	SET	172	RSET	213	=
132	CLS	173	SAVE	214	<
133	CMD	174	SYSTEM	215	SGN
134	RANDOM	175	LPRINT	216	INT
135	NEXT	176	DEF	217	ABS
136	DATA	177	POKE	218	FRE
137	INPUT	178	PRINT	219	INP
138	DIM	179	CONT	220	POS
139	READ	180	LIST	221	SQR
140	LET	181	LLIST	222	RND
141	GOTO	182	DELETE	223	LOG
142	RUN	183	AUTO	224	EXP
143	IF	184	CLEAR	225	COS
144	RESTORE	185	CLOAD	226	SIN
145	GOSUB	186	CSAVE	227	TAN
146	RETURN	187	NEW	228	ATN
147	REM	188	TAB(	229	PEEK
148	STOP	189	TO	230	CVI
149	ELSE	190	FN	231	CVS
150	TRON	191	USING	232	CVD
151	TROFF	192	VARPTR	233	EOF
152	DEFSTR	193	USR	234	LOC
153	DEFINT	194	ERL	235	LOF
154	DEFSNG	195	ERR	236	MKI$
155	DEFDBL	196	STRING$	237	MKS$
156	LINE	197	INSTR	238	MKD$
157	EDIT	198	POINT	239	CINT
158	ERROR	199	TIME$	240	CSNG
159	RESUME	200	MEM	241	CDBL
160	OUT	201	INKEY$	242	FIX
161	ON	202	THEN	243	LEN
162	OPEN	203	NOT	244	STR$
163	FIELD	204	STEP	245	VAL
164	GET	205	+	246	ASC
165	PUT	206	−	247	CHR$
166	CLOSE	207	*	248	LEFT$
167	LOAD	208	/	249	RIGHT$
168	MERGE	209	↑	250	MID$

is used in conjunction with a table of routine addresses starting at 6178. This table has a two-byte address for each processing routine, arranged in the same order as the token table. The address for FOR, for example, would be found at the second location in the table (6180/6181). The addresses may be found by the usual PEEK(N) +PEEK(N+1)*256.

Knowing the structure of BASIC statement lines can be very helpful when you're designing programs to process BASIC programs themselves. Such things as appending two programs, merging two or more programs, compiling lists of the variables used in a program, renumbering programs, and other **utility** functions are all possible when we know the structure of Level II BASIC operations.

Suppose that we want to detect all occurrences of the REM statement in a program, for example. We may wish to leave REMarks in while we're debugging a program, but to delete all REMarks automatically after the final version of the program has been produced. (If there ever is a final version!). The first step in this process would be to scan each statement line for REM tokens. The code below does exactly that and lists all line numbers containing a REM token.

```
1000 CLS                                'clear screen
1010 PRINT "REMARKS AT LINES:"          'title
1020 NL=17129                           'first BASIC line
1030 REM FIND NEXT LINE #               'remark for test
1040 A=PEEK(NL)+PEEK(NL+1)*256          ┌'find address of next line
1050 REM FIND STATEMENT LINE #          │'another rem for test
1060 B=PEEK(NL+2)+PEEK(NL+3)*256        │'get current line #
1070 REM IF NEXT LINE IS ZERO, DONE     │'third remark
1080 IF A=0 GOTO 1200                    'go if end of program
1090 REM BYPASS NXT LINE,ST #
1100 NL=NL+4                            'point to text and tokens
1110 C=PEEK(NL)                         ┌'get text byte
1120 REM IF C=0 END OF LINE             │'a remarkable program
1130 IF C=0 GOTO 1180                   │'go if end of line
1140 IF C=147 PRINT B                   │'if remark token pr line #
1150 NL=NL+1                            │'point to next text byte
1160 GOTO 1110                          └'peek at next line
1170 REM GET NEXT LINE #                'last remark
1180 NL=A                               'from start of line processing
1190 GOTO 1040                          └'go to process line
1200 PRINT "DONE"                       'must be done
```

The Search for Variables

Continuing with our investigative analysis of Level II . . . We've seen how BASIC lines are stored, and we've looked at the token format. Let's next see if we can deduce something about variables and arrays. We know from our work with VARPTR that we can easily find the location of a simple variable. If we have two variables, A and B, for example, we can print their locations by

```
2000 CLS                               'clear screen
2100 A%=333                            'dummy variable
2200 B%=666                            'another dummy
2300 LA=VARPTR(A%)                     'get first location
2400 LB=VARPTR(B%)                     'get second location
2500 PRINT "LOCATION OF A=";LA,"VALUE OF A=";(PEEK(LA)+PEEK(LA+1)*256)
2600 PRINT "LOCATION OF B=";LB,"VALUE OF B=";(PEEK(LB)+PEEK(LB+1)*256)
```

Using a technique such as the above, we can easily trace simple variables as they are assembled in RAM. We can also use the same technique on array variables. VARPTR will also find the location of the elements of an array, as shown in the code below, which prints out all 34 locations of A(0) through A(33). It can be seen

that all array locations are **contiguous**—that is, in a block—and the
first element is first in the block followed by the second,

```
3000 DIM A(34)            'dummy array
3100 FOR I=0 TO 33        ┌'setup loop for location
3200 B=VARPTR(A(I))       │'find locns of elements
3300 PRINT B              │'print locations
3400 NEXT I               └'loop
```

and so forth (*Guard, arrest that reader for making that snide remark
about simple writers!*).

What is the layout for multi-dimensional arrays? By means similar to the above, we can find out that multi-dimensional arrays build
data as shown in Figure 12-5. The code to illustrate the memory
arrangement for two dimensions is shown below.

```
4000 DEFINT A                                   'define integer
4100 DIM A(2,2)                                 'establish 2-d array
4200 FOR J=0 TO 2                               ┌'loop for one dimension
4300 FOR I=0 TO 2                               │┌'loop for second
4400 PRINT "I,J=";I;",";J,"VARPTR=";(VARPTR(A(I,J)))
4500 NEXT I                                     │└'continue
4600 NEXT J                                     └'continue for first
```

Arrays are built directly below simple variables. Knowing the
array structure makes possible such things as creating machine-
language subroutines to perform a "super-fast" sort or search of
data in arrays or to perform high-speed matrix conversions.

String variables have been discussed in Chapter 3. VARPTR can
be used to find the location of any string. The argument returned
for VARPTR ("string") points to a three-byte block containing the
string length and the two bytes of the string location. Strings are
located in one of two areas, either the string space area above the
stack but below the MEMORY SIZE? reserved area, or in the
BASIC statement line itself. As we saw in the graphics chapter, a
simple string of the form A$="THIS IS A STRING" will have an
address equal to its statement line location. A string assembled from
concatenation, CHR$, or other methods will be in the "dynamic"
string area.

Houston, We're Going to Change the DCBs on Our TRS-80 Before the EVA . . .

Ah, acronyms and abbreviations! Would any computer system be
a true system without them? A DCB is a **D**evice **C**ontrol **B**lock, and
any TRS-80 BASIC programmer subsequently caught using the full
name will be stripped of his number 2 pencils and display work-
sheets. In many computer systems, it is convenient to group parameters relating to an input/output device in a single block. One of

the reasons for this is to enable a *logical* device to be easily changed to a *physical* device. Suppose that in our TRS-80 system we normally print out on the *logical* PR device or printer output device. The actual *physical* device associated with the logical printing function may be a Quick Printer I. If our installation also has Baudot tele-

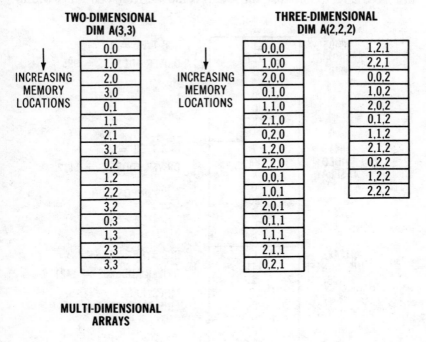

Figure 12-5. Multi-dimensional array formats.

typewriter, we can quickly substitute this device for the Quick Printer I by changing some variables in the PR DCB. The alternative to this would be to change all instructions associated with printing within the ROM instructions themselves. Since this would involve "burning in" a new ROM, you can see that the DCB method is much to be preferred.

There are three DCBs in Level II BASIC associated with the keyboard input, video display, and line printing logical functions. The DCBs themselves are located in RAM at the locations shown in Figure 12-6. Data to initialize the DCBs is moved from constants within

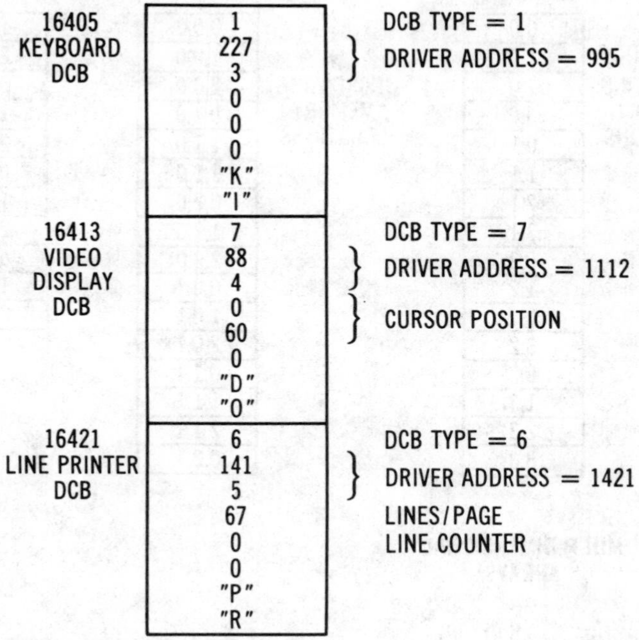

16405 KEYBOARD DCB	1 227 3 0 0 0 "K" "I"	DCB TYPE = 1 } DRIVER ADDRESS = 995
16413 VIDEO DISPLAY DCB	7 88 4 0 60 0 "D" "O"	DCB TYPE = 7 } DRIVER ADDRESS = 1112 } CURSOR POSITION
16421 LINE PRINTER DCB	6 141 5 67 0 0 "P" "R"	DCB TYPE = 6 } DRIVER ADDRESS = 1421 LINES/PAGE LINE COUNTER

Figure 12-6. DCBs.

the ROM code on power-up (data for the DCBs starts at ROM location 1767). We can easily substitute a new keyboard input routine by POKEing the proper address values into locations 16406 and 16407. Of course, the catch is that the new keyboard routine has to be coded in machine language and stored in RAM at the specified address. Similarly, we can "vector off" the video display and line printer functions into new routines by changing their addresses. Other parameters within the DCBs may be interrogated during BASIC program execution. We have seen one example of this in Chapter 4 when we examined and modified the running line count in the line printer DCB to effect a "top of form" action. As a further example of DCB use, let's change the driver address in the video display DCB to enable a printout of the data on the screen. The following code will perform this action.

```
5000 A=PEEK(16414)          'get display byte
5100 B=PEEK(16415)          'get second display byte
5200 C=PEEK(16422)          'get printer byte
5300 D=PEEK(16423)          'get second printer byte
5400 POKE 16422,A:POKE 16423,B   'put dis drvr address to lp
5500 POKE 16414,C:POKE 16415,D   'put lp drvr address to disp
```

After this change is made, any LIST or PRINT action will go to the system line printer rather than the display. A possible application for this is to switch between screen and line printer for program output without having to add "LS" for "LPRINT". The system can be returned to the normal configuration by swapping the two sets of addresses once more. Some characters that are valid for the display will not be valid for a line printer, so you may make the above changes at your own risk. (*You can apply for ACME Data/Program Insurance to protect your programs and data from such catastrophic risks. Insurance void in those states with stringent fraud laws.*)

Keyboard Kapers

One very interesting subject that we should discuss because of its potential use is the keyboard operation in Level II BASIC. As you know, the INKEY$ function returns the string value of the keyboard key that has been pressed. It is possible to bypass the routine that does the decoding and read the keys directly. This is best done by a machine-language routine, but there are several interesting BASIC applications. Let's see how the keyboard functions.

Figure 12-7 shows a simplified diagram of the keyboard. A row of keys may be read by addressing 14337, 14338, 14340, 14344, 14352, 14368, 14400, or 14464. The value returned is dependent upon the column of the key pressed. Table 12-2 shows the values returned for addresses of various columns. Suppose we address location 14344. Possible values we can get back are 1 for x, 2 for y, and 4 for z. If more than one key is pressed simultaneously, we may also get a merge of several values. If we press x, y, and z together, we get a 7. The following code detects key press in the x, y, z row.

```
100 CLS                     'clear screen
200 A=PEEK(14344)           ┌'test x,y,z keys
300 IF A=0 GOTO 200         └'loop if nothing
400 IF A=1 PRINT "X" ELSE IF A=2 PRINT "Y" ELSE IF A=4 PRINT "Z"
500 GOTO 200                'go for next key
```

Try quickly pressing a key and holding the key down for some time. With a quick key press, it is possible for the BASIC routine

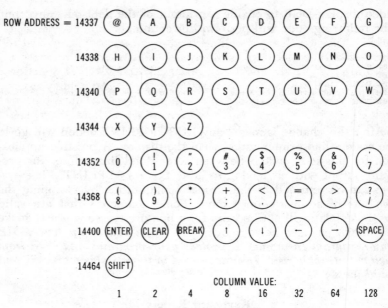

Figure 12-7. Keyboard operation.

Table 12-2. Keyboard Decoding

14337	@/1	A/2	B/4	C/8	D/16	E/32	F/64	G/128
14338	H/1	I/2	J/4	K/8	L/16	M/32	N/64	O/128
14340	P/1	Q/2	R/4	S/8	T/16	U/32	V/64	W/128
14344	X/1	Y/2	Z/4					
14352*	0/1	1/2	2/4	3/8	4/16	5/32	6/64	7/128
14368*	8/1	9/2	:/4	;/8	,/16	-/32	./64	//128
14400*	ENT/1	CLR/2	BRK/4	↑/8	↓/16	←/32	→/64	SP/128
14464*	SHFT/1							

*Lower case shown only

to miss a key; it simply is not fast enough to detect a key that is held down for perhaps 1/50th of a second. When the opposite condition is tried, it appears to the routine that the key has been continuously pressed. Because of these limitations, "scanning" of the keyboard is best done at a machine-language level. However, this decoding scheme may be used for such things as fast game control where a key is simulating a real-time control, to produce a "repeat" function for certain keys such as cursor movement keys, or to assign "function" keys to keys that are not normally translated, such as the "SHIFT" key (the shift key produces a 1 if pressed when address 14464 is read).

Another easy way to obtain a repeat key function is to zero the RAM **buffer** used for the keys. The buffer is made up of seven locations, each location corresponding to a keyboard row, as shown in Figure 12-8. If the location corresponding to the row in question is zeroed after detecting a non-null string for the INKEY$ function, INKEY$ will return another character if the key is still being pressed. Normally, INKEY$ will not return another character until the key is released and repressed. The code below circumvents this problem for the x, y, and z keys, but the scheme will work for any row of keys by zeroing the proper buffer location.

```
10 A$=INKEY$              'get character
20 IF A$="" GOTO 10       'loop if null
30 PRINT A$               'print input char
40 POKE 16441,0           'reset buffer
50 GOTO 10                'loop
```

Cassette Operations

We saw in the last chapter how we could interface to some of the machine-language cassette routines. The cassette reads and writes data at rates of 500 **baud,** which represents byte (character) data rates of 62.5 bytes per second. Data is transferred between the Z-80 and cassette a bit at a time; subroutines in Level II BASIC ROM read a bit at a time and assemble 8 bits into a byte or take a given byte and convert it to a stream of 8 bits for output. The byte data rates of 62.5 bytes per second are marginal for BASIC operation, and interface to the cassette routines should be done in machine language. The addresses for the machine-language routines for cassette operation are located as shown in Table 12-3.

Tape operation is controlled at the most basic level by three bits, as shown in Figure 12-9. Two of the bits control the actual signal level sent to the AUX jack of the cassette tape recorder. The third

Table 12-3. Machine-Language Cassette Routines

Location	Routine	Action
530	Define Cassette	Defines cassette number and turns on cassette. Cassette number, 0 or 1, must be in A register before entry.
662	Find Leader/Sync	Bypasses zero leader and finds sync byte in preparation for read.
565	Read Bytes	Reads one byte from cassette. A register holds byte on exit.
504	Turn Off Cassette	Turns off current cassette.
647	Write Leader/Sync	Write zero leader and sync byte.
612	Write Byte	Write byte to cassette. Byte must be in A register before entry.

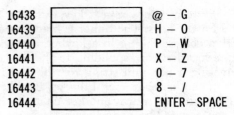

16438	@ – G
16439	H – O
16440	P – W
16441	X – Z
16442	0 – 7
16443	8 – /
16444	ENTER – SPACE

Figure 12-8. Keyboard buffer.

bit controls the REM(ote) jack on the cassette tape recorder. A fourth bit not connected with tape operation controls the 32/64 character mode of the display. All of the four bits are controlled by a BASIC OUT statement. Executing an OUT with an "address" of 255 will address the four bits of the cassette/mode select "latch."

To see how this works, try the following code. It will turn on the cassette and then turn it off after a 10-second delay.

```
2000 OUT 255,4        'turn on cassette
2100 FOR I=0 TO 4600  ┌'for a while
2200 NEXT I           └'loop for delay
2300 OUT 255,0        'turn off cassette
```

The code above sets the third bit in the cassette/mode select latch. This bit controls closure of the cassette relay.

The two bits normally used for audio output to the AUX input to the tape recorder can also operate under BASIC control. The sequence to write out a pulse during machine-language operation is to write a 1 (01), write a 2 (10), and then restore a "0" level by writing a 0 (00). We can write out to the cassette under BASIC by "toggling" these two bits after first turning on the recorder.

```
3000 OUT 255,4        'turn on cassette
3100 FOR I=0 TO 5000  ┌'record for a while
3200 OUT 255,5        │'output one level
3300 OUT 255,6        │'and now the other
3400 NEXT I           └'continue
3500 OUT 255,0        'turn off cassette
```

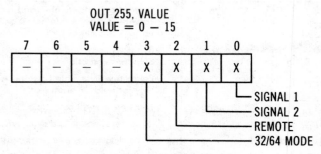

Figure 12-9. Tape operation.

Although we could make a somewhat "tighter" loop by multi-statement lines, this is about the most efficient we can get. The resulting pulses make up a square-wave tone as shown in Figure 12-10. The best we can do under BASIC timing constraints is a low-pitched tone that sounds similar to a buzz saw. The same technique can be used with machine-language code to produce much higher-pitched tones.

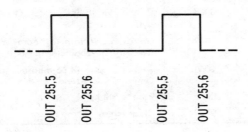

Figure 12-10. "Square-wave" output.

The code above illustrates an important point. We had to set the REM bit (value=4) on, and we had to keep it on when we output values to the other two bits. Consequently, we output a 5 instead of a 1 (1 or 4) and a 6 instead of a 2 (2 or 4).

The resulting tone produced by the code above could be fed into an external audio amplifier for signalling purposes. (*When you hear the buzz saw, change the printer paper . . . .*)

There's one bit left in the cassette/mode select latch, the mode select. Turning on this bit with a 1 sets the 32-character mode, while turning it off sets the 64-character mode. The normal method for setting this mode is to execute a PRINT CHR$(23), "set 32-character mode." Unless this method is used, the (software) display driver will get confused about the mode and only every other character will be displayed. It is not recommended to turn on the mode select bit alone in BASIC. (If you **must**, PEEK at location 16445, OR in an 8 value, and POKE the result back to 16445 after an OUT 255,8.)

Further Investigation Shows . . .

Would you like to investigate Level II BASIC further? The first action to take would be to invest some time in a study of Z-80 assembly language using the Radio Shack Editor/Assembler and TRS-80 Assembly-Language Programming. Then, follow the clues to the assembly-language routines such as the DCB driver address, the addresses of the statement processing routines in the 6180 table, and

Table 12-4. Level II Processing Routine Addresses

Location		Processing
Decimal	**Hexadecimal**	**Processing**
43	002B	Get character from keyboard. Do not wait for input. On exit (A) =character or 0 if no key press.
51	0033	Display ASCII byte. On entry (A)=ASCII byte.
59	003B	Output byte to line printer. On entry (A)=ASCII byte.
73	0049	Get character from keyboard. Wait for input. On exit (A)=character in ASCII.
96	0060	Timing Loop in 14.66 millisecond increments. On entry (BC)=Delay #.
102	0066	Reset system.
457	01C9	Clear screen, home cursor.

Table 12-5. Communication Area Addresses

Location		Number of Bytes	Description
Decimal	**Hexadecimal**	**Bytes**	**Description**
16405	4015	8	Keyboard DCB
16413	401D	8	Display DCB
16421	4025	8	Printer DCB
16438	4036	7	Keyboard Buffer
16445	403D	1	Out FF Status
16544	40A0	2	Start of String Data Pointer
16546	40A2	2	Last Executed Line Pointer
16551	40A7	2	Input Buffer Pointer
16554	40AA	3	Random Number Seed
16607	40DF	2	Default Entry Point for SYSTEM/
16633	40F9	2	Start of Simple Variables/End of Program Pointer
16635	40FB	2	Start of Arrays Pointer
16637	40FD	2	Start of Free Memory Pointer

others. Without detailed explanation, we'll provide some hints in Table 12-4 for some Level II processing routines that may be called in assembly language or simply in BASIC. In addition, Table 12-5 supplies some of the interesting "Communication Area" variables that may be accessed for BASIC operations.

Index